The Caribbean

The Caribbean

THE GENESIS OF A
FRAGMENTED NATIONALISM

FRANKLIN W. KNIGHT

New York · Oxford University Press

Copyright © 1978 by Oxford University Press, Inc.

Library of Congress Cataloging in Publication Data

Knight, Franklin W
  The Caribbean, the genesis of a fragmented nationalism.

    (Latin American histories series)
  Bibliography: p.
  Includes index.
    1. Caribbean area—Economic conditions. 2. Caribbean
area—Social conditions. 3. Caribbean area—Politics
and government. I. Title.
HC155.K58   972.9   76-51715
ISBN 0-19-502242-4
  ISBN 0-19-502243-2 pbk.

Printed in the United States of America

This reprint, 1980.

To
W.J.K. and I.M.K.
with Love

Contents

Maps

Tables

Introduction

Ever since the entry of man into the Caribbean region there have been two contradictory patterns at work. One trend has been toward homogeneity, the other toward diversity. Such are the common trends of all societies and cultures at all times. Groups are either coming together or falling apart, playing out at varying speeds the age-old struggle between centrifugalism and centripetalism, the priorities of the individual against the requirements of the group. At the collective, or group level, the victory of one force, however temporary, creates one type of society, state, or nation. But no victory results in a permanent situation. Today's dominant nation forms tomorrow's client sub-state.

The victory of centripetalism establishes large nation-states or confederations, albeit sometimes artificially contrived and precariously maintained. Within the western hemisphere, Canada, the United States of America, Mexico, Venezuela, Brazil, and Argentina are the results of the dominance of a politically strong center to restrain the irridentist forces of the periphery. But all these nation-states were themselves parts of larger political groupings, called empires. On the other hand, the independent states of the Caribbean, Central America, and the Andean region demonstrate the failure of the cohesive forces of centripetalism. The eventual results of group conflict—whether in the form of maxi-nation-state or mini-nation-state—are more often the consequences of chance than of historical laws. Circumstances are forever changing, and to individuals and groups alike, what appears logical and desirable one moment soon ceases to be so the next.

Yet both the nation and the nation-state are merely convenient forms of identification along a spectrum, ranging from the narrow, local self-consciousness—termed in this book, *patriachiquismo*—to the vast empire. No one has so far been able to ascertain the precise time at which a local self-consciousness transforms itself into a national sentiment. Nor can anyone incontrovertibly assert why some forms of diversity seem at one time to be a political asset and at others, a political liability. The Caribbean is caught up in the movement of political consciousness, but it is not at all certain that all the units are moving simultaneously in one direction or the other.

In treating the Caribbean region I have made certain assumptions, which, I hope, will not be outrageously unfamiliar to anyone who has read about, traveled to, or lived in the area. The major assumption is that while the separate units pass through the same general experience, they do so at different times—hence comparisons of the Caribbean should be systadial rather than synchronic. Another assumption is that the sum of the common experiences and understandings of the Caribbean outweigh the territorial and insular differences or peculiarities. To speak therefore of Haitian, Jamaican, Cuban, or Caribbean characteristics should not be to speak of them as mutually exclusive; the first are merely variations or components of the last. Yet another assumption is that the forces that have resulted in the balkanization of the region have varied more in degree than in kind. This assertion, however, does not imply any underestimation of the accumulative impact of historical traditions, linguistic forms, administrative differences, and general ignorance. To deny these differences would be to deny the political realities of the Caribbean. The separate political identities of the Caribbean are as patently strong as they are inescapable. They can no more easily be banished by the written word and wishful thought of an historian than the denial of any politician can banish his action.

Political boundaries do not necessarily make, or conform to, cultural boundaries. The concept of the Caribbean endorsed in this book emphasizes cultural commonalities rather than political chronology, without neglecting the importance of the latter. In my view, the region comprises one culture area in which common factors have forged a more-or-less common way of looking at life, the world, and their place in the scheme of things. All the societies of the Caribbean share an identifiable *Weltanschauung*, despite the superficial divisions that are apparent. The difference in belief, values, and attitudes of the Trinidadian and the Guyanese is perhaps no greater than that between the English and the Welsh, or the Castilian and the Andalucian. Moreover, the Caribbean peoples, with their distinctive artificial societies, common history, and common problems, seem to have more in common than the Texan and the New Yorker, or the Mayan Indian and the cosmopolite of Mexico City do in their respective nations of the United States and Mexico.

This history traces the genesis of the Caribbean from a decidedly international Caribbean and New World perspective. Many other histories are written from the viewpoint of European and imperial affairs, rendering the transformation of the region as a coincidental by-product of other, presumably larger, and more important events. Such histories do not deny that the Caribbean had its day in the sun. But, to change the metaphor, the history of the Caribbean was written merely as an act within a play. Here the act is the play, the main event. It is, of course, valid to view Caribbean history from the political and economic perspective of Africa, Europe, or mainland America—especially for Africans, Europeans, and mainland Americans. But the validity of that view cannot, and should not invalidate the local perspective. This is the only conscious "slant" that this history provides: to look from the inside out (for someone on the inside) is not only legitimate, it is the only view.

One further admission is necessary. The criteria for dividing this history rest more on socio-economic considerations than on political ones. It begins by reviewing the processes of social formation in the Caribbean, and it culminates with the political factors (or realities) which impinge on the social and economic structures. It is a history, therefore, without designated heroes and significant dates—though some concessions have been made with a political chronology. This is a deliberate act. The heroes are what the Cuban poet Nicolás Guillén would call *Juan Nadies*, or common folk, too numerous to mention; the significant dates are not specific years, but varying periods slipping almost imperceptibly by. Such has been the history of the Caribbean and the nature of change in that part of the world. The history of the Caribbean is the examination of fragments, which, like looking at a broken vase, still provides clues to the form, beauty, and value of the past.

The research and writing of this book leaves me greatly indebted to a number of institutions and individuals. The Research Institute for the Study of Man made available its magnificent collection on the contemporary Caribbean, and its director, Dr. Vera Rubin, combined a generosity of spirit, intellect, and charm which I found pleasantly contagious. The Latin American, Portuguese, and Spanish Division of the Library of Congress provided excellent facilities for more than two years, while Mrs. Georgette Dorn and Mr. Everett Larsen pampered me. The Johns Hopkins University Seminars provided a preliminary audience for some of the early chapters, and the keen verbal exchanges forced me to clarify some of the earlier thinking. Walter and Margret Bauer, Fernando and Françoise de Mateo, and Anne Perotin-Dumon all extended material kindnesses at a crucial moment. In addition, I derived much help from the following colleagues and friends: Margaret Crahan, Philip Curtin, Jack Greene, Barry Higman, Asunción Lavrin, and Johanna Mendelson. Edward Cox corrected my thinking on the Eastern Caribbean, and kindly allowed me access to his research and provided a quotation which he had transcribed from the British Public Record Office. Ingeborg Bauer Knight and Sheldon Meyer have been models of patience, tolerance, and understanding while making suggestions which I have tried to meet. I do remain, however, entirely responsible for all errors and shortcomings of this work.

The Caribbean

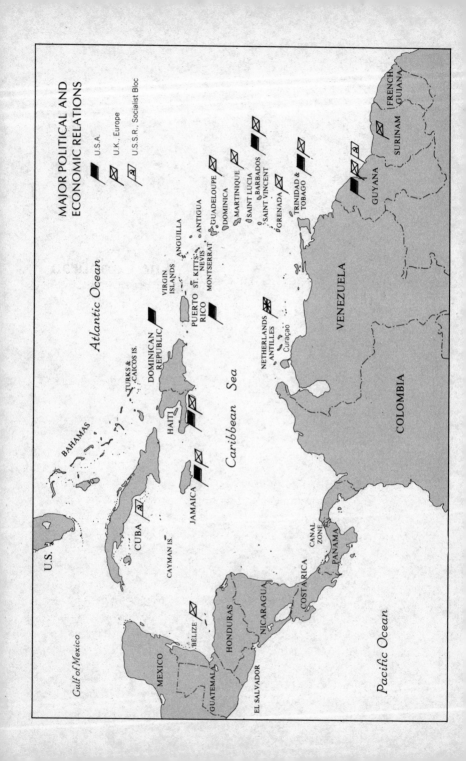

MAJOR POLITICAL AND
ECONOMIC RELATIONS

U.S.A.

U.K., Europe

U.S.S.R., Socialist Bloc

Chapter 1 • The Political Geography
of the Pre-Hispanic Caribbean

They very willingly traded everything they had. But they seemed to me a
people very short of everything.

Christopher Columbus,
Thursday, October 11, 1492

The physical geography has been, from pre-Hispanic times to the present, one of the dominant and inescapable influences on the pattern of Caribbean life and society. The thousands of islands vary in size, and stretch like an inclined backbone from the Florida peninsula to the slanted northern coastline of South America. These islands are the irregular, jagged breakers of the Caribbean Sea, the entrance to the Gulf of Mexico. Altogether they span an area from longitude 59 degrees west to longitude 85 degrees west, and range from roughly latitude 10 degrees north to latitude 25 degrees north—almost totally within the northern tropics, if one excludes the northern Bahama Islands. But the distances from island to island are not very great. Nor, with the possible exception of Cuba (more than 44,000 square miles) and Hispaniola (more than 27,000 square miles), are the islands very large. Some islands, and parts of the others, have steep, rough, and disconcertingly inhospitable terrains—as is the case in Dominica, Grenada, Montserrat, Guadeloupe, northern Hispaniola, eastern Jamaica, and southeastern Cuba. Some islands are flat, such as Barbados and Antigua; while central and western Cuba reveal broad vistas of gently undulating mountains punctuating gradually sloping plains. Some islands are precariously miniscule, such as those in the Grenadines, Anguilla, the Bahamas, and the Cayman islands. The larger, northern islands—Cuba, Jamaica, Haiti and the Dominican Republic, and Puerto Rico—form the Greater Antilles. The smaller, eastern islands form the Lesser Antilles. During the days of sailing ships, the more northerly ones were called the Leeward Islands, and the easterly ones, the Windward Islands, although for administrative purposes, quite a few have been transferred from one to the other jurisdiction, and the designations have continued to the present day.

The Caribbean islands all lie within an eminently salubrious environment, conducive to the growth of populations, and the development of complex societies. The islands had been inhabited for a very long time before the arrival of Columbus, although no firm date can be established for the first arrival of man.

In general the soils of the larger islands contain coral limestone pockets of varying fertility and sandy loams. The soils are easily cultivable once the dense tropical forest covers have been destroyed or removed. Rainfall is constant: adequate to abundant during the long rainy season from May to November, with quantities varying from about 30 inches on the leeward plains to approximately 200 inches in the forests of the windward mountains. Light showers infrequently moisten the dry, often hot "winter" months. Temperatures, which fluctuate between 70 degrees fahrenheit and 90 degrees fahrenheit throughout the year, combine with the rainfall to provide a long growing season and a pleasant harvest. The living can be easy for the acclimated and the natural beauty is most alluring.

Nevertheless the alluring natural beauty tends to obscure the accompanying physical hazards of life in the Caribbean: the frequent hurricanes, the diseases, the volcanoes and earthquakes, the limitations of physical size, the violent floods which often accompany the destructive hurricanes, and the insects make the area a difficult environment of tantalizing magnetism.

The difficulties and frustrations of perpetuating a cohesive and sophisticated society preceded the arrival of the Spanish explorers and conquerors of the late fifteenth century. The history recovered by persevering archaeological research supports some useful generalizations about the pre-Hispanic populations and the type of societies which they had fashioned when they were overtaken by the series of events beginning in 1492.

No reliable estimate exists for the indigenous population in 1492. None could have been made. Christopher Columbus, who gave as good a description of the early inhabitants as any other, was understandably vague or misleading on the numbers of the groups he met. Bartolomé de las Casas, who later gained considerable notoriety as the originator of the anti-Spanish "Black Legend," produced incredible figures which ought not to be taken seriously. The majority of the early first-hand reporters could not estimate populations. Crowds tended to look far larger than they were; and the relative inaccessibility of the interior precluded demographic description before the ravages of the early contact of Europeans and Americans had taken their toll.

The indigenous population of the Caribbean probably did not exceed three-quarters of a million, the great majority of whom lived on the island of Hispaniola. Such an estimate is debatable of course. But it seems highly unlikely that a larger population could have been supported by the community organizations that the first Europeans described. Moreover the process of immigration from the South American mainland was relatively recent, and no population explosion had taken place in the islands. Cuba, the most westerly of the islands, had about fifty thousand persons living there. Hispaniola, by virtue of its size and central location (therefore, probably of longer settlement and social development), might have had approximately half a million persons. Jamaica had several thousands, probably not exceeding twenty thousand. Barbados, Antigua, and some of the smaller islands were not permanently inhabited. Very few islands had the population concentrations found on the mainland.

Three different types of people comprised this relatively sparse population at the end of the fifteenth century: the Ciboney, or Guanahuatebey; the Taino Arawak; and the Carib, from whom the region and sea derive their name. These were the earliest societies in the Caribbean, and in some cases these people were the ancestors of the present population. They were not peoples without problems. Indeed some of their social problems were not different in nature from the problems of the later societies of the region. It is important that in 1500 they were trying to come to grips with their environment in many creative ways. In some respects they were succeeding; in others they were failing. But these early inhabitants present the baseline of understanding about the region and its societal genesis. They ought not to be neglected. The fact that we have yet to unearth more information about the indigenous inhabitants is no excuse to ignore them. For all people have a history. And while all history is not necessarily recorded in books, every history is recorded somehow, somewhere. Some people leave their history in their pottery and their paintings. Others in the statues, sculptures, tools, and buildings they make. This is their history; their peculiar blend of myth, custom, beliefs, and philosophy; their articulation of reality and the transcendental. We may not understand it all, but we ought to respect it, and seek diligently and unceasingly to comprehend it.

And so from archaeological evidence—often from negative criteria —we can partially reconstruct the societies and cultures of the past whose world was transformed by the accidental discovery of Christopher Columbus and the other peripatetic Europeans who came later to the New World.

The Ciboney were probably the oldest culture group in the islands. Ciboney sites have been found scattered throughout Cuba and the southwestern peninsula of Hispaniola. Columbus encountered some of these people when his expedition first touched the island. Unfortu-

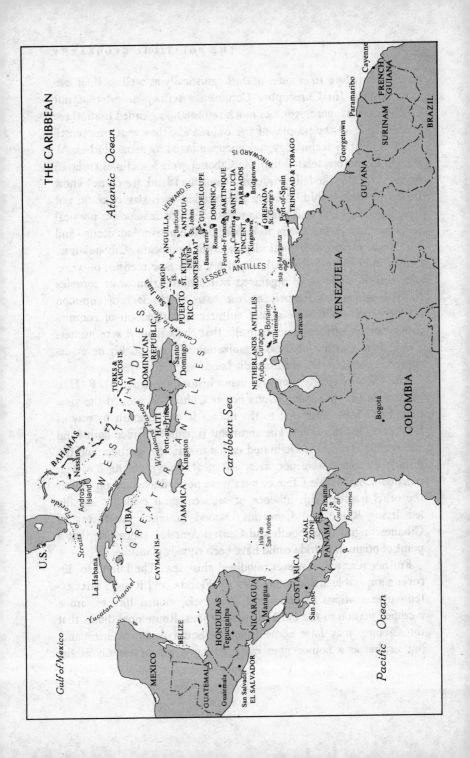

nately the failure to communicate linguistically as well as their evident poverty (in Christopher Columbus's terms) meant that not
much time was spent with, nor much information gleaned from, these
people. Like all the peoples of the out-islands, they were unsophisticated in military technology and unencumbered by many clothes. Although Columbus related that the Ciboney were sometimes enslaved
by the Arawaks, the fellow inhabitants of the island, we do not know
their true relationship. We can suggest that such slavery could not
have been the arduous relationship with a severe demand for physical
labor that the Spanish were to impose on the native Americans—and
which was extended dramatically by other Europeans. Ciboney middens already examined reveal no pottery, domestic utensils, or weapons, and no evidence of organized ritualistic religion or of complex
social organizations. Largely on the basis of the lack of common
artifacts used for the social and cultural reconstruction of communities, one hypothesis presents itself: that the Ciboney were hunters
and gatherers with a political organization which probably never developed beyond that of the nomadic band.

The Ciboney clearly present a major historical enigma. M. R. Harrington, in his 1921 study, *Cuba before Columbus*, posited the view
that the Ciboney migrated to the islands from the south by way of
the Lesser Antilles chain. The argument is plausible, since both wind
and current could have facilitated such a maritime migration, and the
distances covered were not, after all, great. One problem, however,
remains. Comparable Ciboney sites were never discovered on any of
the other islands. This absence of archaeological evidence initially
led Irving Rouse and Cornelius Osgood to reject the theory of
Ciboney origins from South and Central America, suggesting that a
point of origin in Florida could have been equally plausible.

Further research, however, modified this view. The failure to dis-
cover comparable artifacts anywhere in Florida, and Rouse's later extensive excavations in Haiti and Venezuela, guided him toward a
modified version of the old Harrington thesis. Rouse now thinks that
the Ciboney may have come from the South American mainland,
but neither as a homogenous migrant group, nor necessarily at the

same time. This position takes into account the geographical history of the area, too. For it is obvious that autonomous evolution of man is all but precluded because of the geological youth of the islands. They therefore had to be populated by a migrant people. This being so, the archaeological data from Hispaniola and Venezuela substantiate such a migration.

Irving Rouse, probably the most authoritative archaeologist of the Caribbean area, uses five steps to verify his theory of migrant peoples: 1) to identify the migrating unit as intrusive; 2) to trace the unit back to its original site or homeland; 3) to determine that the archaeological findings of the unit are contemporaneous: 4) to establish the existence of conditions favorable for migration; and 5) to demonstrate that some other hypothesis such as independent invention or diffusion of traits does not better fit the facts of the situation.

With the above formula it is easy to establish that the Ciboney must have been migrants by virtue of the impossibility of autonomous local evolution, which we have already suggested. The second stage, however, requires an assumption that the term Ciboney covers all the earlier arrivals of preagricultural peoples. Such an acceptance enables us to establish the connection and contemporaneity of the artifacts discovered both in Venezuela and Hispaniola. Migration could have been facilitated by favorable winds and currents, except during the months of November to March. During that season, the prevalence of the northeast trade winds would tend to inhibit, though not totally deter, maritime travel between the southern mainland and the larger Antillean islands.

Of course one accepts these hypotheses provisionally. The possibility—and high probability—remains that at irregular intervals Indians from the Central American mainland could have inadvertently made the passage between Yucatan and the islands where, if their numbers were insufficient and their culture not reinforced, they could have been absorbed into the local societies and the record of their arrival lost. To date there is no positive evidence of any culture impact from the northern part of the isthmus. No firm suggestion, therefore, can be made at this date of contact between North and Central

America and the Antilles during the early stages of the migration of man onto the islands.

Ciboney society was the most simple among the region's pre-Hispanic inhabitants. They were mere troglodytic bands with an unsophisticated artistic ability, despite the shell and stove designs found. They also apparently had no knowledge of ritualistic religion or the cassava culture which existed throughout the other islands and the South American continent. Nor had they developed a complex military technology to combat the intrusions of the later groups. Instead their military strategy involved simple wooden clubs and stones thrown by hand. They were not a militant society geared for warfare.

If the Ciboney remain largely obscured in the historical record, the other two groups, the Arawaks and the Caribs do not. Thanks to the meticulously kept journals of Christopher Columbus, quoted extensively by Bartolomé de las Casas, we have a considerable descriptive account of the Arawaks. Arawakan communities dotted the islands from the Bahamas in the north to the Venezuelan coastline, and they were by far the most numerous people in the region. Columbus picked up an interpreter in San Salvador who was useful all the way to Hispaniola, a reflection on the linguistic uniformity that existed. Arawaks, therefore, occupied all the larger islands of the Antilles— Cuba, which they shared with the Ciboney, Jamaica, Hispaniola, and Puerto Rico—as well as the Lesser Antilles which today comprise the Leeward and Windward chain, and the British and American Virgin Islands. Columbus wrote glowingly of the Arawaks on his first voyage:

"They very willingly traded everything they had. But they seemed to me a people short of everything.

All the men I saw were young. I did not see one over the age of thirty. They were all very well built with fine bodies and handsome faces. Their hair is coarse, almost like that of a horse's tail, and short; they wear it down over their eyebrows except for a few strands at the back, which they wear long and never cut. They are the color of the Canary Islanders, neither black nor white, and are heavily painted. Some of them paint themselves black, others white, or any color they can find. Some paint their faces, some their whole bodies, some only their eyes, some only the nose. They do not carry arms, nor know them. For when I showed them swords, they took them by the edge and cut themselves out of ignorance. They have no iron. Their spears are made of cane. Some, instead of an iron tip have a fish's tooth and others have points of different kinds. They are fairly tall on the whole, with fine limbs and good proportions. I saw some who had the scar from wounds on their bodies and I asked them by signs how they got these and they indicated to me that people came from other islands near by who tried to capture them and they defended themselves. I supposed, and still suppose, that they come from the mainland to capture them for slaves. They should be good servants, and very intelligent, for I have observed that they soon repeat anything that is said to them, and I believe that they would easily be made Christians, for they appeared to me to have no religion. God willing, when I make my departure I will bring half a dozen back to their Majesties so that they can learn to speak. I saw no animals of any kind on this island except parrots.

The Log Books of Columbus, despite their occasional glaring inaccuracies, provide the basis for a closer look at the structure of the Taino Arawak communities that existed in the region at the end of the fifteenth century. Arawakan culture can also be reconstructed and evaluated by ethnographic and archaeological methods, since both the language and the surviving artifacts provide a solid basis for research. Our knowledge and understanding of Arawakan culture is far more complete than it is for the other two groups in the Caribbean at that time.

Julian Steward describes the Arawaks' society as composed of theocratic chiefdoms similar to those found from eastern Bolivia northward through Colombia and Venezuela to the interior of northern Brazil. The Taino Arawak formed one of a variegated group of such peoples, similar in culture though linguistically diverse, which inhabited the region. Unlike their ancestors on the mainland—groups such as the Chibcha, Warao, Yanomamö, Caracas, Palenque, Caquetio, or the Jirajara of the Colombia-Venezuela tropical forest belt—the island Arawaks were not a militaristic people but a hierarchically structured society of manioc-producing agriculturalists.

When Columbus wrote that the people of the Bahamas had "no religion" [*que me pareció que ninguna secta tenían*], he merely meant that the Arawaks were not Christians. But they did have a highly organized religion based on a hierarchy of gods and men. Their religious spirits were called *zemis*, and were represented by icons of wood, stone, bones, or even human remains. Moreover each individual had a pantheon of *zemis*, and the quantity reflected the elevated social position of the possessor. *Zemi* icons resembled grotesque anthropomorphic figures, often with exaggerated sex organs, presumably fashioned according to the supernatural dictates of the owner.

Village chiefs, who varied in power and influence depending on the size of the village community, had the greatest number of *zemis*, and it seems thtat these *zemis* were publicly venerated. The public ball courts found in Cuba and Hispaniola suggest a ceremonial function. But nowhere in the Caribbean did the priest-temple-idol cult develop the aggressive militarism and the proselytizing fervor that characterized that of the mainland empires. Indeed the island Arawaks seem to have been one of the least aggressive peoples in the Americas. The exact relationship between the chiefs, whom Columbus frequently referred to as "kings" (as the Europeans were wont to call all political leaders whom they encountered on their initial voyage into the wider world), and the religious life of the community has never been clearly established. Certainly the chiefs had great power within their communities. Yet the simplicity of their social relations and the openness which they showed to the Spanish brought not reciprocal kindness but deception—and eventually death and annihilation. Columbus was greatly impressed by Arawakan magnanimity when he described how the Arawaks of Hispaniola helped him and his men after the shipwreck of December 24, 1492:

> On hearing the news the king wept, showing great sorrow at our disaster. Then he sent all the inhabitants of the village out to the ship in many large canoes. Thus we began to unload her and in a very short time we had cleared the decks. Such was the help that this king gave us. After this, he himself, with his brothers and relations, did everything they could both in the ship and on

shore to arrange for our comfort. And from time to time he sent various of his relatives to implore me not to grieve, for he would give me everything he had.

I assure your Highness that nowhere in Castille would one receive such kindness or anything like it. He had all our possessions brought together near his palace and kept there until some houses had been emptied to receive them. He appointed armed men to guard them, and made them watch over them right through the night. And he and everyone else in the land wept for our misfortune as if greatly concerned by it. They were so affectionate and have so little greed and are in all ways so amenable that I assure your Highness that there is in my opinion no better people and no better land in all the world. They love their neighbors as themselves and their way of speaking is the sweetest in the world, always gentle and smiling. Both men and women go naked as their mothers bore them; but your Highness must believe me when I say that their behavior to one another is very good and their king keeps marvelous state, yet with a certain kind of modesty that is a pleasure to behold, as is everything else here.

Arawakan settlements, as we have indicated, ranged from single units of many families to towns of one thousand houses, and probably three to four thousand persons. The village houses were arranged around the ball courts, and the straw-roofed adobe hut of the chief, called a *bohío*. Settlements seemed to be in places favorable for agriculture—on the leeward side of the mountains, and somewhat inland. The villagers produced two crops per year of potatoes, sweet cassava (manioc), peanuts, peppers, beans, and arrowroots. Maize was unimportant as a staple food, but their dietary supplement included coneys, agouti, lizards, spiders, and a variety of insects and reptiles. Chiefs reserved the right to eat certain types of iguanas and agouti. The Arawaks had no domesticated animals except a type of mute dog (which was sometimes eaten).

In addition to agriculture, which was the main economic activity, the Arawaks also fished with nets, hooks, spears, and storage pens. If fishing was secondary to crop cultivation, this was not from any dearth of fish in the surrounding seas, as Julian Steward and Louis Faron suggest. Not only are Caribbean waters quite shallow in some places—and well-known fishing banks still survive around the Bahamas, Cuba, Jamaica, and Hispaniola—but fish are plentiful throughout the region. What appears more probable is the subordination of fishing to the successful pursuit of agriculture. Moreover the society was adequately maintained by its agriculture, and considered fishing a form of "luxury" undertaking, providing nutritional balance and variety.

The political unit varied considerably in the Caribbean. A chiefdom, over which ruled a *cacique*, consisted of villages or a single village of families. In 1500 Hispaniola had six chiefdoms for its estimated population of 500,000 inhabitants, while Puerto Rico had eighteen for its estimated population of 45,000. Apparently the chiefs had considerable authority and prestige but no real political power—and political competition was quite unimportant among these peaceful people. Chiefs officiated over village rites and ceremonies. They led the singing, dancing, and festivities in return for the privileges of special houses, superordinate *zemis*, elaborate titles of address, distinctively large canoes, specially prepared food, and colorful dress and body ornamentation. But as a political or economic elite the *caciques* were chronically weak. They could requisition men and food for military enterprises. They settled intervillage disputes and organized communal work. But they had no special training, no special skills which could establish them as a cohesive, self-perpetuating elite with a distinctive *esprit de corps*. Above all the chiefs received no tribute which amounted to accumulated wealth. The entire political structure was inadequate to mobilize resistance to the constant marauding pressure of the Carib invasions originating in the eastern chain of islands. All in all the social structure contained some weaknesses which had to be modified if the type of society were to survive—and these structural weaknesses preceded the advent of the Spanish and other Europeans.

Matrilineal inheritance characterized Arawakan society. Bride price, bride service, and polygamy were social customs. Postmarital residence was patrilocal. In the absence of an heir of the female line of a chief, succession could be by one's son or by female relatives. Likewise heirs of chiefs who showed no promise for leadership were rejected in preference for a locally elected member of the common people. Arawakan society, therefore, had its internal flexibility and mobility.

Apart from the ceremonial ball courts, the other main cultural artifacts were pottery and gourds, which show some progressive stylization and sophistication, particularly from the larger communities of Cuba and Hispaniola. In general the Antillean pottery also bears strong resemblances to that found in northeast Venezuela. The men of Gonaive Island had some regional reputation for their woodwork, while the men on Hispaniola demonstrated some minor metalurgical skills. But from the European point of view, as reflected in the Columbus journals, the Arawaks were "a people short of everything."

"A people short of everything" was patently a European description reflecting differences of culture and material wealth. Antillean society appears to have been self-sufficient in its simple needs. Luxuries were few, the parasitical elite class was small, and the food base was perfectly adequate to support the existing population. Carl Sauer concludes that "in productivity the West Indian native economy cannot be rated as inferior." It is not surprising, therefore, that trade between the islands, or with the mainland, was limited, and was restricted to bartering pottery for ornamental gold. In any case the economic and commercial trading aspects of Antillean society are imperfectly developed in the literature about these communities. Assumptions of interisland or island-mainland trade derive mainly from the almost uniform response of the Arawaks to the persistent Spanish queries about the source of the gold that they wore on their bodies. They all indicated that it came from the east. But this is a highly inadequate basis for any assumption of regular trade as we understand the term.

The rapid disappearance of the Arawakan population during the first century of Spanish colonization in the Caribbean does not mean that this group failed to have any impact on the future of the area. In the first place it is a fair assumption that a goodly number of early Spanish settlers mated with the Arawakan women and procreated. Some demographic impact must have taken place. Such miscegena-

tional offspring could quite easily have been absorbed into the main-
stream of Spanish colonial society in the same way that they were
accepted and absorbed on the mainland. Secondly the Indians taught
the Spanish about herbs, food crops, and housing. Tobacco, potatoes,
peanuts, manioc, maize, pumpkins, beans, and other crops were cultivated extensively by the Spanish in addition to the crops and animals
they brought from Spain. Finally the Arawaks made an indelible im-
print on Spanish speech, with the additions of nouns which remain a
part of the language of Castille: words such as *bohío, guagua, cacique,
caney, conuco, guajiro, calpulli.* The failure to survive as a viable sociopolitical entity, therefore, cannot be accepted as valid grounds for the
omission of the Arawaks from historical accounts of the evolution of
the Caribbean societies. Like the unseen force of yeast in dough, the
Arawaks played some role in the Spanish adjustment to the New
World, and consequently to the development of later societies there.

The Caribs comprised the third immigrant group in the Caribbean
islands. Of these fierce, proud, and dignified people, much has been
written, but they are probably no more known than the Arawaks—
and slightly better known than the simple Ciboney (Guanahuatebey).
Although the Caribs survived the Arawaks (or rather, because the
Caribs survived better than the Arawaks), they occasioned a wilder,
more unsympathetic press. Indeed, as Richard B. Moore and William
Sturtevant have shown, much of the writing on the Caribs is replete
with gross inaccuracies or patent contradictions. And Christopher
Columbus began it all.

Hopelessly confused in his geographical direction, firmly convinced
that he was somewhere near the outskirts of China, and quite unfamiliar with the local languages, Columbus gave the names Carib,
Caribbean Sea and islands, and cannibals to the area and its peoples.
Even before he met them, Columbus had been predisposed against
the Caribs by the charges made by the Arawak leader on Hispaniola.
Hernando Colon, son of the famous discoverer, described how the
Arawaks maligned their neighboring rivals residing in the eastern islands, the Caribs, while Columbus was temporarily shipwrecked off
the coast of Hispaniola on or about December 26, 1492:

He then prepared to go ashore, inviting the Admiral to a feast of sweet potatoes and yucca, which are the principal foods, and giving him some masks with eyes and large ears of gold and other beautiful objects which they wore around their necks. He then complained about the Caribs, who captured his people and took them away to be eaten, but he was greatly cheered when the Admiral comforted him by showing him our weapons and promising to defend him with them.

From that day on every reference to the Caribs made by Columbus accused them of eating humans; the connection between cannibal and Carib had been made.

The Caribs were the latest of the three migrant groups to enter the island chain. Their society was from all the early accounts highly mobile. By 1500 they had expelled or incorporated all the Arawakan communities of the eastern Caribbean islands and dominated the region. Perhaps because of their recent occupation their social organization was less complex than that of the Arawaks. When they settled down they selected sites that facilitated both agriculture and fishing. This dual interest in fishing and sedentary agriculture falls within the classification of the Tropical Forest peoples made by Julian Steward and Louis Faron. Nevertheless military strategy might have been one of the determinants of settlement sites. Irving Rouse describes them as living on elevated land to the windward slopes of the mountains near running water. It is, of course, difficult to say why these selections were made: the choices might have been accidental or they might have been an effort to survive the ravages of nature in that hostile part of the world. No grander scheme may have been involved.

Carib houses tended to be small, wooden-framed structures with oval or rectangular thatched roofs, surrounding a central plaza with a communal fireplace. Unlike the Arawaks, the Carib villages had no ceremonial ball courts. Instead the fireplace served the functions of ceremonial center and social gathering place. Household furniture, such as it was, closely resembled that of the Arawaks: small wooden tables, *metates*, griddles, stools, hammocks, gourds, and pottery. The diet, too, remained similar to that of the Arawaks: fish, lizards, crabs, agouti, corn, sweet potatoes, yams, beans and peppers. Men and women engaged in canoe making, beer brewing, basket making, and weaving.

Given the information we have for the Caribs and the Arawaks, it appears that both societies were closely affiliated culturally. Indeed Carib island society recruited its female members from the neighboring Arawaks. This practice must have had tremendous repercussions on the structure of their society, since the socialization of the mixed offspring within the family would have reflected strong Arawak customs and some degree of bilingual and bicultural skills on the part of the women. Moreover the predominance of Arawakan women probably explains the presence of Arawak artifacts in Carib middens.

Further details on Carib social organization, however, are difficult to ascertain. The records and reports of early observers make no mention of inheritance practices, kinship relations, or social ranking and economic organization beyond a few elementary points: land was communally held; canoes and ornaments were personal property; and tobacco served as currency.

The social and political organization of Carib society reflected both their military inclination and their immigrant status. Villages were small and comprised members of an extended family. The leader of the village, often the head of the family, supervised the food-gathering activities, principally fishing and cultivation. He also settled internal disputes and served in a military group of the most experienced and accomplished in that activity, which led the raids on surrounding groups. Raiding, while carefully planned, was an ad hoc activity.

Warfare was the most serious group activity of Carib males, and they had a reputation as the premier fighting force of all the island peoples before the arrival of the Spanish. Their arsenal contained bows, poisoned arrows, javelins, and clubs. Huge war canoes, made from the trunk of one tree, capable of carrying more than one hundred men, made their escapades a threat to the peaceful Arawaks. A successful raid on an Arawak island produced women and children who were captured and taken away to be slaves. Arawak men were killed and sometimes ritualistically cooked and eaten. This ritualistic

eating of the male members of the attacked led to the charges of cannibalism. Less certain, however, is whether the Caribs considered human flesh a staple food item.

Carib religion lacked the elaborate ritual of the Arawak or of the
mainland civilizations. They had no *zemis*. Each Carib had a personal deity which had many representative forms, and to which he
occasionally offered some cassava. Good and evil spirits battled constantly not only within his body but everywhere in nature, and the
society supported *shamans* who attempted to resolve the conflicts of
the spirits on behalf of one or the other.

The differences between Caribs and Arawaks—as among all three
groups of island inhabitants before the arrival of the Spanish—were
differences of degree rather than kind. The Ciboney-Guanahuatebey
had almost been absorbed by the Arawaks; the Arawaks had been
partially expelled and partially incorporated by the Caribs; and the
Caribs must have been undergoing a severe transformation as their
migration became increasingly successful, and the society became
increasingly influenced by the captured Arawakan women. Above all,
the relative lateness of Carib arrival in the islands did not give them
sufficient time to crystallize their social forms and customs. And by
the time that we have detailed ethnographic accounts of these people
by the French in the seventeenth and eighteenth centuries, they had
already been radically acculturated to the reality of European influences.

All the Caribbean peoples were undergoing critical internal change
when the Spanish arrived. Arawakan society, despite its aesthetic
achievements and complex social structure, could not defend itself
adequately against the invading Caribs. But the Arawaks did not simply surrender to the Carib invaders. Some Arawakan communities of
the eastern frontier which were more prone to attacks began to make
adjustments to the new peril. They abandoned their traditional pacific inclinations, and, rather than respond to the Carib aggression
with evasions, made weapons similar to those of their attackers and
fought back. Whether this particular kind of response would have
been more generalized, and whether such response on a general scale

would have averted the Carib domination of the Caribbean, no one can say. But it is interesting to speculate what such Carib domination would have produced. For it would have been more difficult for the Spanish to subordinate an organized, experienced military elite. Nevertheless subordination to the Spanish was inevitable given the differences in technology. But the Caribbean would have had a slightly different historical course in the colonial period. For diseases were, perhaps, the most potent weapons in the Spanish arsenal, and the ability of the Caribs to survive Spanish colonization is closely related to the relative inaccessibility of those people on the fringes of the area to which the Spanish directed their attention.

It is difficult to contemplate the nature of the society which would have emerged had the Spanish delayed their entry into the Caribbean. Carib society, as we have noted before, was also undergoing significant change. J. A. Bullbrook deduces from his archaeological work in Trinidad that the Caribs there had apparently forsaken their "cannibalism" and become sedentary farmers, fishermen, and gatherers. Bullbrook's suggestion derives from the failure to find human bones or spears in the excavated middens. But if the Caribs never ate members of their own community—or better, if such eating was merely ritualistic—then the absence is quite easily explained. Trinidad lay too far to the south and the east of the frontier for the Caribs to reinforce their communities by plunder and pillage. Instead they reverted to the habits and customs of the peoples of the Tropical Forest from where they originated, supporting themselves by fishing and agriculture and modifying their customs to conform with the female branch of their society.

Carib survival in the eastern Caribbean, we have also implied, stemmed from fortuitous circumstances, not from the effective challenge which they represented to the Spanish invaders. The Caribs, after all, were no more hostile than the Aztecs and the Incas of the Mexican and Peruvian highlands, who eventually succumbed to the men on horseback, with their cannons and shields and unrelenting zeal and self-confidence. The Caribs survived for a number of reasons. They inhabited the smaller peripheral islands, and the limited human resources of the Spanish precluded total colonization of the islands and the mainland. The islands themselves lay off to windward, outside the main direction of sailing ships—and outside the main interest of the Spanish after the discovery of gold and silver on the mainland converted Mexico and Peru into veritable meccas for the Spanish. So the smaller islands lost what importance they might have offered at the outset as potential settlement bases for the European intrusion into the Americas.

By the time the English and French arrived, more than a century after the Spanish establishment of its American empire, the Caribs had undergone vast internal social changes, making it difficult to differentiate between the truly indigenous and the creative adaptations from the Europeans. Certainly the Caribs actively borrowed from their new neighbors. The most marked innovations occurred in the technology of naval transportation. Canoe sizes increased, for the Caribs no longer restricted size to the trunk of one tree. Sails were incorporated, fashioned from plaited palm leaves or cotton cloths—a clear imitation of the Europeans. But the military and technological superiority of the Spanish restricted the transferral of these innovations to the eastern islands. Carib society, therefore, became more sedentary than its natural predisposition warranted, and the Caribs began farming the crops imported by the Spanish—sugar cane, oranges, and bananas—and herding the cattle, goats, and hogs introduced by the Europeans. Still the Caribs remained militaristic enough to provide great nuisance value to the colonization efforts of the other European powers in the outer islands during the seventeenth and eighteenth centuries.

But the pre-Hispanic peoples as a group were the first victims of the peculiar characteristics of the Caribbean, of crisis and transition. The physical geography of the islands conditioned their society and their culture as it would those who succeeded them. Responding to external forces, these island peoples have been especially vulnerable to influences from the outside, and their society has been more a reflection of eclectic adaption than original creation. Peopled from the mainland, the region later became the center of European political, economic, and social attention, and the receiving zone of the largest proportion of involuntarily emigrated Africans. The cycle of influence would turn to the American mainland again, but the pattern of crisis and transition remained an integral aspect of Caribbean social development. For the original inhabitants, however, the arrival of the three caravels from Spain in 1492 meant inexorable doom.

Chapter 2 • Settlements and Colonies

The Indians [shall] live in community with the Christians of the island and go among them, by which means they will help each other to cultivate, settle, and reap the fruits of the island, and extract the gold which may be there, and bring profit to my kingdom and subjects.

Queen Isabella to Nicolás Ovando,
December 20, 1503

The first intrusion into the complacent indigenous tranquillity of the Caribbean came from the restless, bellicose Spanish. Driven by the internal effervescence and the centrifugal forces which were then engrossing western Europe, the Spanish set out to establish a trading post empire patterned closely after the Portuguese model. The four voyages of Christopher Columbus fortuitously discovered a whole New World, and set in motion a chain of events whose profound consequences gave new directions to the histories of Europe, Africa, America, and Asia.

But the lands and the people discovered by Columbus on the dispersed Caribbean islands had neither the commodities nor the in-

clination to trade in ways to which the Europeans were accustomed.
For King Ferdinand and Queen Isabella the idea of trade quickly
faded. If wealth were to be derived from the overseas empire, it would
be wrung from the inhabitants or produced by the directed industry
of Spanish colonists. The first Spanish plans, prognosticated on the
error that the Caribbean was an Asian sea, lasted seven years. In those
seven years Columbus had made three voyages, discovered the paths
to the mainland, started a settlement on Hispaniola, and created a
viable beachhead for later Spanish-American activity. An inept ad-
ministrator and an incurable romantic, Columbus produced neither
riches nor peace in the New World. Queen Isabella, despite earlier
promises, replaced him with the firm Francisco de Bobadilla in May
1499; and in 1502 she sent Nicolás de Ovando with a motley group
of about twenty-five hundred to reinforce the Spanish hold on Hispaniola and the Indies. The arrival of Ovando marked the first turning point in the history of the Spanish Caribbean. Semiprivate entre-
preneurship, which brought great rewards to the Portuguese, gave
way to a selected, coordinated, and highly centralized policy of immigration and colonization. The theory and hopes of successful trading posts yielded to the reality of settlement. The *reconquista* moved
to America.

After 1502 Spanish governors went out to the Caribbean—and later
viceroys went to the mainland. These governors received their orders
from Spain, and while they retained, of necessity, the flexibility of
nonobedience common to all peripheral bureaucrats, they nevertheless were responsible first to the *Casa de Contratación,* and then to
the Council of the Indies. The original instructions given to Ovando,
and repeated frequently afterwards, included prohibitions against the
admission to the colonies of Moors, Jews, converts to Roman Catholicism of either group, Protestants from northwestern Europe, and
gypsies of any variety. The Spanish colonies were designed to be orthodox and unified in religion, and Castilian and Spanish in culture and
nationality. Castilian exclusiveness, however, was a fiasco from the
beginning. Neither the Spanish Crown nor the colonial governors
could prevent converted Catholics from going out to the Indies, and

after the unification of the crowns of Spain and Portugal in 1580 an increasing number of Jews moved across to Spanish America and the Caribbean from the Portuguese imperial possessions.

Royal government did not prevent the wandering of free-lance explorers in the Americas. But it indicated an end to the linear expansion of feudal powers from Spain to the Americas. No other individual ever got the power originally conceded to Christopher Columbus—although the Cortés grant came close—and all subsequent explorers and conquerors felt the proximity of the Spanish colonial administration. Hispaniola was not only a Spanish colony, it was also the private domain of the Castilian monarchs. Hispaniola—and later Cuba and Puerto Rico—became important recruitment bases for the expeditions to *tierra firme*. The islands might have been, like the metropolis itself, poor in people. Yet in a short time they provided an abundance of familiar Castilian animals and local and imported fruit —horses, mules, cattle, pigs, sheep, goats, figs, maize, melons, oranges, yucca (the local manioc), peppers, pomegranates, sugar cane—in excess of that available in the mother country.

Until 1509 Santo Domingo—or as the Spanish then preferred to call it, Española or Hispaniola—remained the focus of Spanish interest and their only true settlement in the Americas. There the native pre-Hispanic population had been pacified in a long campaign during the summer and autumn of 1503, in which Ovando, Diego Velasquez, Juan de Esquivel, and Ponce de León exercised the unrestrained barbarity which the three were to extend to Cuba, Jamaica, Puerto Rico, and Florida. Local Indian leaders were executed, and the remaining adults distributed in *encomienda* grants among the conquering Spanish warriors.

The pacification of Española undoubtedly diminished the prospect of further Indian uprisings, but it also undermined the agricultural productive capacity of the local inhabitants and considerably reduced the available population liable for distribution in *encomiendas*. Nevertheless the Spanish were determined to settle, as they had previously in the reconquered Moorish lands in the south of the peninsula. They therefore established fifteen towns strategically located along-

side, or near, both the preexisting Indian pueblos and the newly discovered gold mines. Of the fifteen towns, ten—Santo Domingo, Azua,
San Juan de la Maguana, Buenaventura, Salvaleon, Santa Cruz,
Bonao, Concepción de la Vega, Santiago, and Puerto de Plata—were
founded in the eastern part of the island, in what comprises nowadays
the national state of Santo Domingo. The other five were west of the
Neiba river, carved from the former Indian territories of Bainoa and
Guacayarima, and today corresponding roughly to Haiti: Puerto Real
on the site of Cap Haïtien; Lares de Guahaba, north of Gonaïves;
Verapaz just north of Port-au-Prince; Salvatierra de la Sabana near
Les Cayes; and Villanueva de Yaquimo near Jacmel. These fifteen
towns got their coat of arms in 1508.

Many names, later to become famous in the annals of sixteenth-
century Spanish expansion, were associated with some of these early
towns established by Ovando. Alonzo de Ojeda, who came out on the
second voyage of Columbus, explored the Guianan and Venezuelan
coast, discovered the pearl fisheries at Margarita, and retired to
Villanueva to engage in the dyewood trade. Vasco Nuñez de Balboa,
the first European to view the Pacific from the Isthmus of Darien,
was a farmer in Salvatierra, as was Diego Velázquez, the conquistador
of Cuba. Ponce de León settled in Santa Cruz along with the curious
encomendero Bartolomé de las Casas. The former discovered Puerto
Rico and later lost his life in Florida. The latter wandered about the
Caribbean, then returned to Spain to be "Protector of the Indians,"
and gadfly in the Court of Charles V. Hernán Cortés and Francisco
Pizarro lived in Azua, and Juan de Esquivel, the explorer of Jamaica,
came from Salvaleon de Higuey.

By 1508, according to Troy Floyd, Española had a population of
approximately twelve thousand Spaniards, and its economic base had
been stretched to the limit. The rule of Ovando, then drawing to a
close, had been generally peaceful and attractively prosperous. The
preceding years represented the acme of Caribbean prosperity prior to
the advent of the sugar industry. But already the Hispanicism of the
Caribbean had begun to manifest itself.

The basis of the economy so successfully developed by the able, if severely harsh, Ovando revolved around mining and agriculture. Mining centered upon the towns of Santiago, Concepción de la Vega, Bonoa, and Buenaventura. The labor as well as the foodstuffs, hides, and other accessories came from the surrounding towns, Puerto de Plata, Santa Cruz, and Salvaleon de Higuey on the north coast, Azua and Santo Domingo on the south coast, and San Juan de la Maguana in the extremely fertile valley of the Yaque del Sur river. The eastern port towns also supplied the mines by transshipping through the nearby ports of Santo Domingo—in 1509 a rather bustling city—Puerto de Plata, and Santa Cruz. The Spanish introduced their animals, which multiplied so rapidly and roamed so freely that they soon became pests, greatly outnumbering the population, and often destroying the cultivated *conucos* of the Indians and Spanish. Wild pigs took over the forests, and cattle and horses dominated the plains in such profusion that pioneers found abundant meat in the interior, as did the later runaway slaves. Indeed it was the ready availability of these animals that gave rise to the transient, transfrontier society of buccaneers during the late sixteenth and seventeenth centuries. The most abundant food crop was the yucca, or cassava, a high-yielding, surface-feeding pre-Hispanic tuber. Wheat, one of the few imports that failed to prosper in the tropics, was scarce, so cassava bread rapidly became the standard fare for settled colonists or transient sailors.

The pattern of the society existing in 1509 in Española also presaged the future for Spanish colonization in the New World. At the top in social esteem and in political power wielded through the village councils were the arrogant Spanish settlers. These were a variegated group, dominated by Andalucians. Peter Boyd-Bowman calculates that 60 percent of the colonists leaving officially for the Spanish Indies originated in Seville, with a substantial proportion of the remainder coming from the infertile, semidesert, and relatively unproductive Extremadura region. Most provinces of Spain had representatives among these early emigrants, although very few came from Galicia, Navarra, Aragón, Cataluña, Valencia, Baleares, Murcia, the Canary Islands, or the new zones created from the recently reconquered kingdom of Granada. At the same time, despite the royal prohibitions, more than 140 foreigners obtained legal permits, including 44 Portuguese and 61 Italians. Contrary to popular belief, only a few of these immigrants were criminals. A substantial number were decent, honest, hardworking individuals who went out to seek a fortune or to find a better life. Many of these colonists distinguished themselves as leaders in the early history of the Caribbean, although most, in common with others of their class, were illiterate. But literacy was not a prerequisite for political office, upward social mobility, or the pursuit of wealth. The Spanish men who ventured to the Indies represented a cross section of their metropolitan society and a wide range of the medieval motivations for territorial expansion and military strife.

Until 1519 the Spanish Caribbean tried desperately to assume the sociopolitical profile of a new Andalucian territory. Apart from the town councils, where the colonial *vecinos* were represented and were administratively equal to any other mainland Spanish town, the *encomienda* closely approximated its Iberian antecedent.

The Spanish Church became prominent during the period of Ovando's governorship in Santo Domingo, and at least seventy-eight priests—mainly Franciscans and Dominicans—sailed to the Indies during the first two decades. And like the rest of the immigrants, these priests also represented all the regions of Spain. Of the first seventy-eight in the *católogo de pasajeros*, Boyd-Bowman identified the following regional origins: twenty-two from Andalucia, seventeen from Old Castile, eight from New Castile, twelve from Extremadura, nine from León, one each from Catalonia and the Basque region, and six non-Spaniards.

The early migration was a microcosm of Spanish society transplanted to the Antilles. Entire families moved with wives, children, and servants following the men to maintain the structure and organization of the expansion taking place since the middle of the fourteenth century on the southern Iberian frontier.

But in the Antilles there was a major difference. The cultural gap between Spanish and Arawak never approximated that between the Spanish and the Moors. The symbiotic relationship attempted by the

Spanish assumed a dominance to which the indigenous technology was grossly inferior. The Spanish relatively quickly and easily reorganized the Indian communities, divided the families into *encomienda* grants of perpetual servitude, and exacted tribute in gold, labor, and food supplies. This reorganization as well as the tributary exactions facilitated the rapid extermination of the local population.

For the Spanish the ruthless efficiency of Ovando facilitated the economic success of the colony. For the Indians it was an unmitigated disaster. The large number of Spanish arrivals strained to the breaking point the productive capacity of the indigenous *conucos*. The greater demand for food could not be satisfied under the circumstances. The discovery of gold in Hispaniola led to demands for Indians to work in the mines and placers, withdrawing an ever increasing number of individuals from the cultivation of food crops—an activity the new arrivals seemed to spurn. In addition the growing number of uncontrolled, semiferal animals frequently destroyed the fields of food crops. Above all the stipulations that required the Indians to work for periods of eight consecutive months in the mines and placers did not leave sufficient time for the proper pursuit of agricultural practices designed to increase the available supply of food. The Spanish could not expect large numbers of workers and a consistently high yield of cassava and yams, however ideal such a situation would have been. Of course it is possible that Indians willfully neglected their *conucos* in revengeful anticipation of Spanish discouragement and eventual withdrawal from the island. If so they unwittingly contributed to their own extermination. For it was the Indians rather than the Spanish who proved more vulnerable to the ravages of disease, debilitation, and scarcity in the first two decades of the Conquest.

As Ovando prepared to surrender his mandate in 1509, he might have been proud of his accomplishments on Española. His had been a term of unprecedented and perhaps unequalled success. He had replaced chaos with order, completed the subjugation of the entire island, established fifteen permanent towns, boosted the production of gold, dyewood, and local provisions, and converted Columbus's failing, sporadic attempts to colonize into a permanent settlement.

Nevertheless the colony had reached a critical turning point. The once populous regions had become sparse. The large numbers of Indians which Diego Columbus presumably counted, and Bartolomé de las Casas insisted with characteristic hyperbole to be "more than 3,000,000 Indians on the whole island," had largely disappeared. The *encomienda* yields started to decline, as did the gold output of the mines. Food, apart from meat, became scarce, although probably not as scarce as labor. Both to local Spanish settlers and to the Spanish King Ferdinand—appointed regent of the Indies by Isabella on her deathbed in 1504—the situation was alarming and demanded drastic action. The immediate solutions lay in finding new Indians to work on Española, diminishing the size of the local Spanish population, or getting the Spanish to work to maintain themselves. The first two solutions were adopted. There is no evidence that the third received either serious consideration or sustained application.

Though the enslavement of the Indians of the neighboring islands had always occurred, it had never been pursued as a policy of state. Isabella had approved it with reservations, carefully insisting that only the most warlike and recalcitrant Indians should be enslaved. To Isabella the Indians were her vassals. To Ferdinand they were the indispensable link with public and private wealth. If the decline of the local populations jeopardized the continued economic vitality of overseas kingdoms, then there could be no other alternative than to introduce new Indians. These new Indians would only come as unwilling slaves. Of course Ovando, in proposing the general enslavement of the Indians, used two arguments of considerable weight with his king. He reasoned that the other islands were "useless," since they had no known deposits of gold; and that the enslavement of such Indians facilitated their conversion to Roman Catholicism. The dichotomous goals of gold and God were reconciled in slavery, and the decimation of the local population which had taken place in Española spread throughout the Caribbean from the Bahamas to Trinidad.

The socioeconomic salvation of Española could not be accomplished only by the introduction of servile Indians. The resident Spanish population had to be reduced. And so began the restlessness which has become a fixture of colonial society in the Caribbean to the present day, as the Spanish settlers moved on to the neighboring islands. Yet in so doing, the *vecinos* of Española were merely giving impetus to the exploration continuously going on since Christopher Columbus accidentally happened into the Caribbean Sea. By 1509 the Spanish-American center of gravity was leaving Española.

In rapid succession the Spaniards spread far afield in the Caribbean. Juan Ponce de León went to Puerto Rico in 1508 and quickly organized the Indians into gold miners, placing them in *encomienda* to the *vecinos* of the two towns he founded: San Juan de Puerto Rico on the northeast coast and San Germán on the west coast near the Mona passage. Puerto Rico produced sufficient gold to make Ponce de León one of the richest men in the Americas within a year. But the demographic price was high, for the Indians died even more rapidly than in Española. Ponce de León, rich and restless, moved on to Florida, where the local Indians did unto him as he had previously done to so many in Española and Puerto Rico.

In 1509 Nicolás de Ovando and Diego Columbus organized slave-raiding expeditions to the Lucayan Islands, which the English later called the Bahamas. The population was easily "pacified" and quickly decimated. The same year Juan de Esquivel began the reduction of Jamaica, the third largest island in the Caribbean chain. Jamaica, like the Lucayas, produced no gold, but possessed an adequate supply of Indians, who were transported to Española and sold as slaves or indented into serfdom. A small number of Spanish settlers moved to Jamaica and started a grazing economy on the coastal plains which ultimately produced the feral herds the English attackers so casually destroyed after 1655.

By 1511 Spanish expansion reached Florida and Cuba. In the latter, Diego Velázquez renewed his military confrontation with the Indian warrior Hatuey, who had fled from western Española. Having defeated Hatuey, Velázquez, surrounded by some familiar faces like Pánfilo Narváez, Hernán Cortés, and Bartolomé de las Casas, proceeded to establish seven towns and divide the local population in *encomienda*. The seven towns were Asunción, later called Baracoa,

Santiago de Cuba, Bayamo, Puerto Príncipe, Trinidad, Sancti-Spíritus, and Havana, then on the southern side of the island. Within three years the conquest and occupation of Cuba was complete. The future of the colony seemed secure and the island replaced Española as the premier overseas possession of Castile. Velázquez wrote to the king in 1514: "The hogs which we carried with us have multiplied to thirty thousand . . . and this island is so bountiful that it could provide sufficient food for Tierra Firme."

Diego Velázquez served as governor of Cuba until his death in 1524. It was a period of enormous prosperity for the governor and for those colonists who found the large deposits of gold that had eluded Columbus. Indeed the royal fifth amounted to 21,000 pesos in 1517, indicating a production for that year in excess of 100,000 pesos.

The prosperity of Cuba did not endure. By 1518 the colony was already rife with dissension, and the successful campaign begun in Mexico the following year reduced it to the status of a supply base for the war bands of Tierra Firme. Throughout the sixteenth century the colony virtually stagnated, challenged by pirates, ravaged by hurricanes, plagued by diseases, and depopulated by the magnetic pull of Mexico and Peru. Cuba played second fiddle to the gold- and silver-producing mainland colonies for the succeeding centuries, and only its strategic location saved it from total eclipse. Havana, moved to the fine, protected harbor on the north coast, became the vital collecting point for the transatlantic convoys moving between the Spanish Americas and home.

For more than a century Spain enjoyed the undisputed dominion of the Americas, sending out explorers, settlers, and priests to wander hither and yon. They settled where they could, moved where they liked, fought when the occasion arose, either against the Indians or among themselves. Some went for gold; some for glory; some for God and king. Many died; a few got rich; an undetermined number returned.

It is extremely difficult to compare the quality of life in the Indies with that in the metropolis. In general the quality of life in both for the vast majority of the population was poor. Cities in the Indies were mere glorified villages of crude huts and ubiquitous squalor—except where indigenous laborers could be coerced into building impressive churches and magnificent palaces. Death was frequent; and nature deceptively violent. But conditions appeared more difficult than they probably were to those Spaniards who wanted facsimile representations of what they left behind in Iberia. Moreover the settlers rapidly learned to spurn agriculture and value only precious metals, prodigally destroying cattle, forests, and local Indians with callous abandon, both on the islands and on the mainland.

The physical hazards of life, however, were assuaged by the fecundity of the land and salubrious climate as well as the almost limitless political freedom which distance imposed on the Americans. And from a demographic point of view, the relatively few Spaniards who went out to the Indies increased impressively. By 1570 the Spanish Antilles had twenty-four predominantly Spanish towns with a white population of approximately 7500, an Indian population of about 22,150, and a new heterogenous group of Africans, mestizos, and mulattoes amounting to around 56,000. The Spanish had been amazingly productive in fortuitously replacing the people they had wantonly destroyed. As the period of Spanish monopoly drew to a close in the Caribbean, the pattern of society began to assume the form that made the area variegated in people and culture. The unusually prescient could have seen the ominous signs in the figures of 1570: Spanish settlements in Indian territories had a population composition of roughly 9 percent Spanish, 26 percent Indian, and 65 percent African or mixed. If the Spanish desired viable colonies of loyal vassals to the Castilian Crown, then they would have to produce the population themselves. For the rapid diminution of the Arawaks and the irresistible attraction of the mainland colonies of Mexico and Peru contributed to a severe population decline in the Caribbean. Neither Spanish laws nor Spanish immigrants could effectively counter the dramatic depopulation. Moreover the zeal to expand on to the eastern Antillean islands evaporated, leaving adequate room for other Europeans to enter and found settlements of their own.

Despite the papal rulings of 1493, which divided the world into two spheres of influence pertaining to Spain and Portugal, the legitimacy of such claims appeared extremely hollow. Indeed the misgivings concerning legitimacy seemed to have permeated the two Iberian courts to such an extent that they reinforced the partition in an additional secular agreement signed at Tordesillas in June 1494. To Spain belonged all lands and peoples west of an imaginary line drawn 370 leagues west of the Cape Verde Islands. Considering the geographical information of the day, it was a reasonable compromise. Portugal retained the significant hump of South America which gave her vast amounts of Brazilian dyewood and protected her sailing route to India. Spain reduced the competition for what it thought was the shortest route to the Asian spice islands. The other European monarchs disliked the arrogance implied in such a division but could do very little about it.

For more than a hundred years no seriously organized European threat to the Spanish and Portuguese monopoly of the New World developed. Individual privateers such as the Elizabethan Englishmen Francis Drake, Walter Raleigh, and John Hawkins, sometimes with official benevolence attempted to establish rival semiprivate colonies in the Americas. The French tried to do the same during the sixteenth century with equal lack of success. Domestic political unrest and lack of nautical resources precluded a major state operation during either the troubled reign of Elizabeth I or the regency of Catherine de Medici. Moreover, Spain became the dominant European political and naval power with the election of Charles V as Holy Roman Emperor in 1519, the loyalty of the Low Countries to Spain until 1568, and the victory over the Turks at Lepanto in 1570. But while the Spanish could successfully discourage the permanent settlement of others overseas, the continuous harrassment of Spanish shipping and the relentless plundering of Spanish-American port cities forced drastic reforms which eventually made non-Spanish settlement feasible.

The architect of the defense of Spanish America in the sixteenth century was Pedro Menéndez de Avila, the most powerful—and the most successful—Spanish colonial bureaucrat between 1550 and 1574.

Menéndez attracted the attention of the Spanish court as the commander of the fleet returning from the Indies in 1555-56. Obviously a leader of great ability, loyalty, and energy, he successively became captain-general of the *Armada de la Carrera de Indias* in 1561, adviser to the Crown, 1564-66, *adelantado* to Florida in 1565, and governor of Cuba in 1567. His major impact on Spanish America, especially in the Caribbean, was two-fold. First he recognized the limited capacity of the Spanish to settle and protect all the Americas. He therefore reinforced the enclaves by the construction of fortifications and the stationing of garrisons at strategically selected sites: Cartagena, Santo Domingo, San Juan de Puerto Rico, Santiago de Cuba, and Havana. A fortification was also built in Florida. The selection of these sites implied that the rest of the region would be given only minimal protection, and that the islands themselves were of secondary importance to the gold- and silver-producing areas of Peru and Mexico. Second Menéndez regularized the system of protected convoys as the main basis of maritime communication between Spain and the Indies. To supplement the convoys he created a small armada of swift, armed vessels permanently based in the Caribbean with the duty of attacking pirates and discouraging non-Spanish interloping in the region. The system worked efficaciously as long as Spain was stronger than its enemies. And until the death of Philip II Spain appeared strong, for its enemies were divided and distracted by internal problems.

By the early seventeenth century, the enemies of Spain were no longer divided and disunited, and in short succession they penetrated the perimeters of Spanish America. Within the first two decades the French had explored a great deal of eastern Canada and set up a fur-trading empire along the Saint Lawrence basin. Samuel de Champlain roamed over areas of Quebec, Ontario, and New York State, while Étienne Brûle explored Lake Erie and floated down the Susquehanna river to the Chesapeake Bay. The *coureurs de bois* eventually took French influence far afield in the great American Midwest, and down the mighty Mississippi River to the Gulf of Mexico. At the same time English explorers, encouraged by merchants and courtiers rapidly spread English influence along the Atlantic coast from Massachusetts to Virginia. By 1620 the northwest Europeans had reconnoitered a vast expanse of the Americas outside the principal sphere of Spanish influence, and, apart from the hostile Indians, they liked what they saw. Although they could not challenge Spain in Middle America, they discovered that Spain could not repel their efforts in North America.

Yet North America had a rather hostile climate, especially in winter, which made it discouraging to all but the boldest of pioneers. It had the prospect of a refuge, but not of the type of commercially viable colony that Europeans strongly felt contributed to the grandeur of Spain. Along with the probing expeditions beyond the northern perimeter of Spanish settlements, therefore, there were some sallies into the vital umbilical region of the Spanish Caribbean.

The English, French, and Dutch attempted to establish colonies in the Guianas between 1595 and 1620. The Dutch finally prevailed in 1616 along the Essequibo river and in 1624 along the Berbice. The loss of life in the tropics, as in North America, was discouragingly high, but the conviction that great wealth could eventually be obtained prevailed and was sufficiently strong to fuel the desires of merchants and politicians. Finally in 1624 the English gave up in Guiana, and under the direction of Thomas Warner, a survivor from the Guiana campaigns, turned their attention to the Lesser Antilles. St. Christopher in the Leewards had the dubious distinction of being not only the first English colony but also the first French colony in the Caribbean.

The early settlements had to contend with hostile Indian neighbors, summer hurricanes, fevers, and periodic Spanish attacks, but somehow they managed to survive, and, with reinforcements from Europe, to expand. The 1620's were the crucial years. But the Spanish, engaged in the Thirty Years War in Europe and trying to administer not only their own but the Portuguese empire, found themselves increasingly less able to prevent these peripheral settlements. Moreover, the truce with the Dutch, signed in 1609, expired in 1621, and the Dutch mobilized their considerable naval resources to continue

the struggle against Spain. The Dutch West India Company, chartered in 1621, aggressively took the fight to the Spanish Indies, destroying the Spanish Atlantic fleets and supplying Spanish trade centers with Dutch products. In 1624 the Dutch captured Bahía and
controlled the northeast of Brazil for thirty years. In 1628 Piet Heyn,
an employee of the company, took his convoy to Cuba and captured
the entire Spanish silver fleet outside Havana just as it was leaving for
Spain. This strategy severely disrupted Spanish military and commercial activity in the Caribbean and permanently crippled their imperial
defense built by Menéndez. Dutch control of the tropical Atlantic indirectly facilitated the successful penetration of other northwest
Europeans.

Between 1630 and 1640 the Dutch seized the minuscule islands of
Curaçao, St. Eustatius, St. Martin, and Saba in order to expand the
commercial activity already centered on Araya and Cumaná. Meanwhile the depletion of the Spanish fleet made the Spanish colonists
even more eager than before to engage in illegal trade with any for-
eigner who appeared in their ports. By 1640 the Dutch were clearly
the most successful traders in the Caribbean with settlements in
northeast Brazil, Guiana, and New York (then New Netherland),
and lucrative trading posts in six strategically located Caribbean islands. The importance of the Dutch role in vanquishing Spanish in-
vincibility can hardly be overestimated. "It was Dutch action in the
Caribbean," wrote John Parry, "which enabled [the French and English American] settlements to take root and grow. Dutch victories
strained the overtaxed resources of Spain almost to breaking point,
and provided a naval screen behind which the English, the French,
the Scots and the Danes, without much danger of Spanish interference, could build up their colonies in a long string down the Atlantic
coast from Newfoundland to Barbados."

With Spanish military capacity crippled in the Caribbean, the English and French quickly extended their holdings. The English occupied Barbados and, along with the Dutch, St. Croix in 1625; they
took possession of Nevis in 1628, Antigua and Montserrat in 1632,
and St. Lucia in 1638. An attempt to settle Tobago in 1625 failed,

and the Caribs destroyed the St. Lucia settlement in 1641. The English settlements were sponsored by rival chartered companies using influential court politicians like the Earl of Carlisle and the Earl of Pembroke to secure conflicting patents for ill-defined areas of the Caribbean. These conflicts over jurisdiction led to early disorder in the colonies. At the same time the French advanced their settlements under the auspices of the *Compagnie des Iles d'Amérique*, chartered by Cardinal Richelieu in 1635 and ordered to take over the struggling colony of Pierre D'Esnambuc on St. Christopher, and to expand French settlements on any island not previously held by Europeans. In return for some very liberal privileges, the company had the arduous task of settling at least four thousand Roman Catholics in the French Antilles within twenty years. The company settled Martinique and Guadeloupe, and thus gave France a permanent interest in the Caribbean and a base for expansion to St. Bartholomé, St. Martin, Grenada, St. Lucia, and western Española.

The English and the French, unlike the Dutch, were serious about transplanting Europeans who would grow tropical staples—tobacco, cotton, sugar cane, and anything else they could produce—and develop a reciprocal trading relationship with the metropolis. In this way the colonies could become viable, semiautonomous communities and attractive recipients for what was then commonly considered an increasingly superfluous European population. In the early stages of each colony tobacco became the cash crop, and a type of free trade with the Dutch salvaged many a faltering enterprise. The Dutch, until the second Anglo-Dutch war of 1665-67, were, after all, the main promoters of commerce in the Caribbean, far excelling all others in knowledge of agricultural techniques, transportation facilities, financial terms, and general economic sophistication. Unlike the Spanish settlers of the early sixteenth century, the northwest Europeans had no large host populations to supply food, instruct them in techniques of tropical survival, and become slaves and servants. The settlers during the initial phases of colonization in the seventeenth century found themselves either on isolated and uninhabited islands like Barbados, or among hostile warrior groups like the Caribs on Martinique, Gua-

deloupe, Tobago, and St. Lucia. Survival depended on self-help and
trial and error. The colonists cleared the forests and cultivated their
crops by themselves, or with the contractual help of indented servants
in the English islands and *engagés* in the French. Colonial life was
extremely difficult and often short. But the mere fact of a multi-
national form of colonial life in the Caribbean had tremendous consequences for the region and the European powers. During the two
centuries after 1625 three important transformations occurred pertaining to the relations of the region to the wider world.

By the end of the seventeenth century Spain had clearly lost its
hegemony in the Caribbean. That was the first great change, slowly
evolving since the late sixteenth century when the aggressive assaults
of interlopers had forced an imperial policy of strategic retrenchment
and armed fleets. As early as 1604 Spain recognized the right of England to trade in the Caribbean. By 1648, at the treaty of Münster,
Spain tacitly recognized both her loss of the Thirty Years War in
Europe and the eclipse of her global power. She granted the Dutch
those colonies they had occupied overseas, freedom to trade in the
Caribbean, and freedom to practice their own religion. Philip IV,
having recently lost the Portuguese segment of his empire, could no
longer make demands on his European competitors. Nor could the
internal political affairs of European states be separated any longer
from their overseas involvement. Peace in Europe and peace "beyond
the line" of amity became integrally related.

The manifest naval and military weakness of Spain emboldened the
English to change their policy after the late 1640's. Before that the
English had followed the policy of trading along the African coast
and establishing colonies of Europeans outside the effective range of
Spanish reprisals. By the 1650's, however, the English, acting on the
advice of the renegade Dominican friar, Thomas Gage, planned a
massive assault on the Spanish Caribbean aimed at wresting the major islands as a prelude to carving the mainland. That was Oliver
Cromwell's famous "Western Design." Based on the original lofty
aims of the expedition—to conquer Hispaniola or Cuba as a base for
commerce, and to displace the Dutch in the Caribbean—the plan

was a monumental fiasco. The English, still woefully ignorant of conditions in the New World, found that the strength of the Spanish-American fortifications and Dutch dominance at sea exceeded their estimations. The English managed to capture the relatively undefended island of Jamaica. If the Spanish-American empire could not be forcefully seized, Spain was powerless to prevent incursions, and at the Treaty of Madrid in 1670 she surrendered Jamaica and accepted the de facto possession of the other English colonies. When Spain also accepted the French settlements in the Lesser Antilles and on western Hispaniola at the Treaty of Ryswick in 1697, "Adam's will" was redrawn: the world no longer belonged to the Iberian monarchs. And by the end of the century the English and French had effectively duplicated the Dutch commercial system with their own overseas imperial possessions.

The second consequence of the successful challenge to Spain was a series of social and economic revolutions on the islands of the Lesser Antilles as well as on Jamaica and Saint-Domingue, as the French called their part of the island of Española. (The Spanish began to refer to the island in the seventeenth century as Hispaniola; and to their eastern section as Santo Domingo, in keeping with their practice of calling islands and colonies after the chief port city.) The nature of these revolutions will be examined and discussed in chapter four, but the essential characteristic was the conversion from colonies of settlement based on mixed small farming, and seminomadic cattle ranching, into full-fledged, dependent plantation colonies integrally related both to Europe and Africa. As these colonies were transformed from obscure havens for restless refugees from a divided Europe to economic areas designed for the production of tropical staples, they also changed profoundly in political importance. No longer was the Caribbean an area of marginal importance to the Spanish empire. Instead, until eclipsed by India in the nineteenth century, the Caribbean islands became the most valued possessions in the overseas imperial world, "lying in the very belly of all commerce," as Carew Reynell so aptly described Jamaica.

The settlement experiment failed for two related reasons. The region could not compete with the mainland as a lure for free citizens seeking land and a new style of life, and a free mixed economy could not be sustained. For more than forty years the northwest Europeans had attempted to establish random settlement colonies throughout the Americas. Everywhere they had paid a frightfully high price in human terms. Everywhere they faced enormous, often crippling difficulties: hostile Indians, antagonistic Spanish, unfamiliar climates, new fatal epidemics, failing harvests, and illusive riches. The frontier conditions of tropical and temperate America took their toll equally, but it was the temperate climate that Europeans found more conducive to re-creating the type of society they either had, or wished for.

By the middle of the 1640's the English and French settlements in the eastern Caribbean faced the same crisis that the Portuguese and Spanish had encountered in Brazil and the Caribbean a century before. An acute labor shortage jeopardized the success of a viable agricultural economy. Barter arrangements with the Indians collapsed, as did outright Indian slavery. Tobacco competed neither in quality nor quantity with the mainland product. And the exodus of the released indentureds and *engagés* to the mainland or to join the marauding bands of transfrontier buccaneers exacerbated the labor shortage. One buccaneer, William Jackson, easily recruited 500 men from Barbados and 250 from St. Christopher to join his free-lancing band, and 1200 Barbadians moved to New England. Moreover the unsettled state of English domestic politics precluded the sustained political and commercial attention necessary to succor the fledgling colonies. French domestic politics was more stable, but French imperial colonization, with the possible exception of St. Christopher, presented equal discord. In addition to the scarcity of labor, the French colonists had the burdens of poor administration and the rapaciousness of the local merchants—grievances which would explode during the revolution of 1789.

The third consequence of the new situation resulted directly from the other two. The acquisition of possessions in the Caribbean forced the northwest European states to articulate elaborate theories about the relationship of colonies to the mother country, and to try to implement these ideas in order to control the wealth and power which such colonies afforded to a metropolis. The theory and practice of imperialism closely resembled the dilemma which the Spanish had confronted—if not adequately resolved—a hundred years before in the aftermath of the conquest.

The organizational structure which the Europeans fashioned for their empires responded to their perceived needs as well as the actual circumstances of the seventeenth century; but it prevailed, with only minor modifications, until the late nineteenth century. These structures did not vary greatly among imperial divisions, having been conscious imitations of the most successful aspects of the expansive empiricism of the age. The basis of these schemes rested on the delegation of public functions to private corporations or associations such as the Dutch West India Company, Richelieu's *Compagnie des Iles d'Amérique*, or any of the numerous charters given to Roger North, William Courteen, or the Earl of Carlisle. All charters and companies involved in American exploration, trade, and colonization blended the political activities of the medieval guilds and corporations in Europe with the cooperative stockholding concerns of the Italian and Dutch cities. They therefore possessed three characteristics: financial support through joint-stocks, with the stockholders receiving a share of any profits; political supervision in their sphere of influence; and some economic monopoly from their chartering government.

These characteristics could be seen quite clearly in the charters granted to the French *Compagnie des Iles d'Amérique*. With Cardinal Richelieu as its major sponsor and stockholder, the company got a charter in 1635 to develop parts of the Americas "not previously held by any Christian prince." In 1642 Richelieu won an extension of the charter, giving the company control over all islands they could capture or settle between the equator and latitude 30 degrees north, exclusive trade with these territories, privilege to import the produce of the islands into France duty free, and complete jurisdiction to appoint governors and the governor-general. Not only were these extensive privileges awarded, but the Crown promised letters of ennoblement to any settler who transported fifty men to any uninhabited island and lived there for two years. The extent of the powers awarded to individuals and companies in the late sixteenth and early seventeenth centuries reflected the relatively weak position of the monarchies of the various competing Europeans. Joint-stock companies with informal government control facilitated the execution of imperial policies that would be too unpopular either at home or with neighboring states. Methods changed when the monarchs felt themselves stronger.

The overlapping political and economic aims of the various states were handled by a series of institutions that did not reveal fundamental differences across imperial boundaries. Of course some proved more successful than others, and some exhibited greater efficiency over a longer period of time. But the goals of controlling trade and fractious colonists required only a few firm measures.

At the end of the seventeenth century it is clear that the *Consejo de Indias* handled the imperial political coordination for the vast Spanish overseas empire. For the Portuguese the *Conselho Ultramarino* performed similar administrative functions, as did the English Parliament, the French Ministry of Navy (after the bankruptcy of the company in 1649), and the Dutch *Heren XIX*, the board of directors for the West India Company responsible to the four provincial governors.

Local political control was somewhat diffused. In the Spanish colonies it resided with the captains-general, the *audiencias*, and the *cabildos* or local town councils. The English distributed local control among governors, assemblies of property-holding colonists, and patentees, who could appoint some governors. The French reorganization of the colonial structure under Colbert in 1664 gave local control to governors appointed by the newly chartered West India Company (in effect a front for the French government), and aided by appointed councils. Planter interests gained representation by their appointment to the local councils. The Dutch, who had less ambitious aims for settler colonies, merely appointed local governors to supervise the commercial and other affiliated interests in their colonies.

Economic direction and control fell within three portfolios: overall economic planning for the empire coordinating economic schemes with the prevailing interests of the metropolis; local control of trade; and management of production. The *Casa de contratación* and the *Consulado* of Seville had the highest responsibility for overseas Spanish trade, although by the seventeenth century most trade to and within the Indies passed out of effective Spanish control. The English Parliament exercised a similar function for the English empire, with the Board of Trade responsible for advice on policy matters. The French Ministry of Finance made policy, with advisory input from the commercial companies funneled through the Chambers of Commerce. And although the Dutch West India Company was not solely a commercial enterprise, it had control of overall economic planning.

The domestic and overseas *consulados* controlled trade at the local level in the Spanish imperial system, and managed production, sometimes in collusion with the local town councils. Local merchants and private shippers, however, handled this operation in the three rival non-Hispanic systems in the Caribbean, although nominally the Dutch West India Company supervised their American affairs. Similarly the supervision of staple production was entirely in the hands of the local planters. In theory any English subject could organize his own trading enterprise within the empire as long as he did not violate the Navigation Acts designed to ensure metropolitan domination of trade.

The formal imperial structures, however, could not prevent vertical commercial association. In practice the administrative systems failed to function efficiently from their inception. A number of factors contributed to this. States made exceptions to the general rule when such exceptions were in their interest, such as the licensed trade, or *asientos,* granted in violation of orthodox mercantilistic principles. Public officials frequently bought their offices and found that the perquisites of office increased more by noncompliance than by adherence. Laws propounded on general principles often required local, commonsense applications. Communication between the home office and the periphery was slow, and subject to conflicting political vagaries. In the final analysis the administrative bureaucracies could be no more responsible, sensitive, and effective than the metropolitan governments, which in that age were demonstrably short of those qualities.

The formal relationship between the European metropolises and their American colonies became increasingly more complicated as the nature, circumstances, and values of the colonists were subtly transformed through time. The novel experiences of the successive waves of immigrants fashioned the changes between European society and American society. But perhaps the greatest single element in the structuring of this separation was the involvement in slavery, the slave trade, and the conversion from colonies of true settlements into zones of economic exploitation.

Slavery was not unfamiliar to the European social experience when Christopher Columbus, Juan de la Cosa, Amerigo Vespucci, Juan and Sebastian Cabot, Pedro Alvares Cabral, and the other brave explorers of the fifteenth and sixteenth centuries broadened the Atlantic horizons of their fellowmen. Slavery in the Mediterranean basin had been commonplace in the fifteenth century, and continued to be practised until the nineteenth century. Spanish and Portuguese merchants bought and sold Africans in a number of Iberian port-cities, especially Huelva, Cadiz, Seville, Málaga, Valencia, and Barcelona. The Iberian market for slaves, however, was relatively small, absorbing annually perhaps no more than 200 individuals—not all of whom were Africans. Communities of exslaves and their descendants formed in these southern Iberian cities. These communities included a varied number of groups of diverse origins: Moors, Jews, Syrians, Lebanese, Egyptians, Russians, and Canary Islanders.

In the Mediterranean world where slavery flourished most, slaves were an important commercial commodity. But slavery was not so important a part of general commerce or society that national governments became unduly interested. Nevertheless, Christopher Columbus was sufficiently impressed by the potential economic value of slaves to take some indigenous American Indians as samples back to Spain after his second voyage to the New World, hoping that they would be vendible products. Isabella II, Queen of Spain, refused to sanction this expansion of slavery, and, preferring vassals to slaves, forbade the large-scale and unrestricted importation and sale of her newly acquired American subjects. The moral qualms of the Spanish queen were insufficient, however, to save the native Antillean population. Isabella died in 1504, and by 1510 the inadequacy and reluctance of Indian workers created a severe labor problem in the gold mines, pearl fisheries, and farms of the islands.

Africans had accompanied the Spanish explorers and colonists to the Caribbean from the beginning of the age of exploration. An indefinite number arrived with the expedition of Nicolás de Ovando in 1502. By 1516 Spanish-speaking Africans—most likely born in Spain—had already outnumbered the true Spanish colonists. As Spanish colonialism expanded, so did the need to find individuals who would perform the demanding physical tasks required to clear the forests, plant the crops, attend the animals, build the cities, work the mines, and seek the pearls. Spanish colonists themselves were not sufficiently skilled, sufficiently available, or sufficiently willing. The Arawaks, coerced to perform, died in large numbers, while the Caribs demonstrated such a vigorous opposition that the majority were left alone. The Spanish Crown abandoned the cautious scruples that had inhibited the selling of non-Christians in their American possessions, and in 1518 Charles V sanctioned the monopolistic commerce of non-Spanish-speaking Africans shipped directly to the Antilles. The trans-Atlantic slave trade then began in earnest. For the succeeding century the number of Africans increased steadily. As each colony became subdued, the Indian population dwindled. As the Indian population decreased, the African component increased. African slavery preceded the establishment of the plantation economy, the development of the *ingenio*, and the monocultural dominance of sugar. After 1530 the number of Spanish-speaking Africans declined drastically in the Caribbean as metropolitan policy prevented their legal export from Spain, and as earlier arrivals followed the general exodus of colonists to the mainland.

The supply of slaves became a major concern. Spain, by the treaties of Alcaçovas (1479) and Tordesillas (1494), had surrendered to Portugal access to the African coastal trade for an undisturbed hegemony of whatever she encountered within the western Atlantic. With Africa—and in the first century of the trade, the Guinea coast—providing the majority of the marketable slaves, the Spanish-American colonists had little recourse but to depend on others for their legal slaves. The attitude of the Spanish Crown was that slaves could be supplied in a controlled, monopolistic fashion, supervised just like any other commercial activity by the *Casa de Contratación*.

Lorenzo de Garrevod, Duke of Bresa and an intimate of the young Spanish King Charles, was the first licensed American slave trader. Awarded the monopoly to supply 4000 Africans within four years, exempt from custom duties, Garrevod quickly realized the difficulties and disadvantages of initiating direct trade between Africa and the Americas. Apart from lacking the capital for ships and goods of exchange, Garrevod and the Spanish had no contacts, and no protection along the African coast. Garrevod then sold his contract to a consortium of Genoese merchants for 25,000 ducats. The merchants in turn resold the permission, probably illegally, to individuals who were in a better position to effect the purchase and transportation of Guinea slaves to the Americas—Portuguese sea captains, sailors, and factors—making a profit on their investment of 275,000 ducats. The slave trade had become lucrative business, with considerable gain for speculating middlemen. By 1528 Charles realized that there could be a profit for the Crown, too. He sold the monopoly, then regarded as an *asiento*, to two front-men for a powerful German banking firm, Heinrich Ehinger and Hieronymous Seiler. With the monopoly, the Spanish Crown tried to fix both the flow of Africans—1000 per year—and the selling price at the point of delivery—40 ducats per *pieza*, or unit of labor, roughly equivalent to a physically healthy male adult. Unfortunately, the American colonists found, not for the last time in their history, that both the legal number and the legal price were breached with impugnity.

In 1537 Charles granted an *asiento* to Domingo Martínez and Cristóbal Francisquime of Seville in which they pledged to supply 1500 Africans to the Indies in return for a one-time payment of 9750 ducats to the Crown, and the usual exemption from the levy of customs duties. The Sevillians resold their monopoly at the usual profit. By the middle of the century, the Crown assumed the direct award of contracts, or *licencias*, to individuals as well as groups of merchants and shippers, gently escalating the price of the permit as the demand increased and the Crown's fiscal situation became steadily less secure. The individual permits afforded a magnificent opportunity for illicit trade. Foreign interlopers, like the Englishman John Hawkins, found that anyone who could get slaves off the African coast could easily dispose of them in the Americas regardless of the requirements of the king of Spain and the *Casa de Contratación*. To stem the increase of illicit trade, Philip II reverted to the monopoly system in 1586, vesting the delivery of slaves in a number of Portuguese firms until 1640. Although the Crown gained a large and steady income, the Americans remained unhappy both with the number and price of the slaves delivered. Moreover, the period saw the beginning of a boom for interlopers.

In 1640 Portugal regained its independence from Spain and lost its preferred position as chief supplier of slaves to the Americas. During the period after 1518, approximately 75,000 Africans had been shipped to the Spanish Americas, amounting to about 60 percent of the total trans-Atlantic slave trade.

Conditions in Europe, in Africa, and the Americas, however, had changed considerably with respect to national politics and international slave trading. Spain no longer held the dominant political and military position in Europe; England and the Netherlands were no longer Roman Catholic in religion—which made commercial intercourse with those countries tantamount to endorsing heresy—and France and Spain were at war. Spain, therefore, was in a weaker position than ever before to regulate the trade to her American possessions. In Africa slave trading had emerged as a sophisticated system of commerce, highly organized, and with accepted rules of conduct on the part of Africans and Europeans. The area of the trade had expanded along the coast, as well as far into the interior, making the recruitment and exchange of slaves a complex, multifaceted operation along an interlocking system of client relationships. Almost every European state, except the Spanish, had factors, forts, and contacts along the African coast, with the Dutch ascendant until the end of the seventeenth century. In the Caribbean, the Spanish hegemony had been effectively broken as the French, English, and Dutch established footholds in the eastern Caribbean islands, and along the maritime coastlands of the North Atlantic. More colonists meant more work; and more work required an even greater demand for Africans than before. After 1640 the Spanish colonists became only one sector of the American slave market, and received, until the nineteenth century, an ever declining proportion of the Africans sold in the New World. Moreover, by 1640 the sugar and plantation frontier had reached the Caribbean, creating an "economy world" which Philip D. Curtin has called the South Atlantic System. The Atlantic world of plantation agriculture, big business, international commerce, and slavery was born. For the next two centuries it would expand in all directions. The modest requirements of Spanish colonists in the early sixteenth century had become an insatiable demand by the beginning of the eighteenth century. The Caribbean colonies became slave societies.

Chapter 3 • Patterns of Colonization in the New World

We have not only eaten all the cattle within twelve miles of the place, but now almost all the horses, asses, mules' flesh near us so that I shall hold little Eastcheap in more esteem than the whole Indies if this trade last, and I can give nor learn no reason that it should not here continue; so beside this we expect no pay here, nor hardly at home now, but perhaps some ragged land at the best, and that but by the by spoken of, for us general officers not a word mentioned.

Anonymous soldier, Jamaica, November 1655

At first glance it is difficult to reconcile the wide variety of cultures and societies that developed in the Americas between 1492 and 1800. These colonies, as already indicated, arose at different times, in different geographical areas, under the auspices of different European national patronage. Beginning with the initial expeditions of Columbus and Cabral, the Americas went from an Iberian monopoly to a territory theoretically mapped out by and for the emerging nation-states of Europe. At one time or another the English, French, Dutch, Danes, and Swedes colonized America—or rather, some part of the

Americas, since the impact, though tremendous, produced relatively small enclaves of occupation. These enclaves survived by forging ingenious relationships with one another, with the local indigenous populations, and with their parent society in Europe. In time the colonies all reflected the accumulated experience of these contacts.

Until the end of the eighteenth century the predominantly European society was merely one form of society and culture in the wide spectrum. In Spanish America, Brazil, and the Caribbean, significant and vital indigenous communities continued to exist alongside the Europeans, ranging in size and social sophistication from the Tupi and Puelches, to the Mayo, Maya, and Yaqui. Also present at one time or another were the semi-European cultures that had developed during the period—buccaneers in the Caribbean, Gauchos on the plains of the Rio de la Plata, Llaneros in the interior plains of Colombia and Venezuela, and Maroons just about everywhere.

The genesis and interrelationship of these societies have been conventionally viewed through ethnocentric European lenses, with the consequent distortion and obscurantism of not only the general pattern of evolution but also the common prevailing impact of geopolitical and geophysical factors. I would like to try to reverse this convention of regarding the Caribbean as a sidelight of European history. The European communities and cultures are the focus, but in ways that limit considerably their variety, and that diminish the value of particular national origins. Indeed this internal American perspective discerns merely two enduring types of European colony in the region between 1492 and 1800: the colony of settlers and the colony of economic exploiters.

To Europeans of the fifteenth and sixteenth centuries, America was the great unknown. Physically isolated from the contiguous Afro-Eurasian land mass, it was the essence of that virginity which so obsessed the curious, expansive, irrepressible intruders of that day. Yet Europeans have always been ambivalent about the meaning of America. And the American impact on Europe, though unmistakeably broad and continuous, has been, to use John Elliott's adjective, "uncertain."

America was undoubtedly a novel and challenging ecological envi-

ronment for the newcomers. Its flora and fauna were different. Its social and economic structures were unfamiliar. Its populations lacked
the common epidemiological immunities of the eastern side of the
Atlantic. Its existence, topography, and geopolitical realities challenged, where they did not refute, the most basic conventional wisdom of the Europeans—theories concerning time, geography, society,
theology, philosophy, and aesthetics. Naturally each traveler saw
America as he wanted, within the framework of his inherited cultural world view.

Christopher Columbus died thinking that he was certainly on the
outskirts of China, and wondered why the Antilleans were such "an
extremely poor people." His concept of a Spanish trading post empire, patterned after the Portuguese experience along the African
coast, died with his early settlement in Hispaniola, and the de facto
revocation of his grandiloquent titles by the astute Isabella.

Bernal Díaz del Castillo, that charming chronicler of the most astounding military success of Spanish arms, saw America as the new
venue for an updated crusade, merging the religious assumptions of
his medieval age with the pragmatic aims of his modernizing monarch. For him the American venture was "to serve God and his majesty, . . . and to get rich, as all men desire to do." He died an op-
timistic pauper in the wilderness of Guatemala, dazzled by his deeds,
but oblivious to their consequences.

Charles V, understandably impressed by the papal pronouncement
of *Sublimus Deus* of 1537 that Indians were rational beings, sought,
through the instrumentality of the New Laws, to subordinate the
ubiquitous brigandage of the indefatigable *conquistadores* to the or-
ganizing structure of the Spanish corporate state. This political re-
trieval on the part of Charles V coincided with the aims of João III
of Portugal to convert Brazil into a true colony rather than a geographical reference point on the way to India.

By the middle of the sixteenth century both the Spanish and Portuguese had decided to establish types of colonies in the Americas
that failed to conform to their preconceived notions of an overseas
empire but were not entirely removed from the general European tradition of settlements beyond the frontier.

In every respect, then, the earliest Caribbean settlements were microcosms of metropolitan society. The expedition of Nicolas Ovando to settle Santo Domingo in 1502 represented a continuation of the pattern of the *Reconquista* with its curious combination of military posturing and material greed for land, wealth, and servants. In the wake of the explorers, opportunists, and free lances came a complete cross section of Spanish society, ably described by James Lockhart in *Spanish Peru*, and *The Men of Cajamarca*, and Peter Boyd-Bowman in his *Indice Geobiográfico*—hidalgos, clerks, artisans, merchants, priests, and members of the lower orders of society. A substantial proportion of these men and women manifested little or no desire to return to Spain. Of course the fact that a great number came from the depressed towns of Extremadura and western Andalucia made a one-way ticket even to the American unknown a rather pleasant prospect. Similarly the early English settlers in Thomas Carlisle's Barbados, John Smith's Virginia, and John Winthrop's Massachusetts represented a continuation of the "plantations" in Ulster, Wales, and Scotland—the expansion and domination of an English social structure within an English polity.

Initially the institutions and the ideas of the colony paralleled those of the metropolis. The American frontier offered space and opportunities to create a quality of life and an environment superior to that left behind. This pattern of expansion incorporating goals of economic amelioration and political and social relaxation—if not elevation—was, after all, closely associated with the eastern expansion and consequent modification of Western European feudal society during the Middle Ages. The ethnocentric Roman Catholicism of an absolutist monarchy in Iberia prospered in Hispaniola, New Spain, and Peru. The *fazenda* and the *Senado da Camara* held together early Brazilian colonial life. And Englishmen in Barbados reflected all the political and religious vicissitudes of the motherland in the early seventeenth century.

A viable community necessitated a substantial proportion of women both for procreation and for the vital function of socializing the newborn to the norms and expectations of the majority. As soon as the Spanish state inaugurated its policy of subjecting the free lances, it began to assure a continuous and sufficient supply of suitable females. Perhaps more than any other European group, the Spanish invested their womenfolk with all the qualities of social honor and familial responsibility and stability. The Crown not only actively discouraged sexual intercourse with the indigenous population but fostered the migration of family units. According to Peter Boyd-Bowman, of the known 5481 Spanish who immigrated to the Americas between 1493 and 1519, 308 or roughly 6 percent were women. Although this appears to be a small number, it was a fairly representative female population for that early stage of colonization. Richard Dunn found approximately the same percentage of women among the English passengers bound for Barbados in 1635—at a time when Barbados was still trying to promote the settler society. After 1570, in accordance with the declaration of the Council of Trent that marriage was a sacrament, the Spanish Crown forbade married men to journey overseas for periods in excess of six months unless accompanied by their families. The subsequent emigration of predominantly single males from Iberia greatly stimulated the rise of a miscegenated population in the Americas. The Crown did not approve—nor did the laws recognize—the practice of Spanish males in the colonies who mated to suit their fancy.

Yet if the settler mentality responded to the possibilities of America, it was a response tempered by three related considerations operating at three different levels. In the sixteenth century, before the successful penetration of the northwest Europeans and the shattering of the tenacious illusion of an Iberian monopoly of the Americas, these views could be roughly divided into a) official secular; b) official religious; and c) the individual.

The official secular or state policy toward the Americas was integrally connected to the new ideas of national power and the position of the monarchy in the sphere of political power. The absolutist monarchy of Spain considered—and successfully imposed the concept of—the Americas as the personal domain of the king. All Americans, Spanish as well as non-Spanish, were thereby vassals of the Castilian king. The bureaucracy attempted to reinforce this claim, and to destroy any other manifestations of feudalistic autonomy in the Americas. The Portuguese monarchy eventually had the only resources that could make Brazil a viable and secure part of an American empire. The French in the seventeenth century were in a similar position, and early English and Dutch colonization drew their greatest stimuli from individual entrepreneurs. In the fluid political atmosphere of the sixteenth and seventeenth century, each colony needed, sought, and received the patronage of a state, however peripheral such a state was to the main political power configurations of Europe. Eventually it mattered not what the official attitudes to the Americas were. Europeans went forth subscribing fully or partially to the goals of Bernal Díaz del Castillo.

And in accordance with the age, state policy paralleled—when it was not identical with—an official religious policy. The pioneering Iberians had established with papal consent the division of the Americas within their sphere into a Christendom-versus-infidel classification that William McNeill refers to in *The Rise of the West* as the political interstices of the "Eurasian ecumene." Christendom, fraught with multiple political jealousies, broke apart during the wars of the Reformation. The Treaty of Cateau-Cambrésis (1559) accepted the principle that the political head of state determined the general religious denomination of the people. Conformity, however, proved tantalizingly unattainable, and further undermining of the metropolises, such as the religious wars in England and France during the sixteenth century, created fresh impetus to settler communities in the Americas—with the conscious conviction that their microcosm conveyed the best ideals of the old society.

Latin America and the Caribbean were spared the more extreme forms of that religious parochialism that drove John Winthrop and his pilgrims to the rather inhospitable coast of North America. But the domestic English rivalry between Anglicans, Presbyterians, and Arminians affected social relations in Barbados and Jamaica, and Jews found relative security only in the early Dutch settlements— thanks to Spanish-Dutch political antagonisms.

Individuals shared to a greater or lesser degree the official positions of church and state. Nevertheless to admit that church and state influenced the actions and attitudes of individuals ought by no means to be construed as a necessarily harmonious relationship between these groups. Indeed it was with considerable difficulty that the Spanish Crown imposed its authority over the conquering free lances and their descendants in the sixteenth century, or all the established societies dominated essentially by transfrontier groups such as the buccaneers during the seventeenth century. Nonconforming groups of Indians and Africans defied civil authorities until the nineteenth century. Individuals who defied authority, however, did not always form collectives. Nor did all move beyond the effective reach of the established society such as the buccaneers and Maroons. Bartolomé de las Casas and Thomas Gage chose to remain individual dissenters, the former protesting from within the framework of Spanish society, while the latter in one fell swoop changed both his religious and his political affiliation. Las Casas and Gage were merely the extremes of individual dissent in an essentially dissenting age.

The distinction between settler colonies and exploitation colonies was probably best sketched by the jaundiced eye and poisoned pen of that ethnocentric Englishman, James Anthony Froude, regius professor of modern history at Oxford University. Writing in an entirely different context, Froude saw two sets of colonies, one "as offering homes where English people can increase and multiply; English of the old type with simple habits, who do not need imported luxuries," and the other set serving Europeans to "go there to make fortunes which they are to carry home with them." Despite Froude's unsophisticated economic view, the two categories represented the goals of European colonization in the New World. In a real sense these categories represent two points along the kaleidoscope of ideal European colonial activity in the Americas.

To a certain extent every settler society had its exploitation component and every exploitation society its settler dimension. It is important to understand not only the dynamic interchange between these extremes (which often lead to reversals of the pattern) but also the corpus of ideologies that permeated the colony and gave it a sense

of community, a sense of identity. Europeans went to the Americas—
as they did in the wider world—to make a profit if they could, and to
settle if they had to; in the poignant words of the laconic adventurer
and fellow comrade of Hernan Cortés, Bernal Díaz del Castillo: "to
serve God and his majesty, to bring light to them that dwell in dark-
ness, and to get rich as all men desire to do."

Among these islands of contrast within each variant of the European colony in the Americas could be found anomalous individuals
within either settler or exploitation colony. These individuals established families that did not conform to the mold of their imposed
colonial pattern. Some of these families continued for generations,
even centuries—families such as Codrington, Drax, Pickering, and
Hothersall in Barbados; Warner and Jeaffreson in St. Kitts; Warner
and Kaynell in Antigua; Stapleton and Pinney in Nevis; and Price,
Dawkins, Tharp, and Beckford in Jamaica. At randomly selected periods, any of these families, viewed superficially, might appear socially
and politically indistinguishable from any of the prominent settler
families of New England, Virginia, New Spain, or Peru. Nevertheless
a crucial difference can be found in the attitudes that these English
West Indians held toward their territories, or the milieu that they
helped to create and their plantations perpetuated. These families
never ceased to be or to behave like transient English families. They
never ceased to identify closely with English society and the politics
of the metropolis. They prospered in the Caribbean, and that facilitated their reentry into English society. But at no time did they adapt
to the Caribbean.

The bewildering novelty and variety of America severely challenged
the colonists between the sixteenth and eighteenth centuries. The earliest settlements paid a discouragingly high price in human terms.
After a century or so, the dreams of El Dorado had become night-
mares to so many that spontaneous migrations overseas began to decline sharply. It became evident that the wealth of America would
only yield to arduous toil and constant perseverance in mines and
jungles and swampy, mosquito-infested tropical coastlands. The vision of cities of good people everywhere yielded to the geographical

imperatives of the region. Settlement colonies of Europeans would prosper only under climatic conditions roughly similar to those in Europe—in the salubrious highlands of Mexico and Peru, and, much later, on the peripheral lowlands of Brazil and Argentina. The widespread myth of geographical influence on a European population began, grew, and flourished as the source population absorbed slowly the empirical evidence on colonial ventures.

Still the necessities of empire and imperial commerce required the production of staple commodities of high value and small bulk which were most economically produced in the relatively insalubrious tropics. The Europeans repeated in the Americas what trial and error had produced in Africa—a situation where others did the toil and they reaped the profits. The exploitation colony was created.

This type of colony ideally responded to the developing political situation in Europe. Mercantilism was the catalyst of the exploitation colony, merging politics and economics to serve the interests of its expanding states. The role of the Dutch West India company in the Americas was not merely to show a profit to its corporate stockholders but to wage relentless attack on the political might of Spain. This rationale gave impetus to the slogan "no peace beyond the line."

The typical exploitation colony was one in which a minority population of Europeans usually but not always dominated and managed a majority of non-Europeans to produce some export commodity primarily for the European market. Unlike the settler colony, economic motivation became almost the sine qua non for European interest. Unlike settler societies, occupation, social cleavage, and social status tended to be mutually reinforcing and directly correlated to the respective level of participation in the export-commodity production. Almost everywhere these commodities were the tropical staples of tobacco, cotton, sugar, and coffee.

The mining communities of Brazil, Upper Peru, and New Spain were exploitation enclaves par excellence, but their symbiotic relationship to the surrounding settler communities diluted their influence and mitigated their social impact. The mines never succeeded in moving beyond the periphery of settler social and economic relations.

Not so the plantations. Plantations were the fertilizers of the exploitation colony, especially in view of their geographical insularity. For this reason northeastern Brazil (for all practical purposes an island prior to the nineteenth century), northern New Granada, and eastern or Gulf coast New Spain form, along with the Caribbean islands, a natural breeding ground for this type of social organization.

The exploitation colony came into its own in the seventeenth and eighteenth centuries, but the attempts go back to the earliest days of the Spanish presence—to the experiments of Pedro D'Avila's Darien community, and the post-Ovando Hispaniola, or Cortés's Marquesado estates. The *encomienda* system was perfectly compatible with, and conducive to, its genesis. What foiled these early attempts was the demographic disaster in the tropical American world and the exigencies of empire that precluded common Spanish contact with both the African and American fringes of the Atlantic simultaneously. To the very end of empire Spain pragmatically used Indians, Africans, and the lower classes from the metropolis in the economic development of her empire.

The exploitation colonies were typified by the Portuguese in Brazil; the Dutch in Brazil, Curaçao, Aruba, St. Eustatius, St. Croix, and Surinam; the English in Barbados, St. Kitts, Antigua, Nevis, Anguilla, Jamaica, and later Guiana; and the French in Saint-Domingue, Guadeloupe, Martinique, St. Lucia, and St. Vincent. The Spanish belatedly converted Cuba and Puerto Rico from settlement to exploitation colonies in the late eighteenth century, and almost succeeded in Caracas.

The imperial divisions, however, were of minor significance—a fact illustrated by the facility with which territories moved into and out of empires. The characteristics of the exploitation colony followed a logic and a tradition that was created in the twelfth-century Levantine Mediterranean basin and moved inexorably westwards with the changing fortunes of the European Atlantic expansion. Discernible differences occasionally appeared as the colonies responded to the vicissitudes of European political alliances, Western economics, and their own dynamics. These colonies became societies with self-conscious identities no less strong than those of the settler communities, albeit considerably more vulnerable to prevailing winds of economic, political, and ideological change.

Nevertheless it was precisely the distinct ethos of the exploitation society that made it somewhat anomalous in the eighteenth century world. If that ethos was permeated with instability, this was the consequence of the character of the colonists and the characteristics of the locale—character and characteristics that unsettled local leaders such as Edward Long, Moreau de Saint-Mery, and Ludy Nugent; tourists such as Alexander Humboldt and James Froude; and armchair philosophers such as the Abbé Raynall and Cornelius de Pauw.

European settlers tried to recreate and create, to preserve and perpetuate. European exploiters merely held together as long as they could. This difference manifested itself in the physical setting of the colony as well as the conduct of the colonists.

> Kingston is the best of our West Indian towns [wrote Froude in 1888] and Kingston has not one fine building in it. Havana is a city of palaces, a city of streets and plazas, of colonades and towers, and churches and monasteries. We English have built in those islands as if we were but passing visitors, wanting only tenements to be occupied for a time. The Spaniards built as they built in Castile; built with the same material, the white limestone which they found in the New World as in the Old. The palaces of the nobles in Havana, the residence of the governor, the convents, the cathedral, are a reproduction of Burgos or Valladolid, as if by some Aladdin's lamp a Castilian city had been taken up and set down again unaltered on the shore of the Caribbean Sea. And they carried with them their laws, their habits, their institution and their creed, their religious orders, their bishops and their Inquisition.

Froude was, of course, viewing a Havana luxuriating in the fortunes of the sugar plantation society of the nineteenth century. He did not know, and probably did not care to find out, that this splendid vista was of recent creation. Indeed until the late eighteenth century Havana was a rather dilapidated *gran aldea* (large village). More important, perhaps, is the similarity between the early Spanish settlers in Cuba and the early English settlers in Barbados or St. Christopher.

For the early English, like the early Spanish, built and behaved in the Caribbean as they did at home in Europe. "The early West India colonists," wrote the historian Richard Dunn, ". . . tried their best to transfer English modes of diet, dress and housing to the tropics. Scorning to imitate the Spaniards, the Indians or the Negroes [sic] who were all experienced at living in hot countries, they clung determinedly to their own North European styles and standards."

The attempt to perpetuate the settler colony in the British Caribbean failed dismally. By 1650 Barbados and the Leewards forsook their settler destinies to pursue the lucrative path of the tropical plantation society. Those English who remained on the islands—or who came out later—no longer attempted to reproduce English societies of predominantly non-English peoples. As the islands became plantations based on slave labor, the English retained their Englishness, grotesquely flaunting their origins. The divergence with the mainland accelerated as the settler experiments continued, with geographical modifications on the mainland especially in New England, Virginia, and the Carolinas. The plantation society produced a plantation culture, while the settler society produced its own settler culture.

As long as the base population of the colonial venture remained predominantly European, settler societies faced no greater problem than adjusting constantly to the cultural variations produced by time and geography. Until the late seventeenth century, the Englishman born in the Americas was no less "English" in outlook and attitudes than the Englishman born in England. Both shared a set of assumptions and values that, while not homogeneous, had not appeared to either native Englishman or American-born Englishman to be fundamentally different. The same holds true for the French, Portuguese, Dutch, and Spanish.

The "upper-class" English colonist, if he could afford it, still went to England to complete his education. The Spanish-American creole, while educated locally, assumed that the local universities in Mexico, Guatemala, Havana, or Peru were inferior to those in, say, Salamanca or Alacalá de Henares. By 1700 then neither the European power positions nor American colonial self-confidence were clear. The eighteenth century saw both the resolution of political hegemony in Europe on the one hand and the maturation of colonial American communities on the other into the American creole society.

By the beginning of the eighteenth century the pattern of settlement colonies and of exploitation colonies became demonstrably clear. And the subsequent divergence between Europe and the Americas increased in geometric progression. By the end of the century the Atlantic world had become engrossed in a revolution that strained the intellectual legacy of Europe and shattered the imperial tradition throughout the Americas. The Jamaican planter and member of the British Parliament, Bryan Edwards, described that contagious restlessness as "a spirit of subversion . . . which set a nought the wisdom of our ancestors, and the lessons of experience."

Yet Edwards's "spirit of subversion" did not bear the same apprehensions for both types of societies that were developing in the Americas. In general settler societies interpreted this "spirit" in the best liberal intellectual tradition of the Enlightenment as both a good and glorious thing. British North Americans, under the banner of "No Taxation Without Representation," forsook the empire to chart their own political destiny. Political independence, however, failed to destroy the strong cultural links with England and the rest of Europe, and the end of the war in 1783 brought only minor changes in the social structure and the social base of political power in the new state. In Latin America, under the slogan of "*Viva El Rey. Muera el mal gobierna*," the Spanish-Americans dismantled the mainland empire: in the case of South America to implement a more liberal constitution than that offered by the Junta of Cadiz; in the case of Mexico, to thwart the introduction of that liberalism; while the Brazilians established an equal family division between Lisbon and Rio de Janeiro. Everywhere the local oligarchies, like the propertied classes in the United States of America, usurped political power and began to articulate their own ideas about the state, ideas that descended with only minor adaptions from the corpus of European nationalistic and intellectual traditions.

The outstanding exception, of course, was Saint-Domingue, the notorious colony that flourished until 1792 on the western part of the island of Hispaniola. There things deviated both from the centrifugal currents of the settler mainland and the centripetal currents of the other exploitation islands. There the French colonists endeavored to have their cake and eat it—pretending to be simultaneously Frenchmen and French Caribbean colonists. It was a tragic miscalculation. For them 1789 was the wrong time, and Saint-Domingue was the worst place to emulate the ambiguous metropolitan generalizations of "liberty, equality and fraternity." Saint Domingue was, after all, not Mexico or Peru or Brazil or the United States: it was not a settler society with the common understanding or common appeal that transcended class, race, and color, and gave practical significance to a majority. Saint-Domingue was an exploitation colony—the exploitation colony par excellence during the eighteenth century—where the ideological miscalculation that a minority view was the general will led not only to the fratricidal civil war of the mainland but also to a general slave revolt and a race war. Once war broke out power gravitated to the majority of slaves, with the assistance of that exotic tropical disease, yellow fever. As a result the only true revolution in the Americas before the twentieth century occurred in Haiti, when in 1804 Henri Christophe, Jean Jacques Dessalines, Alexander Petión, and countless unknown others completely destroyed the old social order and reconstituted an entirely new polity.

Whether the Haitian revolution was creative—that is, originally conceived—or reactive—that is, responding negatively to the French attempts to reimpose slavery—the hegemony of the slaves represented a logical extension of the leveling down process in a pluralistic society where the intellectual paradigms of the social structure contradicted the reality of day-to-day living. In the unconscious assumptions of the superordinate groups of literate whites and free persons of color in Saint-Domingue in 1789, liberty and equality meant relaxation of metropolitan controls and the removal of the political and legal disabilities of the wealthy *gens de couleur*. To the slaves of Saint-Domingue—unschooled as they were in eighteenth-century rational thought—liberty and equality meant complete freedom from bondage. In the social context of exploitation, both connotations were irreconcilable.

The ambiguities of this situation dissipated the strongly nationalistic manifestions that prevailed in the settler societies by the end of the eighteenth century. The type of patriotism—or more accurately, *patriachiquismo*—that infused the writings of John Adams of New England or Francisco Javier Clavijero of New Spain was a luxury which the Caribbean whites could not afford. Nor was this the consequence of diet and disease and climate as De Pauw, Buffon, and Adams believed. Rather it was the instinctive ambivalence of a group whose hearts and minds remained adamantly European while their bodies responded to the overpowering impact of African ethnic and cultural influences on their brittle plantation world. The creole habits, customs, and outlook so deprecated by Long, Moreau Saint-Méry, and Lady Nugent were contrapuntal to the Europocentrism of the late eighteenth and early nineteenth century. The exploitation society was the true melting pot of race, culture, and belief. Europeans and Africans shared a peculiar world that profoundly affected both groups simultaneously, and the plight of the European-born in such a world or acclimatized to such conditions was this merger. The African component of exploitation colonial culture, in common with the Indian element in mainland settler culture, was an interesting and important variant on the development of American creole culture. These variants, wherever they were found, and however they were composed, were neither inferior nor superior derivatives of Europe and Africa. They were simply different. The extent to which Africans or Europeans affected the operational values and behavior of any society depended on the proportional size, cohesiveness, self-confidence, and mode of arrival of each component group.

The apparently antagonistic ideals of settler and exploitation colonies had far-reaching consequences for the development of creole society in Latin America and the Caribbean, consequences whose impact is often overlooked by the conventional historiographical model of treating the regions in isolated imperial compartments, chronologically divided.

The division of the Caribbean into settler and exploitation colonies facilitates the analysis of the society by incorporating the inherent dynamics of social change. No longer are societies viewed either as frozen entities suspended in time or reactive structures incapable of articulating their own world view. Any systadial—rather than synchronic—description of the region reveals the continuous attempts by all segments of the colonial societies to come to grips with their particular circumstances in ways that gave meaning to their lives and coherence to their communities. The basic divisions in American colonial societies were not between masters and slaves, Iberians and Indians, Europeans and Africans, or Protestants and Catholics. The basic divisions occurred among societies that allowed all groups to react interdependently, each in its own way creating an environment consonant with a vision of man, nature, and society.

In the settler societies the transfer of the conventional institutions of the metropolis provided the model for conformity and socialization. Newcomers could accept such norms, and usually did. Dualities of status and power could exist, although not without internal strains. The settlers were an enclave determined to succeed, and consciously set about discovering ways to facilitate their domination of nature. Settlers adapted freely and pragmatically, however much they deplored such actions. The very success in taming the wilderness lent zeal to what Francisco López Camara describes as "*la conciencia de sí*," gallantly portrayed by Hawkeye in James Fenimore Cooper's *Last of the Mohicans*. If from the metropolitan perspective settler societies appeared centrifugal; from the colonial view those same traits were centripetal, forging a new independent polity.

Exploitation societies, however, lacked a common, unifying institutional basis. They were ad hoc societies—innovative only for self-preservation. Not only were such societies divided, they tended to be divisive, with mutually reinforcing cleavages within the castes. However long the elite remained physically *in situ*, they were psychologically transients, with a myopic confusion of social order and productive efficiency. The most enduring and sometimes the most interesting features of the society were created by the lower classes, who were often told what they could not do but rarely what they ought to do.

Nevertheless the cultural weaknesses and deficiencies of the plantation elite provided an almost unique opportunity for the coerced African element to help fashion a society. And the greatest distinctions within the Afro-American tradition resulted not only from the legacy of demography and diet but also from patterns of colonization, creolization, and Americanization.

This realization of the way societies evolve is a basic requirement to understanding the colonial experience of Latin America and the Caribbean. The region forms one culture area no more subdivided and internally variable than is India, West Africa, the British Isles, Europe, or the United States. The difference between settler and exploitation societies should not be seen in terms of superior or inferior, of better or worse. By doing so one surrenders the positive characteristics of interaction and interdependence to the dictates of nationalism and chauvinism. Of course the "settler and exploiter" division of the colonies by no means exhausts the wide range of social responses to the circumstances of the American frontier. The settler and exploiter divisions merely form the focus of the European colonizing efforts in the western hemisphere, and as such represent not a rejection of the conventional historical parameters but a clarification in the interest of greater objectivity. Moreover the commonalities that linked the Caribbean peoples far exceeded their differences—although some of these differences were, and remain today, extremely important. And nowhere were these commonalities more profound, or more portentous, than in the long experience with the twin yokes of European imperialism and African slavery.

Chapter 4 • Imperialism and Slavery

It were somewhat difficult, to give you an exact account, of the number of persons upon the Island; there being such store of shipping that brings passengers daily to the place, but it has been conjectur'd, by those that are long acquainted, and best seen in the knowledge of the Island, that there are not less than 50 thousand souls, besides Negroes; and some of them who began upon small fortunes, are now risen to very great and vast estates.

The island is divided into three sorts of men, viz: Masters, Servants and Slaves. The slaves and their posterity, being subject to their masters for ever, are kept and preserv'd with greater care than the servants, who are theirs but for five years, according to the law of the Island. So that for the time, the servants have the worser lives, for they are put to very hard labour, ill lodging, and their dyet very sleight.

Richard Ligon,
True and Exact History . . . of Barbadoes, 1653

The seventeenth century witnessed some fundamental changes in the political, economic, and social structure of the Caribbean. This was the century that marked the transition from settler communities to exploitation colonies within the non-Hispanic sphere. The most startling political change was the balkanization of the imperial divisions as the Dutch, the French, and the English successfully defied the might of Spain and established permanent strongholds along the strategic outer periphery of what had for more than a century been reluctantly conceded as the private domain of the monarchs of Castille. After 1700 Caribbean possessions changed hands among European powers, but the region remained cosmopolitan. Economically those early outposts of empire began to assume increasing international importance owing to their conversion into major producers of tropical staples—a conversion in which the older Spanish colonies on Cuba, Hispaniola, and Puerto Rico lagged perceptibly. Socially the Caribbean acquired a racial-class delineation far more complex than the simple divisions of Richard Ligon's "three sorts of men." And the connection between society, economy, and politics was related to the development and inexorable expansion of the Caribbean sugar industry.

As late as 1700—and much later on the larger islands and mainland possessions—the European colonies in the Caribbean constituted growing enclaves with moving frontiers. Until the Peace of Utrecht in 1713 there were two general types of society existing in alternating harmony and discord. The first type comprised the boisterous, violent society of struggling settlers, prospering planters, exasperated officials, machinating merchants, suffering slaves, and ambivalent free persons of color. These were the true colonists who accepted, albeit under duress, the rules, regulations, and interventions of the metropolis, and subscribed in varying degrees to the political integrity of the different imperial systems. The second social type generated by the considerable sociopolitical flux of the times was a variegated group of individuals, commonly considered transfrontiersmen. Such transfrontier groups ranged from the organized communities of Maroons, or escaped slaves, to the defiant, stateless collectivity of buccaneers. These groups—Maroons and buccaneers—were not primarily a threat to settled, organized society, but represented a temporary alternative to the colonial social structure.

The Maroons formed the most successful alternative to organized European colonial society. Born of the resistance to slavery, they were essentially communities of Africans who escaped individually and

collectively from the plantations and households of their masters to
seek their freedom, thereby continuing a tradition begun by the indigenous Indians. The word "maroon" was first used to describe the
range cattle that had gone wild after the first attempts at Spanish
colonization on the island of Hispaniola. Then the Spanish transferred the term to the escaped Indian slaves, and finally to their African successors. In any case, *marronage*—the flight from servitude—
became an intrinsic dimension of American slavery, enduring as long
as the institution of slavery itself.

American plantation society spawned two forms of resistance to
enslavement. The first was the temporary desertion of individual
slaves. This form of escape, called frequently *petit marronage*, reflected a strong personal inclination on the part of the slave to resist
labor, to procrastinate, to defy a master or a rule, or to visit friends,
family, or acquaintances in the neighborhood without the requisite
permission. *Petit marronage* was eventually accepted with due reluctance as one of the inescapable concomitants of the system, and was
punished with less severity than other infringements of local regulations, or other patterns of behavior that jeopardized the social order.
At its most serious, *petit marronage* remained a personal conflict between master and slave.

This was not equally true of the second form of resistance, which
constituted a fully organized attempt to establish autonomous communities, socially and politically independent of the European colonial enclave. This pattern of conduct was potentially subversive to the
entire socioeconomic complex of colonial life. Such communities—
variously called *palenques* in the Spanish colonies, *quilombos* or *mo-
cambos* in the Portuguese, and Maroon towns in the English colonies
—encompassed varying numbers of individuals. They not only survived for considerable periods of time but also represented the eloquent negative expressions of the Africans and Afro-Americans about
the situation in which they found themselves. Organized bands of
Maroons prevailed for centuries in Jamaica, outlasting the determined
communities of Bahia and Palmares in Brazil, Esmeraldas in Ecua-
dor, and le Maniel in French Saint-Domingue.

Detested and vehemently opposed by the European slave-owning

colonists, these misnamed towns taxed the ingenuity and resourceful-
ness of all the participants both for their sustenance and for their
survival. Considering the extreme disadvantages under which the
Maroons labored, it is most surprising that so many communities survived for such long periods of time, often in close proximity to operating plantations. The principal ingredients for success seemed to be
the nature of their social organization and the physical location of the
communities.

Maroon villages were composed predominantly of able-bodied
adults. Bryan Edwards, the Jamaican planter, historian, and later
member of parliament in Great Britain, wrote a curiously admiring
description of the Maroons, which reveals as much about the writer
and his society as his subject:

> Savage as they were in manners and disposition, their mode of
> living and daily pursuits undoubtedly strengthened their frame,
> and served to exalt them to great bodily perfection. Such fine
> persons as are seldom beheld among any other class of African or
> native blacks. Their demeanor is lofty, their walk firm, and their
> persons erect. Every motion displays a combination of strength
> and agility. The muscles (neither hidden nor depressed by
> clothing) are very prominent, and strongly marked. Their sight
> withal is wonderfully acute, and their hearing remarkably quick.
> These characteristics, however, are common, I believe, to all
> savage nations, in warm and temperate climates; and like other
> savages, the Maroons have only those senses perfect which are
> kept in constant exercise. Their smell is obtuse, and their taste so
> depraved, that I have seen them drink new rum fresh from the
> still, in preference to wine which I offered them; and I remem-
> ber, at a great festival in one of their towns, which I attended,
> that their highest luxury, in point of food, was some rotten beef,
> which had been originally salted in Ireland, and which was prob-
> ably presented to them, by some person who knew their taste,
> *because it was putrid.*

Leadership seemed to have been determined by military and political ability, and one of the most successful of the Jamaican Maroon
leaders was a formidable lady called Nanny. Like the mature slave so-

ciety, early Maroon communities revealed a strong masculine sex-dominance. The scarcity of women and the observed polygamy of some leaders forced some unusual practices during the formative years of the community. One such practice was raiding for the express purpose of capturing women. Another was the enforced sharing of females. As the community endured and stabilized, however, the sexual imbalance adjusted itself, especially after the Maroons were able to produce and nurture to adulthood their own offspring. The most successful leaders, such as Cudjoe and Nanny in Jamaica, Macandal or Santiago in Saint-Domingue, combined religious roles with their political positions, thereby reinforcing their authority over their followers. They also showed an unusual understanding of settled colonial society, which facilitated their ability to deal with the white political leaders. Prior to the eighteenth century most leaders tended to be rigidly authoritarian and often needlessly cruel. New recruits to Maroon communities were scrupulously tested, and deserters, wanderers, and suspected spies were brutally killed. Nevertheless, many Maroon villages fell victim to internal feuds or disenchanted defections from the ranks.

Security was the constant preoccupation of the Maroon villages. The physical setting of the village became a prime ingredient in its survival and eventual evolution. All successful villages in the Caribbean depended, at least initially, on their relative inaccessibility. They were strategically located in the densely forested interior of the Sierra Maestra of eastern Cuba, the conical limestone ridges of the Cockpit Country in western Jamaica, the precipitous slopes of the Blue Mountains in eastern Jamaica, the formidable *massifs* of Haiti, the rugged *cordilleras* of Santo Domingo, and the isolated interior of the smaller islands. Where geography was not conducive to hiding, such as in cities, or on very small islands, or less rugged terrain as found in Barbadoes, Antigua, Martinique, or Guadeloupe, *petit marronage* rather than *gran marronage* seemed to be the order of the day.

Given the inhospitable environment, only the most fit Maroon communities survived. Starvation, malnutrition, dysentery, smallpox, and accidental poisoning from unfamiliar leaves and herbs took a high toll of the original Maroons. Moreover the threat of discovery and attack by the organized colonial society remained constant. Cuban and Jamaican colonists employed specially trained dogs to hunt and recapture Maroons, and throughout the Caribbean the activities of large-scale military search-and-destroy missions were sporadic but important. Notwithstanding the hazards, Maroon communities recruited and trained enough manpower to defy local authorities, wage successful wars, and secure their own peace treaties, as did the Jamaican Maroons in 1739 and 1795. Or they secured a modus vivendi with the local communities and recognition from the political authorities as did the Maroons in le Maniel in southern Saint-Domingue.

Successful *marronage* required the concealed cooperation of slaves and other benefactors within settled society. In this way firearms, tools, utensils, and in some cases food, could be secured to help establish the community and subdue the forest. Not only urban Maroons, but also a large number of rural Maroons, gradually developed a semi-symbiotic relationship with the society from which they had withdrawn their support, and revoked their servile status.

Unfortunately it was this very semisymbiosis that proved most lethal to the integrity, cultural distinctiveness, and vitality of Maroon existence. Once the Maroons succeeded in gaining legal or quasi-legal recognition, their structure, internal organization, methods of recruitment, and political attitudes underwent significant changes. In the treaties they signed they accepted severely limited territorial concessions. They also got a legal status. But the price they paid was the surrender of some internal power and control. Runaway slaves could no longer be ascripted to the group, but were handed over to the planter societies—often for a fee. This practice not only restricted the physical size of the community but insidiously undermined the political appeal of the Maroons as a viable alternative to organized slavery. "Following the treaties [between the Jamaican government and the Maroons]," wrote Richard Price in his introduction to *Maroon Societies*, "these same Jamaican Maroons bought, sold, and owned substantial numbers of slaves, hunted new runaways for a price, managed to gain the hatred of much of the slave population, and in many respects may have deserved their common post-treaty nickname, 'The King's Negroes.' " If the Maroons viewed the treaty as a form of collective security, it nevertheless represented a strengthening of the very sociopolitical structure they formerly had despised. Moreover it strengthened the system of slave control by removing, reducing, or otherwise restricting one option of personal escape from slavery to freedom. Maroon communities, by agreeing to the external legal controls on basic aspects of their life, even regarding the succession of leaders, may have done themselves more harm than good. In common with all groups crossing a common frontier, the Maroon societies gradually became virtually indistinct from their neighboring slave communities. Moreover they lacked adequate facilities for long-term economic and social success. Like other transfrontier groups, the Maroons were, like the French Huguenots, ultimately unable to overcome the limitations and internal contradictions of a state within a state.

Like Maroons, the buccaneers were the products of a stage of social evolution in the Caribbean. But buccaneers represented a shorter historical phase, whose period of glory lasted from about the middle of the seventeenth century to the beginning of the eighteenth. This was the period of greatest political and social transition in the Caribbean, of the decline of Spanish influence from the great days of the early sixteenth century and "no peace beyond the line." The boundaries of empires as well as the notions of international law were extremely vague, facilitating fluctuating alliances or associations of European communities within the region. These essentially stateless persons lived comfortably by commerce with the settled communities of European colonists, just as did the Maroons, and with the help of the large numbers of cattle, horses, hogs, and dogs that proliferated on the tropical savannas in the wake of the early Spanish settlement.

It was in this very idyllic existence that legends place the origins of the buccaneers. The word itself derives from the aboriginal Indian custom of slowly drying and curing strips of meat (boucan) over an open fire. This delicious product found a ready market with the increasing number of ships trafficking in Caribbean waters. Small colo-

nies of these hunters and smokers flourished during the middle decades of the sixteenth century on the western parts of Puerto Rico and
Hispaniola, vending hides and boucan to the ships passing through
the Mona Passage and Windward Passage. Over a period of time the
hunters gradually diversified their economic base by adding piracy to
their occupation, and extending their operations to the rugged, but
easily defensible island of Tortuga—relatively safe from the periodic
Spanish search-and-destroy missions, but still very close to the wild
herds of northwestern Hispaniola. Eventually the buccaneers forged
a community, in which the urge for adventure and plunder overrode
the need to settle down. In the Anglophone Caribbean, the term buccaneers adhered to the amorphous group long after they had forsaken
the art of hunting and boucaning. The French preferred the term
corsairs or "flibustiers," while the Dutch called the group "zee roo-
vers." The more successful buccaneers such as Henry Morgan considered themselves to be "Brethren of the Coasts," with allegiance
to no state, and obligation to no laws but their own.

By the middle of the seventeenth century the buccaneers had
achieved international fame and had attracted a motley band
throughout the Caribbean probably numbering a few thousand. Their
recruits came from shipwrecks, deserters from the regular crews of
vessels sailing in the region, fortune seekers, and men and women
repelled by the regimentation and coercion of the sugar plantation
society then rapidly spreading from island to island. But the international importance of the buccaneers undoubtedly increased because
they had the capacity to perform the free-lance attacks on the Spanish
possessions in the Caribbean which neither the English nor French,
then riddled with civil conflicts or domestic political weakness, could
achieve. The buccaneers, by keeping Spain off-balance in the Caribbean, contributed to the permanent success of the non-Spanish attempts at colonization in the tropical Americas. On the other hand
Spain, by trying to destroy the communities of buccaneers—especially
by hitting at their subsidiary economic activity, boucaning—justified
their raison d'être. The myth of Spanish wealth and the reality of
Spanish treasure fleets assembling off Havana and sailing to Europe

each spring merely sharpened the cupidity of an already rapacious group.

Père Labat, the indefatigable Dominican or Jacobin priest who served in the French West Indies from 1694 to 1705 and whose memoirs were published posthumously in 1743, left a rare first-hand account of the organization and political importance of the buccaneers, albeit in their waning days. Labat's account compares favorably with that of Exquemelin, and appears to have captured the attitudes and actions of the buccaneers during their predominantly sea-roving phase:

> "St. Pierre [Martinique], 6th March 1694. We were busy all this morning confessing a crew of *flibustiers* who had arrived at Les Mouillages with two prizes that they had captured from the English. The Mass of the Virgin was celebrated with all solemnity, and I blessed three large loaves which were presented by the captain and his officers, who arrived at the church accompanied by the drums and trumpets of their corvette. At the beginning of Mass the corvette fired a salute with all her cannons. At the Elevation of the Holy Sacrament, she fired another salvo, at the Benediction a third, and finally a fourth, when we sang the Te Deum after Mass. All the *flibustiers* contributed 30 sols to the sacristy, and did so with much piety and modesty. This may surprise people in Europe where *flibustiers* are not credited with possessing much piety, but as a matter of fact they generally give a portion of their good fortunes to the churches. If church ornament or church linen happen to be in the prizes they capture, the *flibustiers* always present them to their parish church.
>
> The conditions of Roving are set forth in what is called *Chasse Partie*. If the vessel belongs to the *flibustiers* themselves, their booty is shared equally. The captain and the quartermaster (who is always second in command on these ships), the surgeon and the pilot receive no more than anyone else except a gift which is given to them by the rest of the crew. As a rule the captain is given a present which is equivalent to three and sometimes four extra shares. The quartermaster is presented with an additional two shares. The pilot and surgeon each receive an extra share and a half: Boys are given a half-share, and the man who first sights the prize wins an extra share.

Other items in the agreement are: That if a man be wounded
he has to receive one *écu* a day as long as he remains in the sur-
geon's hands up to sixty days, and this has to be paid or allowed
for before any man receives his share. A man receives 600 *écus*
for the loss of each limb, 300 *écus* for the loss of a thumb or the
first finger of the right hand, or an eye, and 100 *écus* for each of
the other fingers. If a man has a wooden leg or a hook for his
arm and these happen to be destroyed, he receives the same
amount as if they were his original limbs.

In the case the ship is chartered by *flibustiers*, the owners have
to provision and arm the ship, and receive one-third of the prizes.

In war-time the *flibustiers* are given commissions by the governor of the different islands, who receive a tenth share in the
prizes. In peace-time they were given permits to fish. But either
with or without commissions, the *flibustiers* pillaged the Spaniards, who hanged them as pirates whenever they caught them.

The description of Labat underlined the principal characteristics
of the buccaneers that set them apart from the Maroons as transfrontiersmen. In terms of cultural distinction, the Maroons were
patently further removed from settler society than the buccaneers.
For the buccaneers won the admiration of their metropolitan public,
even though an account such as Exquemelin's history emphasized
the savagery, selfishness, excessive avarice, and utter lawlessness of
that infamous international horde.

The buccaneers were essentially stateless individuals, but they retained strong links with the general culture and society with which
they were familiar. They did not try, as did the American Maroons, to
create a culture and a society. They had their culture, and they knew
their social origins quite well. What they sought—at least for a time—
was freedom from the restraints and obligations of that culture and
society. The leaders of the buccaneers had some "national" identity:
Alexandre Exquemelin was Dutch; Bartholomé Portuguez—the most
famous nonswimmer in the history of the buccaneers—was Portuguese; Rock, the Dutchman, had lived in Brazil; Francis L'Olonnois,
the Cruel, was a Frenchman; Henry Morgan of Barbados—later Sir
Henry Morgan, lieutenant-governor of Jamaica—was born in Wales;
Raveneau de Lassan—in all probability a fictitious character—claimed

to be a French buccaneer. To be sure most buccaneers were not from what was then commonly called the "cultivated classes" of Europe. A large number, among them Morgan, Exquemelin, and L'Olonnois, had served as indentured servants or *engagés* in the emergent sugar plantations of the Caribbean. With the demand for labor outstripping the supply, the later accusation that some of these unfortunate indentureds might have been aggressively kidnapped could be true. Moreover the conditions of servitude engendered an enormous antipathy toward the state not unlike that of the African slaves.

The harsh conditions of indenture produced a physically tough and spiritually callous individual, capable of surviving the exacting and hazardous conditions of international piracy. But this occupation did not dissolve their links with settled society, which often found the buccaneers as convenient a bulwark of defense as the Jamaican planters of the eighteenth century found Cudjoe's Maroons. Moreover the ill-gotten plunder of the buccaneers, lavishly dispensed in the local towns, compensated adequately for their otherwise detestable social manners.

The economic importance of the buccaneers contributed in no small way to their general acceptance among the non-Spanish Caribbean authorities. Clarence Haring in his history of the buccaneers describes the English capture of Jamaica and the entire Cromwellian "Grand Design" of 1655 as "a reversion to the Elizabethan gold-hunt . . . the first of the great buccaneering expeditions." John Milton, Oliver Cromwell's Latin secretary, gave the official justification as a response to the cruelties of the Spanish towards the English-American colonists; their cruelty toward the Indians; and the Spanish refusal to sanction English trade with their empire. Sir Charles Lyttleton, the lieutenant-governor of Jamaica in the early 1660's, proposed six practical reasons for official support of the buccaneers, and these seemed to have impressed the English metropolitan government. Privateering, he argued, provided a number of able-bodied men and available ships that served to protect the island in the absence of a navy. Privateers had extremely valuable information on local navigation, and their practical experience would be invaluable in wartime. The international connections of the buccaneers supplied uniquely rich intelligence on the size, preparation, and potential wealth of Spanish towns and Spanish naval activities. The prizes and currency brought to Port Royal attracted merchants, contributed to the economy, and helped to reduce prices. English colonial authorities lacked the requisite naval force to destroy the bands of buccaneers, and English seamen had such great admiration for the brotherhood that it was doubtful they would zealously support such activities. Finally Lyttleton argued that any attempt to destroy the buccaneers might simply serve to attract their aggressive retaliation on English plantations and English commerce.

Lyttleton knew his buccaneers well, and had perhaps personally profited from his short association with them. In any case he was familiar with their modus operandi. For buccaneers did not usually attack the colony from which the leader of the band originated, nor citizens related in nationality or culture to the majority of the members. In practice, therefore, French privateers, led by a Dutchman, would normally attack only Spanish or English towns and ships; and English buccaneers preferred the spoils of their rivals. Everyone saw the Spanish, however, as fair game. By the beginning of the second half of the seventeenth century, although the lingua franca of the buccaneers remained French, the leadership became English, and, after 1655, the main base of operation shifted from Tortuga to Port Royal. Buccaneer wealth provided a healthy stimulus to the early local economy of the islands. Captain Henry Morgan, admiral-in-chief of the confederacy of Jamaican buccaneers, used his returns from privateering to build a splendid city home in Port Royal, purchase a sugar plantation in the interior, and become the lieutenant-governor of the second most important English Caribbean possession at that time. Apart from the inordinate amounts of bullion and currency which the buccaneers brought and distributed, they dealt in cane, slaves, jewels, silks, spices, wine, and cattle. Buccaneering during the seventeenth century was not only a political weapon; it was also a crude form of imperial revenue-sharing.

Persistent war and conflicts over trade in the Caribbean increased the strategic importance of the buccaneers. Until the late 1670's buccaneers sought formal commissions to engage in privateering raids throughout the region. Ostensibly such commissions made them the legal representatives of the English or French Crown, and their conquests a part of the expansion of empire. But the complicated international situation after the Restoration in England—with Charles II moving toward friendship with Spain, and enmity with France— forced the award of aggressive commissions away from the center of empire to the local governors, whose authority could then be superseded should diplomatic relations so warrant. The legitimate cover of a commission enabled the buccaneers to equip their ships with powder, shot, cannons, and supplies, as well as recruit men. But from the buccaneer point of view, political support was merely a cover—the interests of empire being of minor importance. In this way, Jérémie Deschamps, Seigneur du Rausset, obtained by duplicity simultaneous commissions from the French and the English and successfully played one power against the other for a short period of time, while the status of his "colony" of Tortuga remained ambiguous. Deschamps finally ended up in the Bastille in Paris, where he was persuaded to cede his interest in Tortuga to Jean-Baptiste Colbert's French West India Company for 15,000 livres and his freedom. On the other hand, Henry Morgan was apparently quite upset by the suggestion of Alexandre Exquemelin that he had sailed without a commission, and sought to have the English edition of Exquemelin's history of the buccaneers suppressed. In 1684 Morgan also brought a charge of libel against the publishers, for the lack of a royal commission erased the legal distinction between piracy, which was illegal, and buccaneering, which was not. At stake also was Morgan's new status as a gentleman, knight, influential planter, and respectable lieutenant-governor of Jamaica. By 1684 the golden age of buccaneering was fading fast.

The conditions that had proved most propitious to buccaneering activity ceased after 1770—although it was some time before the signals reached the Caribbean. The political significance of a semi-legal, uncontrolled band to further the cause of colonization yielded to the diplomatic adroitness, increased military strength, and self-consciousness of Louis XIV in France and Charles II in England. Moreover Spain was no longer the power it used to be. The possessions of the French West India Company became true colonies after 1674; and Charles II moved to exercise greater control over the English West Indian islands. Greater supervision of the colonies severely undermined the previous reciprocal relationship between settler society and the transfrontier communities. Lyttleton's analysis was no longer valid. The withdrawal of formal commissions during the 1680's and 1690's meant that the same activities formerly hailed in England and France were condemned as piracy, subject to punishment by hanging. The legal end came with the Treaty of Ryswyck in 1697, when France joined the Dutch (the Treaty of The Hague in 1673) and the English (the Treaty of Windsor in 1680) in agreeing to withdraw official support for the buccaneers. These treaties with Spain, signed outside Iberia, underlined her military decline. Individual, uncontrolled marauding became politically counterproductive to the genesis of exploitation societies based on slave-operated plantations and international commerce. Even nature seemed to support the change. In 1692 Port Royal, the most notorious stronghold of buccaneers, slipped ominously into the sea after a severe earthquake, taking along the house and tomb of Henry Morgan. The activity which had elevated Morgan and Jean-Baptiste du Casse from transfrontier sea rovers to imperial governors no longer prevailed.

The existence of communities of buccaneers represented a stage in the transition from pioneering colonialism to organized imperialism. And the changes in the Caribbean reflected changes in Europe. England, France, and Holland had become strong enough to dictate aspects of their relations with Spain. But the Spanish had not yet become so weak that her empire could be wrested from her. Trade, not the export of people founding microcosmic European societies, became the major preoccupation; and the exigencies of trade demanded not only a new relationship between metropolis and colony but a new climate of international order. This new climate required the control, coordination, and responsibility that was the anathema of buccaneering. Thus while the buccaneering bands displayed their skills, a series of events and circumstances ushered in a new order. Non-Hispanic European states began to expand their political influence by conquest rather than settlement, exemplified by the capture of Jamaica in 1655 and the French advance on western Hispaniola, conceded at Ryswyck in 1697. The French reorganized their empire under Colbert, and finally brought it under the direct control of the Crown in 1774. Spanish-American mainland silver production declined significantly; domestic Spanish industries virtually disappeared; and Spanish merchant shipping drastically diminished in Caribbean ports. By 1686 more than 90 percent of the capital and goods handled on the legal Seville-to-the-Indies trade was controlled by French, Genoese, Dutch, English, and German businessmen (often working through Spanish intermediaries), while an estimated two-thirds of the Spanish-American trade was contraband. At this time, too, the Caribbean region had already been experiencing the revolutionary reorganization of its society, its agriculture, and its commerce. With an understandable delay in the Spanish possessions, the exploiters dominated or expelled the subsistence settlers. The age of sugar and slavery had arrived.

The massive introduction of African slaves and the employment of slavery as the main form of labor organization reflected a major sociopolitical change in the status and role of the Caribbean colonies. The resort to plantation agriculture indicated the failure to re-create viable colonies of Europeans in the tropical islands and lowlands. From about the 1640's, the semifeudal European settler frontier slowly gave way to the rigidly organized, commercially integrated exploitation society of masters and slaves. The slave society transmitted from east to west across the Caribbean brought greater and quicker profits to the private and public proponents of empire than did the former struggling enclaves of predominantly European farming communities.

The eventual adoption of slavery arose from the severe economic crisis of the seventeenth-century Caribbean, and especially from the overwhelming need to establish a more competitively marketable commodity than tobacco as the basis of a colonial economy. After a short period of trial and error, sugar cane emerged as the most valuable potential agricultural crop. Sugar had become increasingly popular on the European market, and the technique of its production had been known in Mediterranean Europe since the time of the crusades. Moreover sugar provided a balance between bulk and value so crucially important in the days of small sailing ships and distant sea voyages. Sugar production and export, however, demanded a considerable capital outlay and a larger, more reliable, and more consistent supply of labor than was available through contracted servants or irregularly supplied African slaves.

The relationship between a colonial export economy and its metropolis demanded a more structured political organization in the interest of trade. The English circumscribed the political independence of the Barbados Assembly in the late seventeenth century, and the French Crown took over direct control of its overseas colonies. A long series of mercantilist trade and navigation laws were passed during the succeeding century regulating the commerce between the European metropolises and their Caribbean colonies. Metropolitan merchants advancing capital and goods largely on credit desired a stable relationship conducive to long-term planning as well as to the security of their investment. Each European state saw enormous potential gain in the employment of its citizens, the development of its industry, and the expansion of its merchant marine through the twin pursuits of trade within the empire and trade with other Europeans and Africans.

From the colonial perspective, however, the priorities were different. As in the metropolis, colonists viewed the relationship between commerce and wealth as direct. Unlike the metropolitan group, they felt the fewer the restrictions on trade, the more lucrative would be the relationship. Colonial planters enjoyed the partial guarantee of the home market for their tropical commodities, but they wanted a steady supply of slaves from Africa and provisions as well as planting equipment from Europe and America. As they became more successful at their pursuits, they realized that mercantilism did not provide the greatest quantity at the lowest prices. On the other hand, free trade implied a state of commercial insecurity (especially with regard to the unsettled competitive politics of Europe) and the removal of the protection and support derived from being part of an empire. These divergent views, ideals, and practices could never be fully reconciled within the context of empire, and they precipitated within the managerial strata of Caribbean plantation society a resentment that grew more bitter with age. Perhaps no aspect of the commercial relationship bred more mutual irritation than the supply and price of African slaves, the most important single ingredient in the economic success of the plantation society.

As early as the 1630's, the bases of a sugar system were introduced to the Caribbean in an attempt to duplicate the Portuguese and Dutch success along the northeastern coast of Brazil. In 1639 the French *Compagnie des Iles d'Amérique*, acting in response to a number of individual entrepreneurs at home and overseas, signed a contract with a Dutch immigrant from Brazil to build a pioneer sugar estate of approximately 3000 acres on the island of Martinique. It was an ambitious undertaking, but, like other such early experiments, it failed from a combination of uncertain finances and an immature infrastructure unable to coordinate the many features of labor supply, agricultural management, and product marketing. Success necessitated at that period international, especially Dutch, support. The Dutch therefore acted as the organizational middlemen of the Caribbean sugar industry, deploying their capital, expertise, transportation, marketing facilities, and slaves throughout the English and French Caribbean. In 1647 the first successful cargoes of sugar left Barbados and Guadeloupe in Dutch ships for Europe. By 1650 the Dutch, confident of available supplies, established a number of refineries on their small eastern islands, a development that pleased the sugar planters as much as it irked the metropolises. For the succeeding thirty years the English and French fought a series of anti-Dutch naval wars in an effort to destroy Dutch influence and improve the efficacy of their own mercantile system.

If the English and French sugar industry depended on the benevolence of the Dutch, the same was not true of the early Spanish sugar industry. On his second voyage Christopher Columbus introduced the sugar cane to Hispaniola, and by the middle of the sixteenth century a number of relatively large estates had begun a lucrative export of sugar to Spain. Sugar production from water-powered mills became an attractive economic alternative to the *encomienda*, since both the supply of Indians and the quantities of gold had diminished greatly. Many partnerships involving the highest officials of the fledgling colony, such as the treasurer Esteban Passamonte, the *fiscal* Pedro Vásquez de Mella, the *contador* Alonso de Avila, and the *oidores* Lebron and Zuazo, imported Africans and participated in the early sugar industry. Diego Columbus had a large estate on the outskirts of the city of Santo Domingo with about forty African slaves producing sugar as early as 1522. Meanwhile Hernando Gorjón of Azua made enough money from the early sugar trade to Spain to endow the *colegio* in Santo Domingo which eventually became the first American university.

Like its Caribbean successors, the early Spanish sugar industry spread throughout the region, island-hopping according to the expansion of settlements and the availability of African slaves. By 1526 Hispaniola had nineteen sugar mills and was importing about four hundred Africans per year. Sugar mills were also established around San German in Puerto Rico and Santiago de la Vega in Jamaica. The gross production of these mills remains uncertain, but their exports totaling several thousand tons went to Spain, Mexico, and Cuba. Most probably as the result of the shortage of available capital, the Cuban sugar industry did not begin until the last decade of the sixteenth century. The first hydraulic mills established in the city of Havana had an export capacity of about three thousand *arrobas* (37.5 short tons) in 1600, sending their product to Spain, Campeche, and Cartagena. Spaniards had produced sugar on estates in southern Iberia, especially around Málaga and Huelva, and transferred the technique to the Americas. But most colonists utilized the sugar cane as a means of making syrup, expressing the juice by a simple manual wooden press or an equally simple, inefficient, rotary animal-powered press called a *trapiche*, and boiling it to the desired state of crystallization. An *ingenio* required both capital and a large supply of sugar cane which were beyond the individual means of most early colonists. As the numerous petitions to the Spanish Crown frequently repeated, a sugar industry needed African slave labor.

Although the Spanish Crown supported the new industry, even to the extent of lending the early Cuban sugar producers 40,000 ducats in 1595, production faltered. The high volume of Brazilian sugar exports to the European market served to depress further the Spanish-American export trade. But Spanish sugar production for domestic consumption remained high and economically attractive in Peru, Mexico, and the islands. Unfortunately the technology of Spanish sugar production remained stagnant, and not until the late eighteenth century did the Spanish return to large-scale sugar production for export.

The supply of slaves, on which any large-scale sugar industry depended, did not develop rapidly. African coastal stations had to be found, trade relations with the Africans established, and the exchange of European merchandise for Africans coordinated. So competitive was the international slave trade that, like the earlier experience of colonization, the private entrepreneurs sought and obtained the full support and military resources of their state to assist them in carving and defending their niche in the system. Thus the English and Dutch fought over access rights to the African ports until the Dutch formally recognized the trading rights of the Company of Royal Adventurers of England at the Treaty of Breda in 1667.

The company, succeeded in 1672 by the Royal Africa Company, was the typical private front for a state enterprise. Chartered by Charles II in 1663 and having members of the royal family among its subscribers, it replaced the commerce in dyewoods, gold, and ivory with the slave trade. Enthusiastically promising to deliver 3000 Africans to the English sugar colonies annually at a cost of £ 17 per head, the company failed miserably in its goal. By March 1664 the company had landed 33 cargoes of 2364 slaves at Barbados, at an average selling price exceeding £ 20. Despite a cost price of £ 3 per African, the company proved neither competitive nor profitable and went bankrupt in 1671.

The Royal Africa Company was only marginally more successful.

The trans-Atlantic slave trade stubbornly refused to be monopolized by either a chartered company or a trading nation. The records of the Royal Africa Company between 1673 and 1684 illustrate the problems inherent in the slave-delivering component of the south Atlantic system. As shown in Table 1, the average selling price of slaves at Barbados, payable mainly with muscovado sugar, varied between £ 12 and £ 20 per slave per cargo, with the highest prices being 29 slaves sold "to a Spaniard at £ 25 per head" in 1681. This was a profitable price to attract private, noncompany traders who did not have the enormous overhead expenses of the company. Given the annual demand in Barbados based on the previous agreement of 1663 to deliver 3000 slaves per year, the performance of the Royal Africa Company fell far short of its promise. Based on the records for twelve years, the company managed to deliver an average yearly supply of only 1356 Africans, and only came close to the required minimum target in 1683 when it brought 2963. Eventually, with its carrying capacity depleted by war, the company resorted to subcontracting its slaves for a fee. Nothing, however, could save the company, and finally in 1698 it lost its legal monopoly of the English trans-Atlantic slave trade.

Despite the constant depredations of war, the importation of slaves expanded rapidly in the Caribbean. The arriving Africans not only completely offset the demographic eradication of the postconquest and settlement period but also contributed to a greater social and demographic variation. Sugar and slavery provided the catalysts for these changes, and during the eighteenth century the Caribbean distinguished itself in the importation of African slaves and the production of sugar. Every colony sought to produce plantation staples, and every successful plantation maintained its own reservoir of enslaved laborers. During the seventeenth century the Caribbean accepted more than 50 percent of all arriving Africans in the New World. That figure increased to more than 60 percent during the plantation heyday of the eighteenth century and declined to a little less than 40 percent as the system began its rapid disintegration during the nineteenth century.

The Caribbean region received approximately one-half of all Africans brought to the Americas during the nearly 350-year span of the organized trans-Atlantic slave trade.

The islands and coastal perimeter of the Caribbean formed the host society for about 5 million Africans—if we accept the total African arrivals in the Americas to be 10 millions. Given the transportation facilities of the time, this constituted one of the greatest migrations of modern times, although the migrants went unwillingly and with no prospect of ever returning to their homelands. The arrival rate of Africans was more than 14,000 per year, with the concentration varying according to the agricultural development of the particular zone. Prosperity, defined in terms of quantity of land under cultivation and volume of tropical staple export, was the most powerful magnet for the African slave trade. But a prosperity based on agriculture tended to be transient. As soil fertility and land availability diminished in each territory, so did the prospect of wealth and the number of slaves.

This correlation between new land under cultivation and high volume of slave imports demonstrated a sequential occurrence throughout the Caribbean involving interimperial as well as transimperial trends. Seen in the conventional terms of the sugar revolution, it is quite clear that the English Caribbean islands tended to experience the first wave of intensification, followed closely by the French, with the Spanish colonies belatedly participating. Barbados was the first English and Caribbean colony to experience the revolution. By 1680 Barbados was perhaps the most valuable tropical colony, and it received the largest supply of Africans. By 1750 Jamaica had superseded Barbados, only to lose its eminence to French Saint-Domingue by 1780. Cuba eclipsed all colonies to become the largest single producer of cane sugar and the "jewel in the Spanish Crown" after 1830. As predominantly monocultural plantation exporters, the Caribbean colonies assumed a commercial importance that transcended the mere buying of slaves and selling of sugar, tobacco, indigo, and cotton. The region demanded such a variety of imports, which not only undermined the structure of imperialist mercantilism but catapulted it into a key element of international trade during the period. The multi-faceted trading system, of which the Caribbean was a part, had connections with North America, Europe, Africa, and South America. From these distant regions came firearms, horses, flour, meat, fish, barrel staves, nails, lumber, tools, slaves, machinery, cloth, and luxury products to supply the economic, dietary, and production needs of the tropical plantation societies.

The so-called "sugar colonies" were never exclusively producers of sugar. But sugar was the mainstay of the export economy. As such the volume of sugar production increased directly proportional to the increase in the slave population. Table 3 illustrates the relationship for a selected number of Caribbean islands for the period of the slave trade and slavery between 1643 and 1860. The gross totals tend to disguise the variations in sugar production as well as the fluctuations in the importation of slaves. They do indicate, however, the rapidity with which the colonies moved into high-scale sugar production. This transformation also produced the social repercussions which will be discussed in chapter 5.

By the eighteenth century "sugar was king" throughout the Caribbean. Ralph Davis graphically noted this dominance in *The Rise of the Atlantic Economies*:

> Sugar production, once it had been introduced, showed a tendency to engulf whole islands in single-crop cultivation, and it created its own form of society whose stamp still lies upon the Caribbean. There were exceptions: the small islands of Grenada and Dominica had single-crop coffee economies for some decades of the eighteenth century, and colonies with great land areas, St. Domingue and especially Brazil, could produce immense sugar crops while still retaining some variety in cultivation. But the value of the Caribbean colonies to Europe came to be in their sugar production. So overwhelming did it dominate island economy and society, so vital was it even to Brazil, that the main features of the life of Europe's tropical colonies are best set out in terms of the movement towards sugar, and the adaptation of society to the needs of its production. After 1660 England's sugar imports always exceeded its combined imports of all other colo-

nial produce; in 1774 sugar made up just half of all French imports from her West Indian colonies; over the colonial period as
a whole more than half Brazil's exports of goods were sugar.
Sugar made up almost a fifth of the whole English import bill of
1774, far surpassing the share of any other commodity.

Sugar and its associated by-products, rum and molasses, accounted
for 81 percent of the exports from the British Caribbean in 1770. The
second-place export commodity was coffee, accounting for 11 percent.
At the same time the French Antilles showed only a slightly higher
variation, with sugar-related exports amounting to 49 percent of exports, coffee 24 percent, indigo 14 percent, and cotton 8 percent. In
1855 Cuba had an overwhelming 84 percent of its export trade in
sugar, with second-place tobacco accounting for less than 8 percent.
The situation varied from island to island, but, except for the de-
signedly free-port trading islands, such as St. Martin, St. Eustatia, and
Curaçao, the situation remained the same. Sugar exports dominated
the economy.

The export-import economy was only one aspect of the local economic structure, albeit a very important one. The mature plantation
complex not only created two societies by the late eighteenth century—one Euro-American, the other Afro-American—it also created
two economies. And like the social division, the two economies coexisted in symbiotic relationship. For if the export of plantation products and the import of consumer articles were major activities, they
were integrally related to the system of distribution and merchandis-
ing done locally by a significant sector of the population.

The import-export trade was more complex than the selling and
shipping abroad of the local harvest. Each colony traded not only
with its metropolis but also with foreigners. J. Stewart aptly indicated
the multilateral dimensions of colonial trade in Jamaica in the 1820s:
"The commerce of Jamaica," he wrote, "may be classed under the
following heads: The trade with the mother country—which is far
more considerable than all the other branches together; the trade with
British North America, and the trade with the island of Cuba and
other Spanish islands, the Spanish Main or Tierra Firma, and other

territories on the American continent formerly belonging to Spain."
In the 1850's Cuba traded with Spain, the United States, England,
Germany, France, Mexico, Venezuela, and Jamaica. Figures for
Puerto Rico in 1843 amply demonstrate how complex external trad-
ing had become by that time. The island exported its products in
British ships to the West Indian islands, England, and Canada; in
Danish, American, Hanseatic, and Dutch ships to England; and in
Spanish ships to Spain and Canada. The exported items included
sugar, tobacco, dry and salted hides, horses, mules, cattle, coconuts,
coffee, beans, tortoise shells, and timber. Imports included olive oil,
brandy, beer, gin, wine, salted beef and pork, hams, figs, fish, raisins,
rice, cocoa, flour, lard, butter, cheese, potatoes, garlic, onions, barrel
staves, lumber, iron hoops, plates and bars, nails, glass, agricultural
tools, soap, utensils, medicines, tobacco, candles, perfumes, and domestic supplies. The absence of a coordinated banking system and
adequate common currencies restricted much of the trade to the form
of a complicated system of barter, in which locally produced goods
were accepted and then reexported along with a variety of coins. This
lack of any systematic banking system, plus the eternal shortage of
coins for small-scale transactions, were perennial complaints of colonists in the tropics.

Strategically located free ports supplemented the direct importation
and export of commodities. Janet Schaw, who visited St. Eustatia on
January 19, 1775, wrote a very graphic description of one of the most
bustling Caribbean free ports:

> We landed on St. Eustatia, a free port, which belongs to the
> Dutch; a place of vast traffic from every quarter of the globe. The
> ships of various nations which rode before it were very fine, but
> the Island itself the only ugly one I have seen. Nor do I think I
> would stay on it for any bribe. . . . The whole riches of the Is-
> land consist in its merchandize, and they are obliged to the
> neighbouring Islands for subsistence; while they in return furnish
> them with contraband commodities of all kinds. . . . But never
> did I meet with such variety; here was a merchant vending his
> goods in Dutch, another in French, a third in Spanish, etc. etc.
> They all wear the habit of their country and the diversity is

really amusing. . . . From one end of the town of Eustatia to
the other is a continued mart, where goods of the most different
uses and qualities are displayed before the shop-doors. Here hang
rich embroideries, painted silks, flowered Muslins, with all the
Manufactures of the Indies. Just by hang Sailor's Jackets, Trou-
sers, shoes, hats etc. Next stall contains most exquisite silver
plate, the most beautiful indeed I ever saw, and close by these
iron pots, kettles and shovels. Perhaps the next presents you with
French and English Millinary wares. But it were endless to enu-
merate the variety of merchandize in such a place, for in every
store you find everything, be their qualities ever so opposite. I
bought a quantity of excellent French gloves for fourteen pence
a pair, also English thread-stockings cheaper than I could buy
them at home.

The other side of the economic coin was the internal marketing
system. This internal economy had two dimensions. The first was
the coastal and retail trade, which took the goods of the large-com-
mission merchants in the principal ports and distributed them via
small coastal vessels of less than seventy tons to smaller merchants
who serviced the planting and free village communities. Again barter
and credit were the major operating media, although all items bore a
discounted cash price. "A wharfinger's receipt for a puncheon of rum,
endorsed by the payer," wrote Stewart, "passes in payment as readily
as a bill or draft would do; so that these articles become a sort of
circulating medium, and it is not unusual for a puncheon of rum, or
other commodity, to pass through twenty or more different hands,
without ever being moved from the wharf-store where it was deposited
by its original owner, into whose possession it may again ultimately
return."

The other dimension of the internal marketing system consisted of
the local markets with their higglers, who supplied the plantations
and free citizens with ground provisions, livestock, smallstock, poul-
try, and eggs. Unlike the other facets of trade, however, this sector
dealt mainly in cash, further accentuating the scarcity of specie in the
colonies. This market was dominated by the free persons of color.
Slaves participated, too, but during the eighteenth century a series of

laws gradually proscribed their economic activities. The Jamaica Assembly in 1711 prohibited slaves from owning livestock or from selling meat, fish, sugar, sugar cane, or any manufactured item without the written permission of their masters. St. Lucia prevented slaves from dealing in coffee or cotton with laws passed in 1734 and 1735. The French Antilles also passed laws between 1744 and 1765 that removed the opportunities for slaves to trade in cattle or engage in the occupation of butcher, while higglering was prohibited on plantations or in the towns. In 1767 St. Vincent forbade slaves to plant or sell any commodity exported from the island. In the 1840's the Cubans restricted the occupations and movement of the free, nonwhite members of the society.

The planter class which formulated the laws restricting the economic activities of the nonwhites were motivated by self-interest. They disliked unnecessary local competition, and economic subordination facilitated the social control of the majority of the population. Nevertheless, the laws could not be enforced, and the gradual collapse of the economic and political worlds of the slaveholders opened more and more opportunities for the nonwhites. By the middle of the nineteenth century nonwhites were, individually and collectively, buying bankrupt and abandoned estates throughout the Caribbean, and peasant economies were competing with the plantation economies for land and labor.

Chapter 5 • Social Structure of the Plantation Society

Virginia and Barbados were first peopled by a sort of loose, vagrant People, vicious and destitute of means to live at home (being either unfit for labour, or such as could find none to employ themselves about, or had so misbehaved themselves by Whoring, Thieving, or other Debauchery, that none would set them to work) which Merchants and Masters of Ships by Their Agents (or Spirits as they were called) gathered up about the streets of London, and other places, cloathed and transported to be employed upon Plantations. . . .

Josiah Child, *New Discourse on Trade*, 1688

The settler plantation complex in the Caribbean region eventually constituted a society. It was a society with some unusual characteristics. Caribbean societies lacked the normal demographic growth of African, European, and indigenous American communities. At times these Caribbean social structures demonstrated traits that appear contrived and erratically eclectic. But they were all extremely dynamic, resilient, and, with certain limitations, unusually creative.

By the late eighteenth century the slave society assumed a distinctive form of its own. Masters and slaves, merchants and shippers, rulers and ruled, free and nonfree, white and nonwhite, all had formed closely integrated, mutually dependent groupings already distinctly divided into castes and classes.

No one group—neither the masters nor their slaves—made this strange world. Rather it was a world that developed as a result of the equal participation of both masters and slaves. To speak of a "world the slaveholders made" provides a catchy, eloquent phrase but does less than full justice to the reality. Masters and slaves together formed a world apart. Time and the exigencies of the plantation export economy hallowed their traditions, calcified their relationships, and froze such views as the inhabitants of the region had of themselves and their role in the universe of production and commerce. Thus it appeared until that world began to fall apart during the nineteenth century.

Before this disintegration, however, some notorious internal ambiguities were manifested. Nowhere were the contradictions more evident than in the structure of caste and classes. The caste system represented the most notable aspect of the plantation society. The typical slave society had three clearly defined castes which were maintained partly by force and partly by legal ingenuity. In ascending order of social status these three castes were slaves, free persons of color, and white persons. Occupation and stipulated legal disabilities patently separated the slave component from the two free components. Within the realm of the free, ethnicity, phenotype, and attributed status largely determined the caste boundaries between the white sector and the other nonwhite sector, subdivided into free blacks and free mulattoes.

This general description sometimes broke down in specific circumstances. The plantation caste system did not possess the notorious inflexibility of the classic Indian caste system. The prevailing ambiguities and inherent contradictions of the plantation structure continually undermined rigidity and permitted vagueness, overlap, and social "passing" on a limited scale along the peripheral penumbra of the two free castes as well as between free colored and slaves.

Caste divisions tended to be vertical and to be distinguished by heredity. Within each caste were internal subdivisions of classes or ranks. Each social class varied in size, function, and the intensity of their acceptance of or hostility to the system. Within the white caste economic and occupational indices figured prominently in designating individual social position and status. With the intermediate stratum of the free persons of color, race and color—or more precisely, complexion and shades of color—determined status and rank. Among the slaves, occupation comprised the single most important consideration in social ranking. Each caste therefore had its elaborate pecking order, a factor that might have contributed to social mobility. Social mobility was possible in two directions: laterally across caste lines; and upward through the ranks.

The conventional demographic profile of the slave society was that of a narrow-peaked triangle, horizontally divided into three sections. The broad base of this triangle represented the vast majority of slaves. Originally these slaves were entirely African- or European-born, but with the passage of years an increasing proportion were born in the Americas—these were called creole or Afro-American slaves. Miscegenation between Africans and all the other ethnic groups also produced a new substratum of individuals usually designated mestizo or mulatto. The middle stratum or band of the triangle formed the small but significant segment between upper and lower, white and nonwhite, slave and free. These were the free people of color, uncharitably referred to by an English colonial governor as "the unappropriated people." The free people of color shared qualities of both the free and the nonfree. Ethnically divided into black and mulatto, like the slaves, they suffered a circumscribed freedom that accentuated their ambiguity and probably contributed to their psychological disorientation. The small apex of the triangle represented the white people. Small in number, diverse in background, this group possessed the economic and political power of the society and exercised an inordinate influence on the local culture.

By custom and often by law any person of European birth or ancestry, regardless of economic circumstance, intellectual ability, or educational achievement, enjoyed a social status superior to that of any nonwhite person. As the plantation system matured throughout the eighteenth century, a concomitant social complex based on the mutually reinforcing cleavages of race, color, and occupation not only manifested itself throughout the Caribbean but became indelible and pervasive. On the plantations as well as in the cities, the color of one's skin fixed both the social position and the occupation of the possessor, with blackness indicating menial and arduous labor and whiteness reflecting superiority and leisure. Such was the situation until the later decades of the nineteenth century, when association with the plantation and its occupational structure no longer provided a reliable index of either caste or class. When that occurred, the plantation society was in an advanced stage of disrepair.

Fully developed plantation societies all exhibited common characteristics. Not only social status but also population composition indicated the degree of participation and the stage of maturity of the particular colony within the context of the south Atlantic system. In general the most vigorous and most mature structures revealed a preponderance of Africans and Afro-Americans. Slaves tended to form the overwhelming majority, outnumbering the free by ratios varying between 2 : 1 to 30 : 1. At the beginning of the nineteenth century the entire population of the Caribbean islands and circum-Caribbean mainland enclaves of Berbice, Demerara, Essequibo, Surinam, Guiana, and British Honduras (now Belize) amounted to about 2 million inhabitants, with about two-thirds of that number being slaves.

Population size and composition fluctuated according to the state of the economy. In times of prosperity the total number of people increased and diminished along with shrinking fortunes, especially among the plantation-owning whites. For example in 1781 the small Dutch island colony of St. Eustatia was both a flourishing free port and a prominent sugar exporter. Of a total of approximately 20,000 inhabitants, nearly 15,000 were slaves working a number of sugar plantations. The English captured and sacked the island and its fortunes rapidly declined. By 1840 the population of St. Eustatia had dwindled to less than 400 white persons and 2000 slaves. The Spanish island of Cuba presented an opposite change. In 1774 Cuba had a population of 171,620, of which only 44,333 (25.8 percent) were slaves. By 1827, with the sugar revolution fairly advanced, the total population increased dramatically to a total of 704,487, of whom 286,942 (40.7 percent) were slaves. The common feature of the sugar revolutions in the Caribbean was the increase of a servile black population at the expense of a free white settler population.

Although the slaves formed the lowest caste stratum of the society, they were just as elaborately subdivided for purposes of occupation and rank as the free castes. The most basic division was along lines of color, between the African and Afro-American slaves—usually referred to as black slaves—and the miscegenated or "colored" slaves, most frequently called mulattoes or *pardos* in the Spanish islands. Slaves of mixed race, however, do not seem to have been a significant factor in the overall slave population before the nineteenth century. By then the healthy increase of the creole element—given a tremendous impetus by the English abolition of their slave trade in 1808—and the sharp drop in the importation of Africans led to a proportionate rise in the number of mestizos.

In 1800 the mixed population on Worthy Park Estate in Jamaica accounted for only about 5 percent of the slave labor force. This percentage does not seem to vary significantly from the general pattern for agricultural populations. In Cuba in 1846 the mulatto slaves amounted to 12,791 out of a total slave force of 323,759, yielding slightly less than 4 percent. Barry Higman finds that the slave registers reveal that the overall mulatto slave population might have been between 10 percent and 12 percent of the total Jamaican slave population in 1820. Such an increased percentage would not necessarily be at variance with the Worthy Park Sugar Estate findings of Michael Craton and James Walvin, since the proportion of the mulattoes would have increased after the termination of the English slave trade. Such a proportion would not be very large, and might have reflected an increased urban concentration of slaves as the Jamaican sugar economy declined.

Urban centers seemed to have produced a greater concentration of mulattoes—slave as well as free—than the plantations. Many travel accounts indicate this. Janet Schaw, the Scottish "lady of quality" who traveled through the West Indies and South Carolina on the eve of the American Revolution, described "crouds [sic] of Mullattoes [sic] . . . in the streets, houses and indeed everywhere" in the town of St. John's, Antigua. Most towns would have offered a similar impression, especially to the eye that could not discriminate between the free and the slave. In Havana, according to the census of 1828, the mulatto slaves numbered 1010 out of a total slave population of 8005, for a percentage of 12.6; but free mulattoes numbered 8215 out of a total free nonwhite population of 23,562, for a proportion of slightly less than 35 percent.

Slaves of mixed ancestry were not generally regarded as good field workers. As a result there was a concentration of these slaves in the domestic, skilled, and artisan trades. But these occupations provided both the exposure and the income that facilitated the movement from slavery to freedom, thereby reinforcing the notion that lightness of skin color lubricated upward social mobility. Consequently slaves of mixed heritage felt that they were superior in rank generally to African and Afro-American slaves, and this sentiment permeated every society where the norms for grace and beauty were those established by the superordinate white sector. Other subtle distinctions followed. Slaves who were born in the Caribbean felt socially superior to their relatives and colleagues who were not. Obviously these creole slaves had some advantages over their African counterparts. They were physically acclimatized as well as mentally socialized to the conduct and routine of the plantations, and in some cases spoke and understood the local languages. Yet this curious creole-African sentiment may have been based only on the reflected impressions and unquestioned acceptance of the prevailing white biases. The white colonists, after all, continuously condemned the Africans as "savages," claimed that exposure to the rigors of the plantation "civilized" them, and in some cases were willing to pay more for locally born black slaves than for recently imported African ones.

Color provided one criterion of rank among the slaves and occupation provided another. Edward Brathwaite, in his study of Jamaica,

divided the slaves into five occupational groups based on the convenient distinction of functions on the plantation and in the economy: field slaves, usually called praedial slaves; mechanic and domestic slaves; slaves working as hired hands; and skilled, professional, or
semiprofessional and managerial slaves. Some of these categories depended to a great extent on the type of society, the size of the category engaged in the activity, and the number of slaves held by the
slave owner. Nevertheless certain common patterns emerged. Field
slaves were generally considered lowest in rank. They were the most
numerous group. Edward Long estimated that about 160,000 of the
approximately 220,000 slaves in Jamaica in 1787 were field slaves, suggesting that more than 72 percent fell in this category. In 1855, at the
height of the Cuban sugar revolution, about 81 percent of the slaves
were registered as rural slaves, indicating an extremely high proportion of field slaves.

But even these field slaves had their own ranking as well as their
own preference for certain tasks. We have fewer records of their pref-
erences and their own determination of their ranks than we have for
their masters. The masters ranked their slaves according to their util-
ity in the production process or their personal needs. On Irwin Estate
in St. James, Jamaica, the slaves were listed in the following order:
first gang, second gang, third gang, tradesmen, pen-keepers, domestics,
watchmen, grass cutters, invalids, young children. The cattle were also
listed in an order that suggested value: working stock, bulls, young
working stock, mules, cows, calves, fattening cattle. Slaves and cattle
were the perennial concerns of the Caribbean plantation owner: their
value, their health, their number, and their disposition. When Rose
Price took personal control of Worthy Park Estate, he divided his 483
slaves into seventeen different categories.

Field slaves were the backbone of the plantation and the economy.
The division into gangs represented the varying degrees of physical
strength and permitted the employment of the gang as a unit,
whether the demands were heavy and rigorous, as they were in the
crop season when the mill operated, or light during the planting season and *tiempo muerto*. Gangs maximized efficiency. The first gang

comprised the most able-bodied males and females, with the second and third arranged in descending order of physical strength and ability. Some planters simplified their groupings, as did J. Stewart, who based his descriptions on his experiences in Jamaica:

> The plantation slaves are divided into three classes or *gangs*, as they are called, according to age and condition. The first gang consists of the ablest of both sexes, from sixteen to about fifty years of age, and are employed in the most laborious of the work; the second gang contains the elderly and weakly men and women, and boys and girls of from twelve to sixteen who have lighter work assigned to them; and the third, or what is called *small gang*, consists of the children from about six to twelve, attended by a female driver, and are employed in weeding the young plant-canes, and other easy work adopted to their strength. In most of the jobbing-gangs the different classes, with the exception of children, are very improperly blended together. When the slaves are rendered unfit, by age or infirmity, for field labor, they are employed in occupations that require little bodily exertion; the men are placed as watchmen over the canes and provisions, and the women to take care of the children, or in other light employments.

Since a great deal of the labor on the estate, from the basic planting to the elaborate preparation of sugar and rum, remained repetitive, newly imported Africans could fit in without considerable difficulty and dislocation. Most purchased Africans, however, began and ended their enslavement working with the field gangs.

One frequently overlooked aspect of plantation slavery was the high degree of participation by women in all aspects of field and factory labor. Plantations in general demanded prime workers and placed their emphasis on able males in the fourteen-to-forty age category. Nevertheless every estate found it expedient to have large numbers of women around both as a form of social control and as a natural consequence of the irregular market supply and normal reproduction process. Sexual imbalance was not very pronounced on large established estates. In Cuba during the middle years of the nineteenth century male slaves in rural areas outnumbered the females by a ratio of slightly less than 2 : 1. In 1857 the official returns for slaves gave a rural slave force of 193,187 males and 114,188 females. Urban slaves showed a slight majority of females, with 34,762 females and 30,848 males. Barbados, one of the first islands to complete its sugar revolution, consistently had more female than male slaves throughout the nineteenth century. In 1832 the island possessed 43,738 female slaves and 37,762 male slaves. Until 1817 males outnumbered females in Jamaica. After that date, however, the female population gradually outnumbered the male population. In 1829 Jamaica had 164,167 females and 158,254 males in a total slave force of 322,421. Extreme sexual imbalance among slaves, then, was a feature of the frontier. As the society matured the imbalance tended to redress itself. As soon as the task of clearing the virgin forests of the tropical lands was completed, women served just as efficiently as men in the daily routine of cultivation, harvest, and manufacture.

In every colony women worked alongside the men in the various occupations. For large established estates women may even have had a proportionately greater share of the field work than men. On the Jamaican estate, Worthy Park, this was certainly the case at the end of the eighteenth century, and there is no reason to believe that the situation did not persist afterwards. In 1789 Worthy Park Estate had a labor force of 339 slaves, 162 female and 177 male. Slightly more than 43 percent of its females (70 slaves) worked in the field gang, while just over 16 percent of the males (29 slaves) did. During the efficient reorganization of Rose Price between 1791 and 1793 the situation remained the same. In 1793 the labor force increased to 528 slaves, 244 women and 284 men. But again almost 44 percent of the women (107 slaves) worked in the fields, while only slightly more than 32 percent (92 slaves) of the men did so. A similar situation prevailed on La Ninfa Estate in Cuba in 1829.

One curious, though probably typical, observation on the female labor force emerged from Barry Higman's study of the Jamaican slave population just prior to emancipation. Higman found that women worked in the fields much longer, on the average, than men, probably corresponding to their longer life expectancy. He also found

few female slaves of color among the field slaves. Indeed the recruitment of black women for domestic work ceased as soon as female
slaves of color could be found.

The relatively low percentages of field labor participation by the
two sexes on Worthy Park Estates indicate a general pattern. The system of slavery did not produce a very efficient process of labor employment. Only about 50 percent of the workhands on any sugar estate
were capable, healthy, able-bodied participants in the field production process. On La Ninfa in Cuba, an 1829 daily register of slaves
showed that of 340 slaves, 26.5 percent (90 slaves) were infants, invalids, or deserters, and only 54.4 percent (185 slaves) were employed
in the fields. More men than women worked in the factory, however,
while an unduly large number of slaves seemed to be in domestic
service, especially while the owners were in residence.

Again the Worthy Park experience was indicative. The great house,
while normally vacant, used two full-time domestics to maintain it.
With the owner in residence, however, the number increased to a
high figure of seventeen slaves. The overseer began with one slave and
within six years, in 1795, had a domestic staff of thirty-six slaves to
serve only six white persons. Domestic slaves tended to form a larger
category of Spanish and French colonial societies than English because of the larger proportion of resident proprietors.

As Edward Brathwaite points out, domestic slaves considered
themselves of a higher rank than field slaves. The masters confirmed
this position by distinguishing the dress and nurturing the civility of
the group and treating—in the most benevolent cases—domestic
slaves as part of an extended family. Banishment to field labor was
utilized as a form of punishment for disobedient or disgraced domestic slaves. One imperial master decreed that his mulatto stable boy
be "stripped of his livery, degraded to a field negro" as punishment
for some unspecified misdeed.

Domestic slaves, like the category of urban, skilled, or semiindependent slaves, had certain advantages denied the field slaves in
general. They had more leisure, were under less coercive control, and
had more opportunities for self-purchase or *coartación* than their rural
fellows. Nevertheless domestic and urban slaves displayed an equal

dislike of slavery and an equal proneness to flee the system as did the field slaves.

Specialist slaves participated in a variety of occupations: they were skilled mechanics, hired hands, and superannuated watchmen and caretakers of children, affectionately called the *criolleras* in Cuba.

Highest in privilege and importance on the estate were the slave drivers and chief sugar makers, whom Matthew Lewis felicitously called "principal persons." The order, loyalty, and productivity of slave forces rested almost entirely in the hands of the slave drivers. Not only did they control the daily routine of any plantation, but they also performed the crucial liaison functions between the Europeans and the Africans. As long as these low-level supervisory personnel were satisfied and loyal, coordinated resistance to the system of slavery could not meet with significant success. In recognition of this fact slave owners tended to bestow special privileges on these slaves. Often they had their own residence, greater rations, and more leeway in the ordinary rules and regulations of the plantation. On sugar estates the skill and experience of the sugar boiler was especially valuable. His keen sense of the proper elaboration of sugar could make the difference between the financial success of the estate and disaster. In terms of purchase price, however, drivers and sugar boilers cost less than those specialists whose jobs made possible the reliable, trouble-free operation of the entire machinery of sugar production: carpenters, millwrights, coppersmiths, coopers, sawyers, and masons. These groups also had a great deal of personal freedom of movement on the estates, and occasionally were hired out to supplement the income of their owners.

Outside the plantations a vast number of slaves plied trades, filled occupations, and participated in the two economies. A number of slaves engaged in higgling, some operating as middlemen between the growers of ground provisions in the rural areas and the consumers in the towns and on the estates. Slaves also operated small coastal boats, or were fishermen, musicians, craftsmen, guides, or ratcatchers. In short any job that provided an income and was not, or could not be, filled by the free population, fell to the slaves.

Some of these occupations gave the slaves tremendous control over their time and their activity, and eventually blurred the legal distinctions between slavery and freedom. For this reason runaways found it quite easy to engage in these occupations as one means of survival until more organized connections could be established. These occupations, connecting as they did the internal marketing economy and the export economy, proved a viable way of circulating the wealth of the society throughout the three castes.

Runaways and individual slaves working independently merged imperceptibly into the lower ranks of the heterogeneous group identified as free persons of color. For this category represented a mélange of somatic images as so many travelers to the Caribbean remarked from time to time. John Stewart, in his anonymously published *Account of Jamaica and Its Inhabitants*, put it this way:

> Between the whites and the blacks in the West Indies, a numerous race has sprung up, which goes by the general name of people of colour: these are subdivided into Mulattos, the offspring of a white and a black; Sambos, the offspring of a black and a Mulatto; Quadroons, the offspring of a Mulatto and a white; and Mestees, or Mestisos, the offspring of a Quadroon and a white. Below this last denomination, the distinction of colour is hardly perceptible; and those who are thus removed from the original negro [sic] stock, are considered by the law as whites, and competent, of course, to enjoy all the privileges of a white. Between these particular *casts*, an endless variety of nondescript shades exist, descending from the deep jet to the faintest tinge of the olive; by gradations which it were impossible to mark and to designate.

Stewart's graphic description neither reflects the full legal distinctions of biological and complexional mutations nor accurately portrays the composition of the group. The Spanish managed to get twenty-five possible hybrid variations, but few outside the esoteric realm of primitive biological specialists bothered to trace bloodlines. The random selections of genetic transmissions frustrated the general desire to have phenotype conform regularly to genealogical heritage. Most designations, therefore, were the simple, visually correct but biologically false, categories of mulattoes and sambos. But the free colored group was not confined merely to persons of mixed African, European, and American heritage. By the nineteenth century, a large number of blacks had become bona fide members of this group. This group was not one of freedmen in the sense that they were all once slaves. Some were the descendants of successive generations of free individuals of unaltered African blood. To describe them as freedmen, with the connotation of a group recently manumitted, is as misleading as describing contemporary creole Latin Americans as Spanish and Portuguese.

The origins of the free colored in the Caribbean were predominantly the miscegenated results of the unions of European masters and their non-European slaves. Gradually the group developed its own internal marital affiliations, procreative impulses, and hereditary continuities. With the passage of time opportunities for self-purchase and other forms of unrestricted freedom allowed fluctuating numbers of African slaves to move upward into the legal category of free persons. Some of these Africans formed unions with persons of mixed ancestry, further contributing to the biological mélange. Others preferred their own kind, thereby continuing to reinforce a distinct, and often distinguished, subcategory of free blacks.

As a proportion of the entire population, the free nonwhite sector varied considerably from colony to colony, and even across time within the same colony. The free colored comprised a high 43.5 percent of the total of the Dutch colony of Curaçao in 1833. In plantation Surinam—likewise a Dutch colony—the free population constituted slightly less than 9 percent of the total colonial society. In Puerto Rico the free colored were 41.3 percent of the island total in 1860, but in Cuba they amounted to merely 15.1 percent in 1827 and increased to only 16.2 percent in 1860. In the English and French colonies the proportion varied between a low of 1 percent in Berbice, later part of British Guiana, and a high of 12.6 percent in the Bahamas in 1810. In Barbados the free colored population represented 6.5 percent of the total in 1834. In Jamaica it was 10.2 percent in 1800. In French Saint-Domingue the free coloreds were 5.3 percent of the total in 1791, and Martinique had a proportion of 5.4 percent in 1789.

The data presented in table 4 provides only a "snapshot" view of the demographic profile of the Caribbean. But "frozen" representations, however graphic they may be, cannot reveal the inherent dynamism of social groups. The history of the free colored population is one of continual response to an ever-varying number of influences through time. One of the most prominent influences on the behavior of the free nonwhite population as a category was the economic fortunes of the plantation-based export economy. But of course fluctuating economic conditions had an equal impact on all sectors of the society.

A few examples illustrate the vagaries of economy and population. During the eighteenth century the plantation economy expanded in Surinam until 1788 when the colony had 591 plantations and 50,000 slaves out of a total population of 55,000 inhabitants. By 1813 the number of plantations had declined to 369, and in 1863, when slavery was abolished, it had reached 210. At the same time the collapse of the Amsterdam exchange in 1773 began an irreversible process of capital withdrawal from agriculture. In 1863 the total population was less than it was in 1830. Other subtle changes also took place. Plantations fell into absentee ownership, with more than 80 percent of the plantations in 1813 (297) forming this category. The number of free, especially among the female mulatto group, increased dramatically. Dutch plantation owners and their families left the colony in large numbers, allowing the Jews to become the predominant element among the white sector; and bachelor whites sent out to administer foreclosed estates accentuated the male-dominant sexual imbalance among the white sector. Between 1768 and 1834 the colored population increased in number from about 3500 to 35,000, a tenfold increase that boosted their proportion from 16 percent of the total free group to about 70 percent. During the same time the white population fell by nearly 50 percent; and the number of slaves—by an entirely unrelated coincidence—nearly doubled. In Martinique, where the plantation economy made a precipitate decline during the Napoleonic wars of the early nineteenth century, the free colored sector increased from 7.1 percent of the total population in 1802 to 24.9 percent in 1835. In Cuba, on the other hand, the plantation economy expanded rapidly between 1774 and 1827, and the free nonwhite sector declined from 20.3 percent to 15.1 percent.

The free nonwhite sector, wherever they were found and regardless of the circumstances under which they flourished, manifested a number of common traits. It tended to be predominantly female, largely urban, and almost self-consciously differentiated from the slave sector. In Trinidad in 1811, 56.7 percent of the free nonwhite population was female, with adult females outnumbering adult males 2830 to 1790. Barbados presented a slightly anomalous picture, with females predominating in all three castes. In 1817, for example, they comprised more than 54 percent of the slave and white sectors, and more than 51 percent of the free nonwhites. Females outnumbered males in Cuba, too, where in 1841 78,843 women outnumbered the men by 3140 and proportionately exceeded the latter by 51 percent to 49 percent. In Demerara and Essequibo adult females outnumbered males 1096 to 487; while in small Tobago the adult women numbered 153 and the adult men 92. In most cases, however, male children exceeded the number of females.

With the exception of Cuba, where there was an unusually heavy concentration of free persons of color in the rural eastern provinces, the pattern of free nonwhite residence tended to be urban. Even in Cuba a far heavier concentration of free colored persons lived in the cities of Havana, Santiago de Cuba, Manzanillo, and Trinidad than in the plantation zones of Cárdenas, Colon, and Matanzas. In Barbados the situation was the same. After 1809 about 61 percent of all Barbadian free nonwhites lived in the parish of St. Michael, and there is a strong suggestion that the majority of this group resided in the capital of the island, Bridgetown. Similarly, more free nonwhites lived in Belize than in the rest of British Honduras during the nineteenth century; and more in Kingston than the rest of the island of Jamaica.

The urban residence pattern fulfilled certain physical as well as psychological conditions for the free colored population. Although some free coloreds figured among the wealthy plantation owners—most notably in Jamaica, Puerto Rico, Santo Domingo, Saint-Domingue, Martinique, and Surinam—most working free coloreds derived their livelihood from trades and services. The cities provided a far more conducive ambience for the pursuit of these occupations than the rural plantation zones. Moreover, as with the slaves, the miscegenated free were generally recognized to be less than ideal manual workers on the plantations. Once the magnetic pattern of urban residence and association was established it could not be easily reversed. The rural exodus might also have had powerful subconscious motivations. The social mores of the Caribbean plantation society consistently denigrated those who did manual and menial labor. Plantation slaves were lowest in social status. Increasing the social distance between slavery and freedom for the Afro-Caribbean population might have meant increasing the physical distance as well.

Yet the flight to the cities, although providing many opportunities for upward social mobility, created and intensified economic and political competition. At the lower end of the economic scale, the free Afro-Caribbean population faced competition from jobbing slaves, often working arduously to purchase their freedom while being indirectly subsidized by their owners. At the upper scale the free nonwhites competed with the artisan, commercial, and semiskilled service sector of the lower orders of the white group. The whites often used their political power, or their access to political power, to define and broaden the economic and occupational gap between themselves and the free colored sector. Laws distinguishing comportment, dress, and residence, or denying the practice of certain occupations, or limiting the material legacy of the free colored population were common throughout the Caribbean. The constriction in the range of occupations, the personal liberty, and the political abilities of the free nonwhite sector tended to run concurrently with the expansion of the plantation economy of the colony. In the eighteenth century, therefore, the French sought to restrict intermarriage across ethnic boundaries and curtail nonwhite participation in shipping and commerce.

These restrictions were introduced to Cuba during the nineteenth century.

The free colored population throughout the Caribbean, then, was a considerably heterogeneous group, struggling to assert itself and gain its identity under a variety of ever-changing conditions. In Santo Domingo, the Bahamas, Bermuda, and a number of the smaller islands in the eastern Caribbean, the local economy remained virtually constant and the social structure remained equally stable in its pattern of slow evolution. Elsewhere the situation was far more volatile, far more dynamic. By 1789 Saint-Domingue had erupted at the height of its prosperity, and the society experienced the first complete revolution in the western hemisphere. The slaves destroyed not only their bondage, but also the symbols of their servitude—the white masters, the large plantations, and the pattern of latifundium. In the early nineteenth century the export economy of the English Antilles was on the verge of collapse. The dominant white minority waged a determined but futile campaign to forestall the emancipation of their slaves and the political participation of the majority of the population. By 1834 both goals were lost. In 1844 the Cuban whites staged a preemptive massacre that virtually decimated the leadership of the Afro-Cuban population and signified the highest point of local racial tension during the century. Despite the monumental handicaps, individuals achieved outstanding success in many spheres of activity. Considerations of class and color might have initiated cohesion of the nonwhites, but their biggest handicap stemmed from the ambiguity of their being neither fully free or plainly servile. The free colored were quintessentially marginal people.

Like the free persons of color, the white sector was also a heterogeneous group. From one perspective the white sector divided along class lines: *peninsulares* and *criollos* in the Spanish colonies, *grands blancs* and *petits blancs* in the French colonies, and "principal whites" and "poor whites" in the English colonies. Every colony had a mixture of national origins and religious denominations within the white ranks. Nowhere was this illustrated better than in the island of Trinidad, acquired by the English from the Spanish in 1797. In

1811 the white population of Trinidad numbered 4353 persons, representing 10 different national origins. Indians totaled 1736, or about 40 percent of the group. English whites numbered 1068, or 24.5 percent. The Spanish were 559 individuals, or almost 13 percent, and the French were 650, or nearly 15 percent. In addition there were 20 Americans, 25 Germans, 4 Portuguese, 18 Italians, 20 Corsicans, and 10 Maltese. But national origin and religious affiliation were smaller considerations than occupation and social rank in determining the status of individuals in the Caribbean. And by the nineteenth century, relationship to the economic and political structure of the plantation was the outstanding criterion for determining class rank and social status.

Every slave society struggled to preserve its carefully delineated hierarchical order, and only reluctantly accepted breaches of social boundaries. The genial Lady Maria Nugent, a creole born in Perth Amboy, New Jersey, of mixed Scottish, Irish, and Dutch ancestry, a loyalist refugee from the American Wars of Independence as well as the wife of the governor of Jamaica, left a classical description of the colonial society in which she lived for five years. Lady Nugent found Jamaican upper-class conduct a source of exasperation and bemusement:

> In this country it appears as if every thing were bought and sold. Clergymen make no secret of making a traffic of their livings; but General N. [her husband, General Nugent, governor of Jamaica 1801-1806] has set his face against such proceedings, and has refused many applications for this purpose. He is determined to do all he can towards the reformation of the church, and thus rendering it respectable. It is indeed melancholy, to see the general disregard of both religion and morality, throughout the whole island. Every one seems solicitous to make money, and no one appears to regard the mode of acquiring it. It is extraordinary to witness the immediate effect that the climate and habit of living in this country have upon the minds and manners of Europeans, particularly of the lower orders. In the upper ranks, they become indolent and inactive, regardless of everything but eating, drinking, and indulging themselves, and are almost entirely under the dominion of their mulatto favorites. In the lower

orders, they are the same, with the addition of conceit and tyranny; considering the negroes as creatures formed merely to administer to their ease, and to be subject to their caprice; and I have found much difficulty to persuade those great people and superior beings, our white domestics, that the blacks are human beings and have souls. I allude more particularly to our German and other men-servants.

It was curious to observe, when we were entering any town, the number of trunks, band-boxes, & c. that were hurrying to the different houses, and the same at our departure, all going back to the country again, and all on negroes' heads; for whenever the ladies go to town, or are to appear in society, their black maids and other attendants start off with their finery in cases or their boxes, on their heads. Trunks of any size are carried in the same manner. In short, everything is put upon the head, from the largest to the smallest thing; even a smelling-bottle, I believe, would be carried in the same way. I have often, on our tour, seen twelve or fourteen negroes in one line of march, each bearing some article for the toilette on his head.

The creole language is not confined to the negroes. Many of the ladies who have not been educated in England, speak a sort of broken English, with an indolent drawling out of their words, that is very tiresome if not disgusting. I stood next to a lady one night, near a window, and, by way of saying something, remarked that the air was much cooler than usual; to which she answered, "Yes, ma-am, *him rail-ly too fra-ish.*"

Lady Nugent's remarkably perceptive observations on Jamaican colonial society could be made, *mutatis mutandis,* of just about any Caribbean colonial society. The "corruption" of the clergy and public officials, the laxity of European moral standards, the stereotypical social behavior of mulatto females, the gluttony (always under the guise of generosity), the prodigal use of labor, and the profligate obsession with materialism could be observed equally in Cuba or Martinique, Barbados or Surinam. There were common behavioral traits of the upper classes of whites in the plantation society which were a clear indication of the effects which the mercantile mentality and occupational servility had on the Europeans overseas. For it was not merely the climate of the tropics but the socioeconomic structure of their own creation that surreptitiously undermined their original Europeanness.

The two basic classes of Euro-Caribbean inhabitants formed four distinct social ranks. At the very summit—and closest to what might otherwise be called an elite—were the noble and seminoble families and the wealthy owners of large plantations. In the Spanish and French colonies some of these noble families had titles that ranked among the most distinguished in their respective metropolises. Cuba, for example, had twenty-nine titled families in 1810, including thirteen marquesses and sixteen counts. Most of these families arrived on the island as true settlers in the sixteenth century, although their titles dated only from the eighteenth century. This was true of the Pedroso, Gonzalez de la Torre, Roxas, Santa Cruz, Cárdenas, Cepero, and Sotolongo families of Havana, the Porcallo de Figueroa, Varona, and Guerra families of Bayamo, the De la Torre family of Puerto Principe, and the Estrada of Santiago de Cuba. Lower members of the nobility also sojourned for various periods in the English islands, brought out by the call of service, pleasure, or the desire for profit. Founding families of the English West Indian plantation society formed, by the late eighteenth century, a core of old planters, whose advice was often extremely influential in the realm of imperial and local politics.

Along with the titled nobility and old plantocracy came a mixed group of wealthy—sometimes nouveaux riches—planters, bureaucrats, senior officers in the military and naval services, and wealthy merchants, often the owners of country estates. The difference between these two strata of the white group was not great. Indeed kin affiliations occurred frequently between these two groups. The most distinguished and dominant Cuban families had offspring who gave valuable service in the Spanish military and bureaucracy. H. P. Jacobs reports in his study, *Sixty Years of Change*, that old planters often sent their sons to fight and die in places such as Spain and Egypt, in the military service of England, convinced that they fought for their king and their country. As Jacobs put it: "The old plantocracy had frequently a deep love for Jamaica and a feeling of responsibility; but they were not completely identified with it. The new plantocracy looked for advancement through Jamaica and through Jamaica alone." Both groups, old and new, formed a powerful alliance defending the economic and political interests of the white planting sector.

Below the old and new planters and their bureaucratic peers came the merchants and professionals such as doctors and clergymen. The expansion of commerce and the complex semibartering nature of the export economy of the period provided the main opportunities for the rise of a prominent and wealthy merchant class. The plantation society was, above all, a major consumer society importing necessities and luxuries from a wide variety of places. Bills of lading for the Port of Havana in 1852 demonstrate the universality of the trade and the diversity of the products. Included in the imports were fine clothes and mirrors from England, Holland, France, and North America; flour, wine, spices, olive oil, and shoes from Spain; codfish and salted meat from New Foundland, New York, Philadelphia, Baltimore, and Vera Cruz; silverware from Manchester and Birmingham; bricks and stones from Toledo; tiles, clay pots, and vases from Puebla, Mexico, and Talavera de la Reina, in Spain. With certain variations in the sources, the list could have been adequate for Curaçao, or Port-of-Spain, Bridgetown, Point-à-Pitre, or Kingston. The merchant groups were a diverse, sometimes socially well-connected class. Some were the scions of great families. This was particularly noticeable in Cuba in the early nineteenth century. Some, especially in the French colonies, were connected to prominent merchant houses in Nantes, Bordeaux, and La Rochelle. Others were simply adventurers of diverse background. Basques and Catalans virtually controlled the Hispanic colonial trade. Jews, Syrians, and Lebanese were prominent in the Dutch and English islands. The most successful merchants who stayed on in the colonies could merge into the planter class. But Jews in some British colonies, while allowed freedom of worship and movement, suffered from certain disabilities. They could neither vote nor serve in the military services until the general enfranchisement of all the free nonwhites, beginning with the Jamaica law of 1830.

Merchants formed a very large and active part of municipal life throughout the Caribbean. They built impressive urban homes and businesses and owned country estates. But they were never as a group regarded as the social peers of the specialist planting class, and it is ironic that in the French and British colonies the merchants were regarded as absentee owners and blamed for many of the economic ills. The nineteenth century modus operandi of the craft necessitated travel, not just abroad to suppliers and customers, but also throughout the island. But it is perhaps unlikely that a greater proportion of merchants than planters retired abroad. Moreover the tone of the cities—Havana, San Juan, Kingston, Bridgetown, or Fort-de-France—was set by the merchant groups who pioneered (albeit with great self-interest) some of the fledgling police and fire protection services that have survived as major municipal occupations. After 1805 merchants consistently comprised more than half of the Kingston Vestry Juror's Lists.

The fourth rank of whites were most numerous. They went under a variety of names, some of which had a pronounced pejorative connotation—*petits blancs*, poor whites, "lesser orders," *campesino, guajiro, mambí*, "walking buckra," and "red legs." The category included small independent farmers, petty shopkeepers, lawyers, tavern and hostel-keepers, day laborers, preachers, teachers, policemen, firemen, bill collectors, commission agents, gunsmiths, blacksmiths, coppersmiths and goldsmiths, druggists, midwives, nurses, undertakers, hairdressers, seamstresses, cooks, gardeners, bakers, barbers, tailors, coachmakers, coopers, undertakers, watchmakers and repairers, shoemakers, sailmakers, wharfingers, shipwrights, cabinetmakers, bricklayers, masons, printers, and stationers. Every type of service required by any society could be provided by these whites, who often competed in their occupations with the jobbing slaves and the free nonwhite population. This motley group also included a small number of unskilled, unemployed, and socially unsuccessful who formed a part of poor white society in every colony. But in general, members of the poorer white classes were employed, industrious, and filled with the hope of enormous pecuniary gain and eventual upward social mobility that formed part of the magnetic attraction of their sojourn in the tropics.

White society was not homogeneous, but it displayed a far greater cohesiveness and unity than any other group. The white sector, after all, dominated all the major institutions of the society. Whites virtually controlled the export economy, dominated the political structure, and set what they presumed to be the cultural norms of the society—although the scathing criticisms of visitors and some long-term residents indicated that white creole culture was a parody rather than a pattern. For the white subgroup reflected the entire spectrum of the European metropolitan society. Edward Long described the white masses graphically in his remarkable *History of Jamaica*:

> The lower order of white people (as they are called here), are, for the most part, composed of artificers, indented servants, and refugees . . . carpenters who never handled a tool; bricklayers, who scarcely know a brick from a stone; and bookkeepers, who can neither write nor read. Many of these menial servants, who are retained for saving a deficiency, are the very dregs of the three kingdoms. They have commonly more vices, and much fewer good qualities, than the slaves over whom they are set in authority; the better sort of whom heartily despise them, perceiving little or no difference from themselves, except in skin, and Blacker depravity. By their base familiarity with the worst-disposed among the slaves, they do a very great injury to the plantations; causing disturbances, by seducing the Negroes [*sic*] wives, and bringing an *odium* upon the white people in general, by their drunkenness and profligate actions. In fact, the better sort of Creole Blacks disdain to associate with them, holding them in too much contempt, or abhorrence.

Such were the peculiarities of the plantation slave society that the conventional class divisions and social distinctions of the metropolitan society largely broke down in the colonies. For the white people, race and color rather than class and nationality became a consoling, fraternal bond. Even when Long wrote in the eighteenth century, he remarked on the fundamental changes that had taken place—the autocracy of the plantation owner had given way to a society of com-

mon law—but the colonial society was only a pale reflection of the
mother country. The essentially frontier conditions of the tropics facilitated a fantastic upward social mobility among the whites that
often made a mockery of class consciousness.

Bryan Edwards, the experienced Jamaican planter and member of
the British Parliament, wrote apprehensively of white colonial social
relations as the French Revolution engulfed the continent and Saint-
Domingue:

> It appears to me [he wrote in 1793] that the leading feature
> [among the whites] is an independent spirit, and a display of
> conscious equality throughout all ranks and conditions. The
> poorest white person seems to consider himself nearly on a level
> with the richest, and, emboldened by this idea approached his
> employer with extended hand, and a freedom, which in the
> countries of Europe, is seldom displayed by men in the lower
> orders of life toward their superiors. It is not difficult to trace the
> origin of this principle. It arises, without doubt, from the pre-
> eminence and distinction which are necessarily attached even to
> the complexion of a White Man, in a country where the com-
> plexion, generally speaking, distinguishes freedom from slavery.

The simple facts of Caribbean life permitted sufficient examples of
the dramatic rise from dismal poverty and humble status to Croesus-
like wealth and the most highly esteemed social rank. Henry Morgan,
the Welsh indentured servant-turned-buccaneer, ended his life as a
respected planter and lieutenant-governor of Jamaica in the seventeenth century. Julian de Zulueta, a poor semiliterate rural Basque,
went out to Cuba in the early nineteenth century, entered the slave
trade, and rose to be the mayor of Havana, a member of the Spanish
nobility, and an advisor to the Crown. There was always some degree
of initial snobbery, and some unease at accepting new members to
the group, but this could be overcome. Lady Nugent found it convenient to act "like an invalid, to keep up the character I have politically adopted" on meeting a group of French refugee ladies in Spanish
Town until she could clarify their social status and determine "what
ladies to receive." Because she was a bit of prude and an official tran-

sient in the society, she probably deliberately exaggerated social distance to bolster her husband's position. It is hardly likely that the other white elite ladies would go to such extremes to display rank with foreign women of their own color. For color alone was a ticket of admission.

The mutually reinforcing cleavages of race and color for the minority whites can hardly be overestimated in the Caribbean. Auguste Lacour, writing of Guadeloupe society in the middle of the nineteenth century, described with cutting precision the ranks within the society as a whole and the congealing effect of color:

> Although the island counted among itself a number of the titled nobility, especially younger sons who had come out to the place in pursuit of their fortune, the nobility was not constituted as in France. Within the white group, the nobility did not exist. The only privilege of the nobility was being entitled to a seat in the *Conseil Supérieur,* and the exemption from the head tax for a fixed number of slaves. What constituted the nobility was not parchment, but color. To the white group, to individuals of the European race, were exclusively reserved all public, lucrative and honorific functions.

Color, therefore, delineated the boundaries of caste and highlighted the distinctions between the "we" and "they." It mitigated the potential class divisions within the whites, especially after the Haitian Revolution demonstrated the ultimate consequences of placing class above caste. Race, color, and bondage were fundamental ingredients in white thoughts about their world in the Caribbean. Unfortunately it was sometimes the only thing they thought about—besides markets and profits.

Race, color, and legal status did not, however, preclude some relationships across caste lines. The masters could no more live without their slaves than the slaves could live without their masters. Each group, the free and the enslaved, the masters and the slaves, the Africans and the Europeans, adjusted to life in the tropical world as best as they could. And this adjustment included an adjustment to each other. The monopoly of power exercised by the white sector on the plantations, in politics, in law, and in the export economy was more apparent than real. In two ways the structure which the whites created was contradictory. In the first place, their success at all levels depended largely on factors entirely outside their control—including the supply of slaves, the price of sugar, and the fortuitous consistency of climate. In the second place, the white master class defined slaves as property but were forced to use them as persons.

Alongside the continuous proliferation of laws establishing the sanctity of private property in Africans and a literature deploring the inherent inhumanity or subhumanity of slaves went an elaborate system of police protection measures fully conceding the basic humanity of the slaves. Slaves, after all, demonstrated equally all the qualities of the whites. They could work as hard, speak the language as well, think as subtly, scheme as cunningly, inflict revenge as maliciously, love as passionately, and subvert society as totally. Other forms of property—land, cattle, equipment, and buildings—could not respond so creatively. Slaves had a life, mind, and culture of their own that induced them to make a parallel response to the situation in which they found themselves.

The exigencies of production, profit, and social order required substantial white supervision of nonwhite society. But this supervision could not take the form of unrelenting coercion or uninterrupted regulation. The white sector delegated authority, recognized cultural differences, encouraged divisions of rank, and employed all types of incentives to minimize the simultaneous disaffection of the majority of the slave sector. The weakness of the white master class provided an agent for upward social mobility. For the fact that the whites could not even provide sufficient women for the adequate sexual satisfaction of the males meant that caste-confined relations even at the most domestic level had to be relaxed. Slave plantation society held an ideal that was far removed from the operational reality of day-to-day living.

The contradictions of the slave society were intrinsic to the social dynamism and social mobility produced by the system. At one level social stratification and mobility initiated explosive pressures of class, color, and race. Theoretically individuals could move upward within the class structure and laterally across the caste divisions. The field slave acquiring a technical skill and polishing his command of English, Spanish, French, Dutch, or Swedish could become a part of the domestic staff of the plantation great house. Or he could join the jobbing gangs of the urban setting. On the contiguous, overlapping, and frequently ill-defined boundaries of race and status some passing could occur. Urban skilled slaves could successfully run away and become free. Free light-complexioned mulattoes could pass as white, and undoubtedly some wealthy ones did, legitimizing their status by judicious bribes, marriages, or general conduct. Even within the upper stratum, newcomers with money and temerity could break into the ranks of the socially privileged, as Morgan and Zulueta did. The slave society, in short, was similar to any other society faced with widely fluctuating economic and demographic circumstances. The dynamism had internal as well as external sources of stimulation.

Nevertheless the fluidity of the structure, especially at the free level, engendered the type of internal class and caste friction that contributed to social instability, and made the slave society a potentially revolutionary society. The slave society during the nineteenth century was equally one of ferment and strife. Its strengths created its inherent weaknesses. A divided society was also a divisive society. Tensions existed within the white groups as well as between white and nonwhite. In Cuba, the most enduring of the Caribbean slave societies, the white groups split basically between Spanish-born *peninsulares* and Cuban-born *criollos*. *Criollo-peninsular* animosity manifested itself in a number of conspiracies throughout the century, flared unsuccessfully during the Ten Years War, 1868-1878, and finally broke the last vestige of the Spanish-American imperial connection in 1898. In 1788 the rift between *grands blancs* and *petits blancs* opened the floodgates of revolution in the French colony of Saint-Domingue, with permanent reversals for French ambitions and the French empire in the Americas. In Jamaica, the political incompatibility between rural whites and urban whites contributed to the constitutional surrender after Morant Bay in 1865. The constitutional crisis at Morant Bay started with a minor riot by some peasants who wanted access to government-held lands following a year of lean harvests across the island. The center of discontent was the north-central parish of St. Ann. But in St. Thomas in the east, an angry mob marched on the court house in Morant Bay while the parish council was in session, set fire to it, and killed a few of the white landholders, including the custos. The disturbance did not spread beyond the parish limits, and the governor of Jamaica, Edward Eyre, declared martial law only for the area. Nevertheless, he used the common religious affiliation of Paul Bogle, the leader of the rioters, and George William Gordon, a leading member of the urban party of Merchants and Free Persons of Color, as the pretext to remove the latter from Kingston to St. Thomas, where he was tried and executed for conspiracy. Eyre grossly exaggerated the nature of the threat to the white established planters, and with the legislature meekly yielding its autonomy, the island reverted to the status of a Crown Colony, ruled as well as governed by an appointed official of the English monarch and parliament.

At the same time, the recurring slave revolts and the constant preoccupation with the possibility of slave revolts exacerbated the antagonistic racial divisions in every slave society. The increased exploitation of slaves at the very period when the institution of slavery was undergoing international moral and intellectual attack—and in some cases physical dismantlement—coincided with the increased nineteenth-century awareness of ethnicity, ethnocentricity, and nationalism. Cultural, ethnic, and economic diversity appeared patently undesirable to adherents of social engineering infatuated with the current ideas of emergent nations.

After more than three hundred years, it was characteristic of the Caribbean plantation slave societies that, just when it seemed they would last forever, they fell apart like tenpins. Corroded on the inside and assaulted from the outside, they passed into history leaving a painful and indelible legacy to their successors.

Chapter 6 • Disintegration and Reconstruction, 1793-1886

Lord Bathurst [might consider] the propriety of communicating to the Governors of the several West Indies colonies that in future no grants will be made to escheated slaves; but that all such persons will be emancipated; with the exception, first, of the aged, secondly, of the incurably diseased, thirdly, of the profligate, and fourthly of those whose ignorance is such as to prevent their earning their own subsistence.

James Stephen to Robert Horton, May 30, 1823

The old order changeth yielding place to new,
And God fulfills Himself in many ways,
Lest one good custom should corrupt the world.

Alfred Lord Tennyson, Morte d'Arthur, 1842

Throughout the Caribbean the nineteenth century represented a long period of disintegration and reconstruction. Slowly the aged vestiges of the cruel plantation slave society yielded to the impatient emergence of a new polyglot society of free peoples. New classes replaced the old. New configurations and new external relationships weakened and sometimes dissolved the distinguishing bonds of empire. By far the most significant development was the growth of a predominantly creole, inward-looking, and primarily peasant group of workers evaluating on their own terms the burdensome legacy of slavery. In freedom these groups fashioned their cultures and their societies in more positive ways than they could have done under the conditions and inherent restraints of slavery.

Naturally each Caribbean colony exhibited certain unique characteristics reflecting the variations in physical size, topography, economic development, population density and composition, and even the historical evolution already alluded to. These characteristics warped but did not break the suggested commonalities that were evident in the development of the region. The Caribbean slave societies, therefore, evolved and disintegrated in a harmony that transcended imperial divisions. Such variations as occurred should not be ascribed primarily to imperial traditions, regardless of the degree to which imperialism impinged on the administrative operation of each colony. Puerto Rico and Cuba were equally Spanish colonies, but their paths during the nineteenth century were not especially close. Barbados, Jamaica, Trinidad, and Guiana were English colonies which manifested great variations in the postabolition period. Likewise the Dutch colonies of Curaçao and Surinam made dissimilar responses to the new age. Metropolitan differences affected, but never determined, the historical course of the abolition of slavery and the rise of free societies.

The abolition of slavery in the Caribbean reflected both the original aims of European colonization and the social structure of each unit. The abolition of slavery, therefore, must be seen as merely one phase—albeit the final one—in the disintegration of the Caribbean slave society, as well as only one phase in the slow evolution of Caribbean society and growth of Caribbean nationhood.

Settler colonies, as we have already argued, represented the deliberate intention to recreate miniatures of the metropolis, with a definite symbiotic relationship. The colonists went out to occupy,

settle, reproduce themselves, and produce whatever the land yielded
in abundance. The colony became their *patria chica*, the region to
which they owed allegiance and with which they forged an identity.
On the other hand, the overriding preoccupation of the exploitation,
or nonsettler, colonies was the organization of labor and the construction of a community geared to the maximum production of
tropical staples, both for the imperial and the international market.
The European component viewed residence as temporary and the
entire society as a transient political and economic extension of the
metropolis, with little or no feeling of identity or community of
interest.

These two aims of settlement and exploitation were neither clearly
articulated nor distinctly separated at any time. One or the other
consideration superseded, or the two coexisted uneasily, as they did
in Curaçao during the eighteenth century and in Cuba and Puerto
Rico during the nineteenth century. Barbados, which originated as a
settlement colony in the seventeenth century, rapidly converted itself
into an exploitation slave society. By the end of the eighteenth century many other colonies—Jamaica, Guadeloupe, Martinique, Saint-
Domingue, Trinidad—had settler components among their European
exploiters. This situation eventually affected the operation of the
slave system and helped accomplish the disintegration of slave society.

The colonial status was an important factor in the Caribbean.
Unlike the circumstances in the United States, where slavery matured
under the auspices of an independent, though sharply bifurcated, nation-state, Caribbean slave societies always had the prevailing influence of an external metropolis. The colonial status made a difference
both in the timing of maturation and the abolition of slavery. Crucial
decisions concerning the colonies were resolved outside the area, in
the metropolitan decision-making body. A general emancipation independent of the whims of the metropolis therefore involved (as the
situation in Saint-Domingue made abundantly clear) reconsideration
of the political status of the colony. For this reason abolition assumed
paramount importance in the internal fortunes and affairs of the European metropolitan powers.

The dismantling of the slave systems can therefore be approached from two angles: the metropolitan dimension and the local perspective. Neither can be fully understood without the other. The conventional emphasis on the metropolitan dimension often results in gross oversimplification of the complexity of slavery and the inherently disintegrating forces of every unfree system.

The metropolitan dimension reveals itself most clearly in three related facets of imperial life: politics, international economics, and the realm of ideas. These three facets operated unevenly across and within the imperial systems, affecting differentially both settler and exploitation colonies. The British Parliament legislated on the issue of slavery without explicity recognizing that the local circumstances in Jamaica varied from those of Antigua. The French muted the differences between Saint-Domingue and Martinique. The Dutch equated the conditions in Caraçao and Surinam. The Spanish reluctantly recognized that Puerto Rico and Cuba varied considerably, their recognition stimulated by ten years of war in the latter colony. Imperial systems acted on general principles not individual cases.

With the exception of Saint-Domingue, the pattern of disintegration of the slave systems followed the sequential order of their establishment. The British abolished legal slavery in 1838, after acknowledging that gradual emancipation as envisaged in 1834 had been a fiasco. The French and the Danes followed in 1848, the Dutch in 1863, the Spanish between 1873 (for Puerto Rico) and 1886 (for Cuba). With the exception of the Spanish colonies, the movement toward the abolition of slavery was symmetrical. The gradual weakening of the economic importance of the colonies undermined their political influence at home, enabling the home parliament to capitulate before the combined pressure of political reformers, imperial free traders, and humanitarian idealists. In all cases the parliaments tried to reconcile what they saw as the divergent interests of metropolis and colony, or colonial slave owners versus domestic political and economic pressure groups.

One important observation overlooked in the histories of abolition from the metropolitan viewpoint is that concern for the slaves—the real victims of the brutal system of slavery—was an incidental part of official policy. The fleeting references to recognition and reparation for the slaves never made an impact when the time for emancipation arrived. Yet the home governments and, above all, the advocates of abolition cannot be accused of calculated malice or hypocrisy. Metropolitan abolitionists were convinced that they were acting in the best interests of the slaves. Yet their adversaries in the parliaments reflected most of those groups in the society that were able to exert direct political pressure. Official responses came as a result of these direct political pressures. The slaves and the vast majority of the Afro-Caribbean population had no way of participating in imperial politics. Representation on their behalf, therefore, came from other groups often with more specific interests to serve.

The British imperial system provided the first metropolitan-directed abolition movement. The abolitionists drew their strength from three areas: the religious community, the British working classes, and the imperialists and free traders. In the colonies the nonconformist churches—Baptists, Moravians, and Methodists—were really fighting for their colonial survival (and a piece of the evangelical action). Their fight coincided with the period when British industry and the English economy were no longer narrowly Atlantic and subservient to the domineering West Indian interest. British capital and British manufactured goods were no longer confined to their empire. The sugar industry accentuated this growing universality of English commercial activity. British West Indian sugar producers by the 1830's were competing with those from India, Mauritius, Cuba, Brazil, Singapore, Java, and the Philippines. The exporters of refined sugar faced the additional competition of a rising beet production both in the United States of America and continental Europe. West Indian production was becoming increasingly uncompetitive both within the imperial system and in the international market owing to its low technological development and corresponding high production costs. Economic considerations fomented hostility to imperial preference and to the economic and political importance of the West Indian planters. This decline was near its nadir when the British Parliament moved to abolish slavery in 1833-34.

The economic factor cannot be easily overlooked in the process of abolition. The English, French, Danish, and Dutch abolition movements coincided with the period of economic stabilization or decline in the respective imperial possessions. Sugar production in Jamaica, the largest of the British islands, remained fairly constant between 1821 and 1832. The median production of about 82,000 hogsheads was considerably lower than the median production for the period between 1799 and 1820. Sugar and rum production for the entire West Indies had declined between 1815 and 1833. A similar situation existed in Martinique, Guadeloupe, and Surinam. Production had remained constant or fallen slightly, while the price of sugar dropped considerably. The situation varied from island to island or from colony to colony, but the predominant trend was toward fewer estates and diversification of products.

The great number of estates sold or deeply indebted to outside merchants and bankers reflected the serious crisis of the export economy. Fifty percent of the 151 sugar estates on the small island of St. Croix were in the hands of creditors in 1841. The plight of the sugar economy in St. Croix found parallels throughout the smaller colonies, especially in the islands. In Jamaica some 50 percent of the 775 sugar estates operating in 1772 had gone out of business by the end of the century. When the English slave trade was abolished in 1807 many estates could no longer recoup their operating expenses, much less repay their creditors. As a result, some 100 estates had simply been abandoned, while another 100 faced debt claims that jeopardized their continuation. From the viewpoint of sugar producers the colonies faced considerable economic difficulties. If colonists did not sell they could not buy. Metropolitan exports, therefore, tended to decline prior to emancipation. Imports into the British Caribbean fell by nearly 25 percent between 1821 and 1833. French exports to Martinique fell by nearly 30 percent between 1841 and 1848, while those to Guadeloupe dropped some 33 percent. The economic figures emphasize only one aspect of the metropolitan-colonial relationship, but they clearly underlined the declining importance of the Caribbean colonies to the industrializing countries of Europe. Obviously the non-Hispanic Caribbean was at the end of an economic cycle in the early nineteenth century.

The Hispanic Caribbean, on the other hand, had only begun to enter the international economic sphere. Sugar production had increased tremendously in Puerto Rico, and Cuba had initiated the modernized, highly technical sugar complex based on steam, railroads, and extended *ingenios*. By 1850 Cuba alone could adequately satisfy the world cane sugar market demand.

Unlike the other European metropolises, however, Spain lagged in industrialization. It could neither supply its colonies with their required manufactured articles and technical equipment nor provide a suitable market for their tropical products. In addition domestic political turbulence rendered Spain incapable of giving the political and administrative control the colonial settler element required. Metropolitan influence in the Spanish Caribbean slave societies in the nineteenth century failed to rival that of the non-Hispanic Caribbean. Despite metropolitan opposition, therefore, Puerto Rico abolished slavery at the request of the colonists. Spanish attempts to mediate in Cuban slave affairs were continually frustrated from the 1850's until final abolition in 1886.

Cuba was undoubtedly unique in the Caribbean experience. By the middle of the nineteenth century Cuba was a prominent contributor to the Spanish treasury. The island provided the principal market for flour from Bilbao and Santander, textiles from Barcelona, and wine and olive oil from Seville and Cadiz. The Spanish merchant community was clearly not in a position to antagonize their best customers by supporting the abolitionist movement that developed in Spain in the late 1860's. The Spanish merchants had no faith in the potential purchasing power of exslaves. Above all they shrewdly calculated that the termination of slavery would probably coincide with the end of the imperial connection and the diminution of their major export market. The Spanish experience varied, with the forces that advocated abolition elsewhere supporting its continuation. That the Spanish metropolis should find itself diametrically opposite to the rest of Europe on the issue of slavery sprung almost entirely from imperial economic and political relations. The economic and political power of the planter class in Cuba during the final phase of slavery was almost tantamount to the English imperial proslavery forces, with the support of the vital cotton-producing colonists of the southern North American colonies, and the French, with the strength of Saint-Domingue. Abolition would hardly have presented the same perspective if the English had not lost their North American colonies, or the French had still maintained Saint-Domingue.

Economic considerations became inextricably bound up with political action extending beyond the internal affairs of the imperial systems. The recognition that sugar production and slavery involved complex international agreements led to the British extension of its campaign to end the slave trade after 1808. Approaches at the separate national levels did not bear fruit rapidly. Spain accepted £400,000 in 1818, and agreed to end the Africa-Spanish Antilles trade after 1820. But Cuban sugar production required African workers, and the Antillean slave trade continued until 1865. The French slave trade continued until the 1830's, and only in the 1850's did the vigorous Brazilian slave trade cease. The abolition of the slave trade was the necessary prerequisite for the emancipation of Caribbean slaves. Pressures to end the trade—which was largely international—were more easily applied than pressures to abolish slavery, which was considered an internal affair. As long as the Cuban slave owners held the upper hand in the political affairs of their island they could retard the external attempts to emancipate the slaves.

The dismantling of the Caribbean slave society in the nineteenth century reflected not merely political and economic considerations but a new intellectual awareness about the nature of man and society. Such ideas had always accompanied the slavery controversy, with humanists, theologians, and philosophers dividing almost equally on both sides of the issue—despite the overwhelming general acceptance of the institution itself. As secular thought moved in the direction of social engineering—most classically expressed or implied in the theories of Comtian positivism, social Darwinism, and Marxism—hostility to the institution of slavery increased. But condemnation of the institution did little to increase sympathy for the slaves. The Europeans expressed concern with the plantation society and the socio-economic complex of slavery mainly because of its relation to their own domestic affairs. Slavery was therefore viewed in relation to European social and technological goals: as an anachronism to the positivists; a sign of fundamental weakness to the Darwinists; or a tool of the bourgeoisie to the Marxists. In its own way each theory included strong elements of ethnocentricity and racism. The important point is that all these theories increased the antislavery sentiment in the metropolis and contributed to the general agitation that mobilized the metropolitan mobs. Even though the abolitionist perspective was Europocentric and reformist, social theorists were undermining the position of slavery in the colonies by including it in the demands for domestic social and political reform. Not surprisingly, therefore, English abolition came in the wake of the great Reform Bill of 1832 and French abolition with the revolution of 1848. Abolition was a by-product of social theories from the metropolis.

In the colonies, on the other hand, abolition and emancipation involved fundamental social problems affecting economic values, social positions, and political reconstruction and realignment. It was not, as in the metropolis, a tangential issue. Moreau de Saint-Méry demonstrated with abundant clarity this revolutionary social awareness when he declared in 1791 that extending the "Rights of Man" to the mulattoes in the French colonies would ultimately extend power to the most numerous. "For if once the slaves suspect," he wrote, "that there is a power other than their masters which holds the final disposition of their fates; if they once see that the mulattoes have invoked this power and by its aid have become our equals—then France must renounce all hope of preserving her colonies." This prophecy applied not to his homeland of Martinique alone but to the larger neighboring colony of Saint-Domingue. The declaration reflected the enormous social tensions under which the colonial slave society existed.

This social tension resulted from the nature of the slave society, for, with the exception of Cuba and Puerto Rico, it presented the spectacle of a small minority of whites dominating a large mass of black and mixed persons. Race, ethnicity, and color were facts of

everyday life, the indelible badges of status and condition. On the eve
of the revolution the white population of Saint-Domingue amounted
to only 8 percent of the total, while Guadeloupe had only 12 percent.
In the 1830's, less than 4 percent of the Jamaican population was
white. The Barbadian whites amounted to around 15 percent. Antigua had slightly less than 6 percent whites. Curaçao had a white
population of slightly less than 25 percent—and 45 percent were
slaves—in 1830. In plantation-dominated Surinam the white population amounted to just more than 4 percent in 1830, approximately
one-half of whom were Jews. In every colony the minority white
population lived in fear of the legitimate aspirations of the free mixed
and slave groups. Only in Cuba, where the white population
amounted to nearly 60 percent of the population in 1870, and Puerto
Rico, where the white settler element was around 51 percent, did the
situation significantly vary. Moreover, as original settler colonies, the
two Spanish Antillean islands had spawned a substantial free mixed
stratum prior to conversion into an exploitation colony.

Throughout the Caribbean the white population, regardless of size,
dominated the administrative machinery of local government, the
militia, and the established churches. Political control ranged from
being very strong in the English colonies, especially in Barbados and
Jamaica with local planter-controlled legislatures, to weak in the
Spanish islands, which were theoretically administered from the
metropolis. But the Spanish colonial administration, noted in principle for authoritarianism, succumbed in practice to the rule of the
local creoles and *peninsulares* in Cuba and Puerto Rico. The local
whites found themselves in a good position to affect the course of
abolition, especially in obstructing the evolution of the entirely free,
multiracial society. Yet dependence on the metropolis, as Moreau de
Saint-Méry pointed out, made the whites extremely vulnerable. Numerically they were weak in relation to the rest of their local community. Their political, economic, social, and ideological commit-
ment to the motherland undermined their ability to forge a confident,
self-conscious Caribbean society based on the diversity of the region.
Such a society, however, far exceeded the potential reserves of origi-

nality and independence of the colonies, even though the Cubans, with Domingo del Monte, Antonio Saco, Cristóbal Madan, and Rafael Labra, moved in that direction during the nineteenth century.

Slavery throughout the Caribbean confronted difficulties from internal forces, too: from the various strata of the society, the demands of the plantation structure, and the necessary local responses to the changing international situation.

Every social stratum manifested the type of discontent and general restlessness that by itself made its members a potentially revolutionary class. As indicated in chapter five, the white classes never represented a homogeneous group, even in those situations where they formed a small minority of the total population. They were a faction-ridden, muted hostile group whose barely contained unity was undermined by the twin forces of class conflict and caste hostility. The divisions between creoles and expatriots was an ancient social one that had, by the nineteenth century, become somewhat anachronistic. Expatriots no longer dominated the economy, and the strengthening sentiments of regional self-consciousness among the native-born whites challenged the notions that birth in the metropolis provided inherent advantages for life in the tropics. The official distinctions accorded those of metropolitan birth, and the occupational distribution that virtually precluded nonlocals from the highest positions of the bureaucracy, accentuated the social distance between the two major white groups. Ironically, although the *grands blancs* behaved like a true nobility in the tropics, their representatives to the French General Assembly after 1789 fraternized and voted with the metropolitan social equivalent, the Third Estate.

The white classes in the nonsettler Caribbean colonies derived their local social position from their relationship to plantation export production and their cultural affinity to what they considered the prevailing behavioral norms of their respective metropolises. Yet each new generation found itself further away from the metropolitan culture and more involved in the scarring competition for status and office. While slavery indicated a major distinction in rank, the abolition of slavery jeopardized the accepted, and to the whites acceptable, social distinctions between the various groups of men. One asset of the slave society to the white classes, therefore, was the ability to disguise social class differences by emphasizing racial caste differences.

But colonial governors found that creoles knew more about the operational procedures of government and were more adept at local politics than the often disease-prone metropolitan recruits. Attempts at political and social cohesion, however, were frequently frustrated by the differences of political philosophy and regional origins of the members of the white elite. Scotsmen, Irishmen, and Welshmen did not necessarily behave more fraternally as individual representatives of metropolitan Great Britain in the far-flung reaches of empire. Basques, Catalans, and Galicians formed clubs that reinforced their *patriachiquismo* in the overseas Spanish colonies in a manner that might have been more exaggerated than in Iberia. And the political consequences of war changed colonies from one imperial sphere to another so that after 1763, for example, generations of solidly elitist French in St. Lucia, Dominica, and St. Vincent found the newly arrived English treating them with undeserved suspicion and contempt. The same attendant snobbery followed the transfer of Spanish Trinidad to the English after 1797. Elite divisions based on religion and culture were not as marked as class divisions within the white group. Metropolitan white travelers to the Caribbean painted a dismal picture of lower-class dissolution, dissipation, and despair, not unlike the descriptions generalized by Edward Long.

Long's negative picture was generally valid for all nonsettler colonies. The condition of the poor whites, however, was not brought about by hereditary social class origins, but by the necessities of the plantation culture with its limited social life, large subordinated masses, and extreme sexual imbalance among both white and black. For the colonies themselves offered little to the lower class of whites except the dubious distinction of being socially superior to all nonwhites.

In the settler colonies of Cuba and Puerto Rico (and in Curaçao) the situation was different. The lower-class whites or creoles were not necessarily economically inferior to the upper-class whites. Indeed they were often more successful and much more attached to the colony which had a life of its own. Cuba and Puerto Rico continued the traditional Hispanic strife—though considerably mitigated—of the Spanish-American imperial rivalry between creoles and *peninsulares*. But more crucial during the nineteenth century was the combined white slave owner-sugar producer resentment to the commercial and political policies of the mother country. As long as slavery existed as a necessary labor component in the sugar enterprise, however, the white groups in the Spanish Antilles supported the metropolis, whose military strength was needed to tip the balance in case of the possible confrontation of the races. The Spanish government exploited this situation of fear.

In economic success as in decline, the colonial white class would have been a restless, if not a revolutionary, group. The metropolitan attacks on slavery did not help the situation, since such attacks exposed both the economic and the social weaknesses of the white position in the colonies. Most European-Caribbean whites admitted that slavery was necessary for the survival of the colonies, especially after the destruction of Saint-Domingue. Thus self-preservation tended to mitigate the mutual hostility between the white groups.

The white attitudes toward slavery took different courses in either settler or nonsettler colonies. In Curaçao and Puerto Rico slavery was not a significant social index for the white person. Slave owners, white and nonwhite, did not feel threatened by revengeful exslaves. The relative poverty of those colonies seemed to have an efficacious equalizing effect on all the population, free and unfree. In Cuba the large slave owners of the western part of the island fought abolition for nearly fifty years. They brought in all the arguments that the nonsettler colonies had made familiar in the history of slavery: legal property rights, threat to civilization, and racial incompatibility. They never succeeded in developing an argument—as had their North American colleagues—establishing slavery as a positive social good. Instead they merely played the game to gain time to develop a large enough population and the mechanical technology which would adjust the imbalance between the high labor demands of sugar and a low labor pool.

The racial fear of the nonsettler whites was more realistic, not only because they were numerically outnumbered by discontented slaves and free persons of color but because the intercaste divisions of the society were under such tremendous strain. It was the impatient demand of the free persons of color on Saint-Domingue that opened the floodgates of the revolution in the colony and eventually led to the overthrow of all the whites and free colored persons. The free colored persons had legitimate grievances—such as the status of the mulattoes—which they wanted redressed. But these demands of the mulattoes ran counter to the white grievances, which emphasized a greater degree of colonial autonomy and a further restriction in the privileges of the nonwhite groups. The outbreak of fighting in the colony, in which both sides employed their slaves, was the ignition for an all-out assault on the social structure of the plantation system. The slaves eventually won the multidimensional war, and set up their own independent republic—the second independent state in the hemisphere.

The situation in Saint-Domingue was not duplicated elsewhere. The whites employed obstructionist tactics to the acceptance of the mulattoes and free coloreds, but by 1832 they were forced to accommodate them in the British islands. The decline of the sugar industry further weakened the resistance of the local whites to the demand of the prosperous blacks for greater participation in the economic and political life of the colonies. The right to vote and sit in the local assemblies, won just before the abolition of slavery, placed the political power of the whites in jeopardy. That they held on to the power and privileges based on their skin color derived not from the dynamics of the local situation but from the operation of imperial politics.

The conduct of the white upper strata of the exploitation colonies during the twilight of slavery provides a good insight into the nature of the colonial elite. The Caribbean slave society was an artificial and novel experience in the history of European imperialism. The stratification based on occupation, race, and color created fundamental inequalities and mutually reinforcing social cleavages that could only be removed by the disintegration of the society. The whites had never considered the colonies their home. They were exiles in the tropics, longing to get back to the society from which they had come. Whenever they could they escaped. And the problem of absenteeism was a chronic one in the British Caribbean. Since they did not see themselves as part of a society distinct from and independent of that of their mother countries, they were forced to defend their existence along a set of rules laid down by the Europeans, and designed for an ethnically homogeneous society. Slavery was not an integral part of European society, and so the Euro-West Indians failed to develop a "home-grown defence" for the institution. In the late eighteenth century they reluctantly accepted amelioration of the conditions of slavery as a compromise position between the status quo and the total abolition of the system. That failed—as did the international sugar market to which they felt irrevocably tied. Finally in the nineteenth century they accepted compensation for their slaves and felt relieved to recover some of their fiscal expenditure with which to face the uncertain economic future. With the exception of Cuba, all the Caribbean societies were intellectually bankrupt at the end of the slavery period. The elites were in trouble—politically, economically, socially, and intellectually—and the metropolis was not very sympathetic.

The slave system was also threatened from below. The slaves had never accepted the institution as a satisfactory medium of salvation. Nor, regardless of the belief of their masters, had they acquiesced in it. The long history of the Maroons in all the colonies bore eloquent testimony to the unquenchable will to be free that permeated every slave-holding society. After the example of Saint-Domingue and the Maroon wars, the restlessness of the slaves throughout the region made the whites even more uncomfortable. In almost every colony the slaves felt that the local whites were deliberately obstructing the course of emancipation, which they were. They also felt, especially when the agitation for complete abolition became intense after the 1830's, that they had already gotten their freedom, which they had not. Violence accompanied the final end of slavery in Cuba, St. Croix, Martinique, Guadeloupe, Demerara, and Jamaica. The slaves made it clear that they meant to emancipate themselves by force.

But even without the forceful pressures of the slaves the slave system was collapsing surreptitiously from within. The vulnerability of the elite to the economic pressures of the international market economy was only slightly reflected in the lower social echelons. The collapse of sugar was not the collapse of the local economies, as the metropolitan politicians and economists thought. The free colored and slave sectors controlled not only many of the intermediate skills and services but much of the local currency that the colonies possessed. Edward Long estimated that about 20 percent of the liquid cash in Jamaica in 1774 was in the hands of slaves, and a fair proportion of the rest among the mercantile community of free nonwhites. Moreover the very nature of the sugar culture presaged a progressive concentration of slaves in fewer hands on larger estates. As the estates collapsed the slaves either got their freedom or were leased out as jobbers. The collapse of the international economy left the planter-producers unable to operate efficiently with large slave gangs whose perennial maintenance was an additional liability. Free, wage-paid seasonal labor became more economical—when the problem of availability could be overcome. The collapse of the economic power of the planters led to the acquisition of many more skills by free men of any color. Alexander Barclay noted that between 1800 and 1826 in Jamaica a whole range of occupations involving sailors on coasting vessels, ship-builders, mechanics, and carpenters had changed from being predominantly slave or white into the control of the free colored community. In the British West Indies the white population had never been sufficient to provide all the services which the colonies needed, and the growing free colored community had quickly filled the void. With the constant exodus of white emigrants to the more lucrative North American colonies or to Europe, the economic position of the free nonwhites was further enhanced.

This process of internal erosion was also evident in the Cuban plantation society of the nineteenth century, even though the white population continued to grow relatively as well as absolutely. The island was sharply divided between the new aggressive entrepreneurs of the western sector and the small-farming settlers of the eastern sector. The western part resembled the nonsettler Caribbean, with its sugar and coffee plantations, slave gangs, and reliance on the export market. Ranching, tobacco growing, and food for local consumption were the mainstays of the eastern part. The external pressures to abolish the slave trade had left the island desperately short of workers, and this shortage had impressed upon the planters the need to find new machines to do the labor for which workhands were lacking. As the sugar industry became increasingly mechanized, the role of the slaves declined, giving way to wage earners and to imported mechanics and engineers who understood the new technology and worked on seasonal contracts. More important, however, was the way in which the new technology increased productivity and made the enormous captive labor force an anachronism. By the 1870's, merely 23 percent of the entire Cuban labor force were slaves. The delayed abolition of Cuban slavery, however, represented a minor variant on the common historical theme of Caribbean slavery. It was not the Hispanic culture but accidental timing that made the difference. Puerto Rico, which had more than 10 percent of its population enslaved, showed a domestic inclination to abolish slavery as early as 1812 but was prevented from doing so by the machinations of the Cuban planters. Imperial politics worked on general principles, not individual cases.

By the time that abolition occurred in the Hispanic Caribbean, slavery had become an embarrassing anachronism in most parts of the New World. Certainly in the neighboring Caribbean islands the institution had already been destroyed. The societies there were far along the way toward making the readjustments to an all-free, majority black society. The United States of America had abolished slavery in 1864 and had fought an agonizing and extremely costly civil war over the issue. The Spanish-American mainland colonies had included abolition among the goals of their political independence. Only Brazil retained slavery as a viable institution, finally abandoning the system in 1888.

The Caribbean slave society depended on its own internal cohesion as well as the political and military goodwill of the decision-making bodies in the metropolis. One way or the other, the slave society

eventually destroyed itself. Not only did it bear the seeds of potential self-destruction in open racial violence and sabotage, but it failed
to establish—as in the United States—a philosophy that could successfully counteract the increasing doubts of humanitarians, economists, and politicians in the home countries. In retrospect it is quite
easy to see that the process of abolition gathered tremendous momen-
tum during the first three decades of the nineteenth century. But at
the time some of the most outspoken abolitionists such as William
Wilberforce and José Antonio Saco thought the final act of emancipation would take place in the distant future.

Abolition in each imperial system depended on the conjunction of
the two opposing elements of external politico-economic reservations
and internal caste and class antagonism. Given the pattern of slave
revolts and rumors of revolts, all slaves in those colonies where they
formed an overwhelming majority could eventually throw off the
bonds of slavery. But the collapse of the system did not depend on
successful revolt, as in Haiti. It could also come, as it did in Puerto
Rico during the nineteenth century, from the general realization of
the upper strata that slavery was not the only method of human subordination and labor reorganization. Moreover with the growing
awareness of capital manipulation and the new sophistication in cost
accounting, it was readily seen that a system of slavery required bal-
ancing convenience and cost. Slaveholders throughout the Caribbean
paid an unduly heavy cost for the dubious convenience of having
their workers when and where they wanted them.

The rise of industrial capitalism proved an enemy of any social system that was inefficient as a mode of production and relatively inflexible to rational planning and cost accounting. It was not a simple
case of slavery creating capitalism, which in turn destroyed its crea-
tor. As an integral part of international capitalism, plantation producers had to be responsive to the whims of their suppliers of capital,
laborers, and markets. Rising cost of supplies and falling prices for
commodities created severe problems for producers. While the price
structure fluctuated, world overproduction tended to drive prices for
sugar, coffee, cacao, and rum below production costs in the British

West Indies. According to Lowell Ragatz, between 1822 and 1833 English Caribbean muscovado prices on the London market averaged only about 30 shillings per hundredweight, while production costs were estimated at more than 24 shillings. Additional transportation costs and import duties meant that the Caribbean producers were selling their product below cost. Sugar was the main commercial commodity, but the downward price spiral of sugar found a parallel in the other tropical crops as well. Coffee prices fluctuated from about 117 to 145 shillings per hundredweight in 1822, to 42 to 83 shillings per hundredweight in 1830, and 75 to 94 shillings per hundredweight in 1833. Rum prices in 1830 were estimated to be 2 shillings and 6 pence per gallon below the production cost.

Caribbean producers faced certain fixed costs, and the wild gyrations of prices returned an unsteady income that left them incapable of making the capital expenditures necessary to maintain equipment, ameliorate the condition of the slaves, or repair damages done by fire, hurricanes, and other disasters. From Anguilla to Jamaica the export economy found itself in straitened circumstances, and increasing numbers of estates succumbed to foreclosure for debt. Moreover it was a situation that fed on itself. The plantation producers often worked on credit, and with the restrictions of credit in uncertain times they found themselves in particular difficulties. But capital investment to increase efficiency, particularly in the quality of sugar produced, did not necessarily bring encouragement and rewards from London. The vacuum pan process that produced a more refined sugar than muscovado threatened the metropolitan producers and jeopardized the rationality of mercantilistic restrictions. The Cubans used the vacuum pan process, but the benefits did not accrue to British Caribbean producers until after 1845, when parliament removed the surtax on "improved" sugar produced in the colonies.

The economic zigzags of the nineteenth century could not obscure the fact that the plantation economy of the non-Hispanic Caribbean was sliding agonizingly down the road to obsolescence and impoverishment. The tragedy was not that production had declined on the main sugar estates—for, with the notable exception of Jamaica, sugar production stabilized or increased slightly after 1838—but the Caribbean area had to produce far more sugar at far lower prices to survive economically in an expanding market and an expanding world production not only of cane sugar but also of beet sugar. This meant that the English and French Antillean producers were, like all exporters, at a marked disadvantage in the supply field since they did not have a monopoly. Moreover after emancipation the political power of the fabled West Indian Interest collapsed, removing the previous imperial protection offered the English Caribbean producers on the sugar market.

By the 1830's the trauma of Haiti had manifested itself everywhere throughout the plantation Caribbean. In Cuba as well as British Guiana, planters predicted that a general emancipation of the slaves would result in the utter destruction of their so-called white civilization, the slaughter of the white inhabitants, and the further catastrophic reduction of the colonies to "rack and ruin." Emancipation came in the British and French Antilles in the 1830's and 1840's, and nothing of the sort happened.

Apologists for the planter class in the British Antilles kept blaming the economic uncertainty on the lack of industry among the Afro-Caribbean population even after the abolition of slavery in 1834 and the termination of the disastrous Apprenticeship System in 1838. Absentee planters in England like Alexander Barclay, a Jamaican proprietor, and unselfconscious racists like Thomas Babington Macaulay and Alexander Postlethwaite—as well as later historians who have repeated their misinformed biases about Caribbean society—simply did not understand the situation. They all believed that the exslaves were exhibiting some congenital defect and would not work, as though they wished to substantiate their previous claims that the whip provided the most efficacious incentive to African labor. Modern research has proved these assertions false. In only a few cases did the exslaves desert the plantations permanently. Planters and their supporters saw the export economy as the only viable economy, and so advocated the coercion and regimentation of the free black population under conditions not far removed from slavery. In some colonies, especially Trinidad and Guiana, East Indians were introduced to bolster the servile plantation labor force and to provide a major stimulus to the expansion of the plantation system after the middle decades of the nineteenth century.

The theory that the black people of the Caribbean were either lazy or inept—or that the societies had collapsed, or the local economies were ruined as a result of emancipation—was both malicious and unjust. It manifests a myopic, European ethnocentric view of the Caribbean that negates the dual economic structure and the multiracial, multicultural nature of Caribbean societies.

For the vast majority of Antillean populations their everyday world was far from synonymous with the fortunes of sugar prices on the export market. Declines in the price of sugar affected them adversely but did not mean the end of their economic existence. The internal economy based on the small diversified farming and local marketing system of the exslaves and lower classes survived vigorously until the series of natural disasters in the 1850's and the machinations of the colonial system dealt them a severe blow. Reversal, however, did not indicate annihilation, and the peasant economy regained its strength toward the end of the century.

The temporary demise of the sugar export economy indeed signaled a new day for the African and Afro-Caribbean peoples. At the time that the Europeans complained of "rack and ruin," the Caribbean colonies witnessed the most dynamic growth of a free peasantry. The dramatic decline in land prices beginning in the 1820's afforded the purchase of numerous estates at bargain prices. Both the affluent free colored and the frugal exslave population took advantage of this circumstance. Where they could, the exslaves formed cooperatives, often under the guidance of religious leaders, and bought estates. Where they could not find the cash, they simply occupied available vacant lands and continued the cultivation of some of the many food crops that the planters and the colonial governments had imported during the eighteenth century to supplement the diet of the slaves.

In the British Caribbean the establishment of these free villages, as they were called, was a conscious act, assisted by the stipendiary mag-

istrates sent out from England to oversee the reconstitution of the
new societies and to provide legal assistance to the exslaves against
the powerful opposition of the planter-dominated local assemblies.
The success of the free village structure, however, depended on the
peculiarities of geography and the fortuitous nature of local politics.

In larger territories like Jamaica, Trinidad, and Guiana, where ample uncultivated and unpossessed land prevailed, the industrious example of the Maroon communities had acted as a powerful magnet
for the servile thousands working on the sugar plantations. After
emancipation a large proportion of the exslaves settled in free villages and began to form a free, agricultural peasantry, relating with,
but largely independent of, the sugar estates. In Jamaica black freeholders increased from 2014 in 1838, to approximately 7800 in 1840,
to more than 20,000 in 1845, and about 50,000 in 1859. In Barbados
freeholders of less than five acres each increased from 1110 in 1844 to
3537 in 1859. In St. Vincent some 8209 persons built their own
houses between 1838 and 1857, and bought and cultivated 12,000
acres of land between 1845 and 1857. In small Antigua 67 free villages of 5187 houses and 15,644 inhabitants were established between
1833 and 1858. The situation was similar in Guiana, where land acquisition by exslaves was one of the most remarkable examples of
West Indian industry. In 1838 the 15,000 exslaves were virtually
landless. By 1842 more than 1000 black families had already purchased over 7000 acres of coastal estate land, valued at more than
$100,000. By 1848 the Afro-Guianese population had bought more
than 400 estates and built more than 10,000 houses for themselves.

The capital investment to buy estates and build houses represented
the ready availability of substantial amounts of cash among the nonwhite population. This cash was certainly not under the control of
the planting classes and was not directly derived from exporting sugar
and sugar products to Great Britain. But the enormous expenditure
on land immediately after emancipation also indicated that Caribbean slaves also had considerable amounts of cash, despite the fact
that the large sums paid by the European mother countries as "compensation" money after independence went not to the slaves but to
their masters.

Small farmers diversified the agricultural exports of the islands. New products such as coconuts, arrowroot, and beeswax and honey became important cash products of the new peasant farmers. At the same time they boosted the production of sugar cane, tobacco, coffee, cacao, limes, and ground provisions.

The new communities and the new crops did not break the strong reliance on the production of sugar for the economic mainstay of the Caribbean region. Part of this attraction was the large profits still to be made from sugar where soils were fresh and fertile as in Cuba, Puerto Rico, Trinidad, and Guiana. The new producers had the advantage of adopting better technology, such as the system of *colonos* and *centrales* in Cuba, where independent cane farmers supplied their crop to huge complex mills which had greater grinding and sugar-producing facilities than they could satisfy. In Cuba, too, the use of railroads accelerated the transportation of canes and shattered the mythical restricting radius of the plantation.

To find adequate labor, the region began to import Asians to work on the plantations, rather than attempting to attract the free local lower-classes with higher wages. Between 1847 and 1871 the Cubans imported more than 100,000 Chinese laborers to augment their slave forces on the sugar estates. Between 1838 and 1917 nearly half a million Indians came to the Caribbean to work on sugar estates. British Guiana imported 238,000; Trinidad 145,000; Jamaica 21,500; Guadeloupe 39,000; Grenada 2570; Surinam 34,000; St. Lucia 1550; St. Vincent 1820; and Martinique more than 6748. Martinique imported 500 Chinese in 1859, while British Guiana imported 14,002 between 1853 and 1879, and Guadeloupe brought in 500 between 1854 and 1887. But the Caribbean was not discriminating in its search for laborers, bringing them from Ireland, Germany, Portugal, Spain, the Madeiras, West Africa, and Japan as well as India and China. The importation of these contract laborers required huge sums of money to pay a daily wage of one shilling and sixpence (in the English colonies) and to provide all those services of housing and medical attention to which the former slaves had been accustomed. Only the most promising colonies could afford large-scale importation. British Guiana invested £360,655 on the importation of about 50,000 laborers from Africa, India, Madeira, and the West Indian islands between 1841 and 1847. The high mortality rate and repatriation costs were discouraging at first. Eventually the immigration scheme succeeded. Land was sold to the Indians, reindenture was made more attractive, and after 1898 the return passage was abolished—unless paid for entirely by the travelers.

Asian indentured labor provided the backbone of the sugar industry in Cuba, Trinidad, and Guiana, and permitted the expansion of production during the nineteenth century. But the crucial differences among the colonies remained the scale of production. In 1792 the average yield per factory had been about 30 tons. In 1894 the yield had increased some 50 times to about 2635 tons per factory, with the largest producers, *Central Constancia*, making a harvest of 19,500 tons—about the yield of the entire island of Jamaica. Cuba produced more than all the other Caribbean colonies combined, with a greater yield of sugar per acre of cane, and a larger average acreage of sugar cane per mill.

Nevertheless the other areas insisted on concentrating on sugar production, and so placed all sorts of penalties on landowning by peasant farmers, or on the cultivation of nonsugar crops. At a time when the British colonies were lavishing money on the importation of Asians, their laborers emigrated to the sugar plantations in Cuba, the canal construction in Panama, the banana plantations in Costa Rica, and to all forms of manual labor in the United States. In 1865, on the eve of the Morant Bay riots in Jamaica, some poor people from the parish of St. Ann, plagued by disease and starvation, petitioned Queen Victoria of England for unused Jamaican land to cultivate peasant crops. The queen refused, encouraging them instead to work "steadily and continuously, at the times when their labor is wanted, and for as long as it is wanted . . . and thereby render the plantations productive." It was precisely such official insensitivity that discouraged the productivity of the peasants and hardened the class antagonisms which exploded at Morant Bay.

Nor did the white population fully accept the reality of the new postslavery Caribbean. As long as sugar remained "king," all social goals were subordinated to boosting production. Little positive incentive was given to develop the arts, inculcate a sense of national identity, or encourage alternate patterns of agriculture. In 1896 the colony of Trinidad spent more money encouraging Indian immigration, more money on medical attention to the plantation laborers, and far more money on prisons and police services than on education. Society in the Caribbean subordinated people to profits. Until the middle of the twentieth century the masses remained excluded from meaningful participation in their societies everywhere except in Haiti. The abolition of slavery and the political changes of the nineteenth century had not reversed the outward-looking, centrifugal forces of Caribbean societies. These remained divided and divisive. But one change was clear: the caste structure had collapsed baring the conflicts of race and class.

Chapter 7 • Caribbean Nation Building, 1804-1970

Cuba could easily provide for a population three times as great as it now has, so there is no excuse for the abject poverty of a single one of its present inhabitants. The markets should be overflowing with produce, pantries should be full, all hands should be working. This is not an inconceivable thought. What is inconceivable is that anyone should go to bed hungry, that children should die for lack of medical attention; what is inconceivable is that thirty percent of our farm people cannot write their names and that ninety-nine percent of them know nothing of Cuba's history. What is inconceivable is that the majority of our rural people are now living in worse circumstances than were the Indians Columbus discovered in the fairest land that human eyes had ever seen.

Fidel Castro, *History Will Absolve Me*, October 16, 1953

The long history of Caribbean nation building spans two difficult centuries. It began spontaneously with the unheralded independence of Haiti in 1804. It continues with the promised political independence of the former British colony of British Honduras and the former Dutch colony of Surinam in the mid-1970's. Throughout the Carib-

bean nation-building has succeeded, not preceded, the creation of the
political state. Only Cuba presents a possible exception, manifesting
a patently discernible nationalism well in advance of its own political
independence. But the sequence of "state first, nation later" has
been perhaps the single most striking characteristic of the twentieth-
century manifestations of constitutional decolonization. It could
hardly have been otherwise in a region where the local inhabitants
almost always lacked the necessary resources to make effective their
legitimate demands.

Yet from Haiti to Surinam there lies an unbroken connection in
the chain of national freedom and independence unleashed in the turbulence of the eighteenth-century world. The historian R. R. Palmer
once described the period between 1770 and 1850 as the "Age of the
Democratic Revolutions," and many historians have accepted this
classic premise. David Brion Davis calls his magisterial study of slavery between 1770 and 1823, "The Problem of Slavery in the Age of
Revolution." The categorization has some validity. For if we look
throughout the Americas and parts of western Europe at that time—
throughout a large area of what has more recently been called "The
Atlantic World"—we find that newly emergent groups relentlessly attacked the accepted structures of political power, and in some places
they achieved remarkable success. In France in 1789 a revolution pop-
ularized the rights of bourgeois man, decapitated the king, and shattered forever the conventional mystique of a semidivine monarchy in
the crumbling dust of the Bastille. In Great Britain in 1832 an in-
timidated Parliament quickly unleashed reform to forestall violent
revolution, eliminated the notoriously unrepresentative "rotten"
boroughs, and in two steps extended the electoral franchise. The
French Revolution and the general restlessness throughout Europe
had its American counterpart. In Europe a wide consortium of groups
reestablished their alliances within national states. In the Americas
states were carved from the former imperial domains, as the ebb tide
of imperialism and colonialism retreated inexorably from Yorktown
on the Chesapeake to Ayacucho in the Andes. All these changes
seemed awfully portentous at the time. It was a disturbed as well as a

disturbing age which Bryan Edwards, the wealthy Jamaican planter and member of the British parliament, described as "an awful period in the history of the world, [and] a spirit of subversion."

The famous revolutions of the eighteenth and nineteenth century created new political forms and undoubtedly brought about unprecedented political changes. Yet the degree to which these significant changes reflected an equally profound change in the social basis of political power remains highly questionable. Very few of the new leaders had ideas incompatible with the old status quo. The masses that made possible the military victories over the English metropolitan forces at Yorktown, or the Spanish imperial army at Ayacucho, derived little tangible political, social, or economic reward for their gallant effort and considerable sacrifice. The long wars of independence that gave birth to the United States of America and the numerous Spanish-American mainland republics from Mexico to Argentina were successful mutinies, complicated with the overtones of civil war.

The history of social revolution in the western hemisphere starts not with Lexington and Bunker Hill in 1775 but less auspiciously in the French tropical colony of Saint-Domingue, which became the independent state of Haiti in 1804. The North American and Latin American wars of independence were political events, almost devoid of significant restructuring of its social classes. Although intrinsically connected with the events in metropolitan France as well as in the United States, the Haitian Revolution sought not merely the political independence of a state but the personal freedom of more than 80 percent of its inhabitants who were slaves. To accomplish this goal, the revolution was necessarily both radical and destructive. The Haitians were forced to destroy the entire socioeconomic structure that was the raison d'être for their colonial existence, and in destroying the institution of slavery they unwittingly voted to terminate their connection with the whole international superstructure which perpetuated slavery and the plantation economy. The implications for the entire Caribbean region were astonishing, and the early nineteenth-century world recognized with abundant foreboding the independence of Haiti as the most radical political achievement of its time.

Haiti, the second independent state of the hemisphere, was politically quarantined, maligned by many, assisted by few. Only after sixty years did the United States of America offer formal diplomatic recognition. Haiti remained poor in material terms, but its people remained strong and free and fiercely independent.

The Haitian Revolution began with a simple event far from the shores of Haiti: the belated calling of the French Estates General by the bankrupt Louis XVI in May 1789. Designed to resolve the economic dispute between the French king and his Assembly of Notables, the affair quickly spread to engulf all Frenchmen. Frenchmen from the colonies hoped that by fishing in the disturbed waters of French domestic politics they could resolve some of their colonial disabilities in a way which would give them more than they stood to lose. For in 1789 those who first declared themselves to be Frenchmen—albeit residents in the colonies, and some even creoles—were the *grands blancs* who had a lot to lose. With boundless enthusiasm and, in retrospect, boundless folly, a small faction of the *grands blancs* composed itself into a Colonial Committee, drafted a *cahiers des doléances* in which the chief demands were for greater home rule and more economic independence, and despatched thirty-one delegates to France. Joined by six absentee planters, the group gained admission, after some initial difficulty, as provisional members of the Third Estate. For pretended noblemen that should have been an uncompromising insult. Nevertheless the delegates took their places, and, when the Estates General reconstituted itself as the National Assembly, they found themselves voting citizens of France. It was a surprising elevation for the colonists, but it represented the pinnacle of their political success. As rapidly as they climbed, so quickly and hard did they fall.

To pretend to speak for Saint-Domingue was a most difficult undertaking, even for a ventriloquist, in 1789. At that time the colony represented the epitome of the successful exploitation slave society in tropical America. The white population of *grands blancs* and *petits blancs* numbered less than 25,000. The free, miscegenated *gens de couleur* numbered about the same. The laboring force, the basis of the wealth and importance of the colony, was a rapidly growing population of African and creole slaves estimated at 452,000 in 1789. The centripetal force of the three geographically disparate regions that comprised the colony—named Northern, Western, and Southern Departments by the colonial authorities—remained the plantations of sugar, cotton, indigo, and coffee, along with the subsidiary activities associated with any such plantation export economy. By the early 1790's the colony supplied about 66 percent of all French tropical produce and accounted for approximately 33 percent of the entire foreign trade of France. The staple-producing *grands blancs*, however, had many economic grievances. Specie was scarce; the barter arrangements for sale placed them at a disadvantage in times of rising prices; and the mercantilist principles of the colonial *exclusif* increased the prices of their slaves while depressing the value of their products.

The price of slaves was a major issue. The wanton waste of servile human lives created an enormous and consistent demand for slaves. Between 1789 and 1791 the colonial slave population on Saint-Domingue increased from 452,000 to 480,000. In 1788 alone the colony imported approximately 29,506 Africans, estimated by Philip D. Curtin in his *Atlantic Slave Trade* to be anywhere from 33 to 50 percent of the total number shipped in the entire trans-Atlantic trade that year. The planters of Saint-Domingue paid more because their demand far exceeded the metropolitan capacity to supply, while their excessive production glutted the metropolitan market. Slave owners denying basic laws of humanity also sought to defy the principles of economics. Every plantation society, however, matured in consonance with the economic fortunes of its export commodities and the role of the local economy in the capitalist structure of the metropolis. In Saint-Domingue the rapid expansion of the slave population, succeeding a decade of consolidation, exacerbated the mutual suspicion and the mutual but usually muted hostility between the castelike divisions of the social structure, thereby aggravating the perennial problems of slave control.

The rapid increase in wealth also aggravated the class problems be-

tween *grands blancs* and *petits blancs*, as well as the race problems between the white sector that feared and distrusted the *gens de couleur*,
especially the wealthy, educated, and culturally polished members of
the nonwhite community. For their part, the free persons of color in
the colony resented their social and political disabilities, especially
as the metropolitan government had begun to circumscribe those
even further during the decade of the 1770's. Nonwhites demanded
that, based on cultural and economic considerations, they be accepted
equally with the white groups, perhaps even be admitted to privileges
denied the nonpropertied *petits blancs*. In 1789 the *gens de couleur*
had won the sympathy of the powerful, radical, recently organized
Société des Amis des Noirs, among whose members were the Comte
Honoré-Gabriel de Mirabeau, Jérome Pétion, Jacques Necker, the
Abbé Sieyès, and the Marquis de Lafayette. Neither the whites nor
the free persons of color as a group recognized the basic human and
civil rights of their slaves. The abolition of the slave trade and the immediate termination of slavery were powerful political weapons of the
Amis des Noirs and its pressure group, the *Colons Américains*, directed by Vincent Ogé and Julien Raimond. But by challenging the
credentials of the thirty-seven delegates from Saint-Domingue, and by
arguing persuasively that such delegates represented merely one faction of the colony, the *Amis* revealed clearly not only the divisions
within colonial society but also the differences between mother country and overseas colony.

The problem for the colonists was that the ideas and language of
the metropolis did not fit the complicated and often ambiguous social structure overseas. The ideals of the French Revolution, vaunted
in the grandiloquent slogans "Liberty, Equality and Fraternity" or
the "Rights of Man," proved enigmatic in the colonies. Nevertheless
each group in Saint-Domingue used the general language of the Revolution and invested it with the particular connotation to suit its own
purpose. A marvelous irony was thus created, allowing each free
group in Saint-Domingue to appeal legitimately to the sense of justice in the National Assembly.

Each sector of the free colonial population accepted the vague gen-

eral slogans of the Revolution to win support in France, but it emphasized only such portions as applied to its own selfish cause. *Grands
blancs* saw liberty as greater colonial autonomy, especially in economic matters, and an end to the commercial restraints of metro-
politan-imposed mercantilism. *Petits blancs* wanted equality—that is,
active citizenship for all white persons, not just landed proprietors or
large slaveowners—and less bureaucratic control of the colonies. *Gens
de couleur* insisted on equality and fraternity with the whites, since
they fulfilled all the qualifications for active citizenship. On the other
hand, both white groups, especially sensitive to the colonial situation,
feared that the political and social acceptance of any nonwhite group
would undermine the system of slavery and the dominance of the
whites. Like any other slave society in any period of history, Saint-
Domingue was an explosive tinderbox. The failure of the whites to
overcome their class antagonism and form a permanent alliance
among themselves, or to subdue their caste hostility and close ranks
with the free persons of color, ultimately proved the disastrous spark
that ignited the revolution.

Armed revolt in the colony began with a united white preemptive
strike against the colonial bureaucrats in Port-au-Prince in April 1790,
and the seizure of the three departmental assemblies as well as the
general colonial assembly which met in the *petits blancs* stronghold
of Saint Marc in the Artibonite valley in the summer of 1790. But the
white union broke down as Colonel Antoine Mauduit, commander of
the French regiment of the regular army in Port-au-Prince, supported
the bureaucrats and forged an alliance with the *gens de couleur*. At the
same time the *grands blancs* failed to gain control of the Saint
Marc Colonial Assembly—the constitution-making body for the entire island—and withdrew to their stronghold in the North Province,
with its local assembly at Le Cap Français. Both white groups armed
their slaves and prepared for war in the name of the Revolution. The
first fighting took place in midsummer of 1790 between the *petits
blancs* militia and the regular troops stationed at Port-au-Prince.
Open warfare was averted, however, when the bureaucrats established
an alliance with the *grands blancs* of the North Province. The colo-

nial assembly of Saint Marc committed political suicide by passing the May Decree enfranchising all propertied mulattoes, thereby alienating the vast majority of whites. The whites of Saint-Domingue temporarily forgot their class differences and forged another uneasy alliance to forestall revolutionary threats of racial equality. The civil war threatened to become a war between the races.

Once the superordinate white group had resorted to violence there was no way the revolt could be contained. Once the moral authority, cohesion, and vigilance of the whites broke down—and that is what happened between 1789 and 1791—the free coloreds and the slaves grasped their opportunity. The absentee free colored people sat out the first two years of the struggle, patiently persuading the National Assembly to pass the May Decree of 1791, sponsored by the *Societé des Amis des Noirs*, equalizing all the free people of the colonies. But the free coloreds had no intention of surrendering their social aspirations for racial solidarity. Vincent Ogé, impatient with the deliberations in France, sailed to the United States, bought some arms, and sailed for Saint-Domingue, where he hoped to rally the colonial free nonwhites. Ogé landed secretly on the north coast but was quickly caught and executed, after being broken upon the wheel. The white repression of the free nonwhites was monstrous in all three departments, and even the French military commander, Mauduit, was assassinated for his unconfirmed mulatto sympathies. The execution of Ogé polarized Saint-Domingue along caste lines. Violence begat violence.

In August 1791 the slaves of the plantation-rich North Province revolted en masse. Within a year Saint-Domingue was experiencing a widespread slave revolt unprecedented in the annals of the history of slavery. After fighting intermittently for nearly two years for *grands blancs, petits blancs,* and *gens de couleur,* the slaves began to fight for themselves and their freedom—but they were careful to do so in the name of the Revolution!

Between 1792 and 1802 chaos reigned in Saint-Domingue. Death and destruction were widespread. At one time as many as seven warring parties were fighting simultaneously: slaves, free persons of color, *petits blancs, grands blancs,* invading Spanish troops from Santo Domingo, a naval assault force of English soldiers, and the French military vainly trying to reestablish peace and control. It was a confused situation. Alliances were as fleeting as they were numerous. The *gens de couleur* alternately fought with and against the whites. The French military fought with as well as against the slaves. As the killing and destruction increased, power slowly gravitated to the majority of slaves, after 1794 increasingly under the astonishing leadership of an exdomestic slave, François Dominique Toussaint L'Ouverture, who had served on Breda plantation in the North Province. Toussaint imposed a semblance of order on the general anarchy.

Ironically the victory of the slaves was a victory for colonialism—and the Revolution in France. By 1794 the leftward drift of the Revolution was unmistakeable. The assembly abolished slavery in 1793 and sent out a revolutionary army and some Jacobin administrators, not to protect the royalist slave owners, but to establish "Liberty, Equality and Fraternity." Léger Félicité Sonthonax, the most implacably zealous of the Jacobin "commissioners," viewed his task to be the total eradication of all vestiges of royalism, even if that meant the ultimate supremacy of the blacks over the whites. With malicious fanaticism he equated all whites with royalism and the counterrevolution and unleashed the black troops on them. With his support the blacks finally broke the back of white resistance at Le Cap Français, capital of the North Province, in 1793. But the role of Sonthonax and the Jacobin army does not detract from the brilliant military leadership and political astuteness of Toussaint. He, more than any other individual, forged the disparate group of fighting slaves into a trained, armed, cohesive military machine. With a number of loyal, able associates such as Jean Jacques Dessalines, Charles Bélair, Henri Christophe, and "General" Moyse, Toussaint rolled up a series of victories in the Plaine du Nord and throughout the Artibonite valley. Within four years he had successfully defeated the French, expelled Sonthonax as well as the British invasion forces, routed the mulatto opposition of the south led by André Rigaud and Alexander Pétion, driven out the Spanish and conquered Santo Domingo, and overcome a widespread revolt against his rule led by Moyse. As a reward he gave the colony a new constitution and made himself governor-general for life.

Between 1800 and 1802 Toussaint tried to rebuild the largely destroyed economy of Saint-Domingue. Hundreds of estates had been sacked and burned in the nearly ten years of civil war. Tens of thousands of individuals lost their lives. The magnificent irrigation system of the Artibonite and the Cul-de-Sac collapsed from lack of maintenance and as a result of the torrential rains of the fall of 1800. Famine and lawlessness stalked the land. But Toussaint established commercial relations with Great Britain and the United States, slowly began to feed his people, restored the operations of the estates, and terminated the wanton massacre of white and colored persons. Although he pledged his loyalty to France, Toussaint acted with the independence of the dictator he had declared himself to be.

All would perhaps have gone well had it remained at that. But a semiindependent Saint-Domingue with a free black population ran counter to the grandiose dreams of Napoleon Bonaparte to reestablish a viable French-American empire. Toussaint had to go; individual freedom had to be rescinded. Napoleon wanted to subordinate Saint-Domingue and restore slavery. His sentiments toward Africans and his loyal governor-general were rather uncomplimentary. He referred to them as "utterly uncivilized men who did not even know what a colony was, what France was" and as "gilded Africans." He dispatched the largest French military force assembled before his peninsular campaigns under the direction of his brother-in-law, General Charles Victor Emmanuel Leclerc, to reconquer the territory. Saint-Domingue was to be brought back to the imperial fold and the status quo restored, as had been done in the smaller islands of Martinique and Guadeloupe. That proved an impossible task. The order to restore slavery cost Napoleon the colony, his American dream, and the life not only of his brother-in-law but also of some 40,000 of the finest French troops, victims both of war and the ravages of yellow fever. The catastrophic military loss severely debilitated the French military capacity in the succeeding years in Iberia and elsewhere in Europe.

The fall of Napoleon began with the reluctant retreat of Leclerc in Saint-Domingue in 1803.

The perfidious exile of Toussaint generated a widespread desperate resistance against which no French army could have prevailed. Christophe and Dessalines directed a resistance movement that was monumental in its savagery and destruction, as neither French nor Haitians gave any quarters. The thoroughness of the struggle between 1802 and 1804—either for reconquest or self-defense—virtually precluded any easy reconstruction period for the newly emergent state and left an insuperable legacy of poverty, ruin, and social division. The fires that forged the birth of the state and the advent of Haitian nationalism unleashed such essentially disintegrative socioeconomic forces that no leader after 1804 found the situation manageable. Individual freedom and national prosperity became incompatible for the masses and provided a severe restriction for the diplomatic option of any successful commander against the French.

No study has yet appeared that examines this important aspect of the Haitian Revolution. But the assumption may be made that, if a substantial proportion of the masses who formed the armies of the blacks and mulattoes in Haiti sensed this incompatibility between freedom and prosperity, then the local leadership of Toussaint, Dessalines, and Christophe was only popular to the degree that they identified with the trend of the majority or generalized an appeal that projected their sympathies as unequivocally antislavery, anti-French, antiwhite, and antiplantation. Dessalines's attacks upon the whites and mulattoes after 1802—in sharp contradistinction to those of Sonthonax earlier—could possibly have been this response, rather than any callous genocidal measure born of racial hatred. Only a violence superior to that of the slave masters could have secured the goals of the popular (that is, the black) revolution in the colony, and such violence required little leadership. Once the masses began to act more from an interest in their own freedom than from any concern for their collective welfare and the prosperity of the emergent state—and this partially accounts for the widespread, spontaneous resistance to the French after 1802—then it seems that neither Toussaint nor anyone else could have significantly affected the future course of Haitian independence.

The declaration of Haitian independence in 1804, then, was a victory for the popular forces, tantamount to a victory of the ideas of Emiliano Zapata and Zapatismo in the Mexican Revolution a century later. The former slaves took over the government and sought to establish their independence in a hostile world. But civil war between blacks in the north under Christophe (until his suicide in 1820) and mulattoes in the south under Pétion divided the society, while the proliferation of small peasant landholdings undermined the economy. After about 1810 plantation products declined precipitously. Sugar exports fell from 141,089,831 pounds in 1789 to 18,535,112 pounds in 1801; to 600,000 pounds in 1821; and 16,199 pounds in 1836. Coffee exports fell gradually from 76,835,219 pounds in 1789; to 32,189,784 pounds in 1826; and then climbed to 37,662,672 pounds in 1836. Cacao exports became erratic, but declined slightly from 758,628 pounds in 1789 to 550,484 in 1836. Cotton exports fell from more than 7 million pounds in 1789, to a little more than 600,000 pounds in 1826; but increased to more than 1 million pounds 10 years later. Indigo ceased to be an export commodity.

A peasant pattern emerges clearly in the considerably expanded and diversified nature of Haitian agricultural production. Crops that could be grown successfully on small plots, and articles that could be produced by individual efforts increased. This was the case with saltpetre, logwood, mahagony, tobacco, hides, gum, ginger, beeswax, honey, coconuts, bananas, castor oil, and cane mats. Peasant production of ground provisions for domestic consumption also increased, as did the semibarter arrangements of the internal marketing system.

Peasant production, however, did not prove attractive to international entrepreneurs. John MacGregor described Haiti through his commercially biased British lenses in 1846 in a fashion typical of the visitors of the nineteenth century:

> From the day on which Christophe expired, down to the present day, a period of twenty-six years, neither industry, nor improvement, nor energetic administration, nor the extension of the

education of the people, nor any progress in the march of civilization, appears in the agricultural, manufacturing, commercial, moral, social, or political condition of the republic of Haiti. The climate, the soil and the pastures, yield almost without culture, sufficient merely to feed a people, too indolent to work for comfort and luxuries.

Without a political and economic infrastructure the peasant production of Haiti could not be harnessed for the general good. Nearly two centuries of independence have not altered the slide to isolation, poverty, and abandonment of that tropical state.

Through the entire nineteenth century, Haiti struggled to assert its independence and define its Afro-Antillean identity. Elsewhere in the Caribbean the various patterns of colonialism continued to flounder amid mixed economic fortunes and changing social circumstances. The anachronistic political structures continued to be unworkable or unrepresentative or both. Created in the floodtide of empire in the sixteenth and seventeenth centuries, they had long ceased to serve their original purpose. As the imperial tide ebbed, it exposed them cruelly at their worst.

The British territories had behaved for a long time as though they were still the original settlements of Englishmen overseas. Charles II had asserted that Englishmen and offspring overseas should "from their respective births be reputed to be free denizens of England; and shall have the same privileges, to all intents and purposes, as our free born subjects of England." Of course in the seventeenth century there still remained the vivid shadow of English settlements overseas. The political structure, therefore, reflected the English model, with the separation of powers among the governor appointed by the king in England, an upper house appointed by the governor, and a lower house elected by freeholders. In England the division had some rationale, and managed to work because it adjusted itself from time to time. In the Caribbean, on the other hand, the situation represented the classical farce of mimic men.

John Parry and Philip Sherlock exposed the essential and inherent dysfunction of an English model in a predominantly African plantation situation when they wrote:

There is this essential difference, however, between the constitution of Britain and of the West Indian colonies—that the English system represented a state in national development, a process in which full power finally passed into the hands of the House of Commons. The West Indian system remained fixed and rigid for nearly two centuries. In England those with or without the franchise were free citizens, and public opinion could be used to compel constitutional change. In the West Indies the free citizens were a small section of the community and it was vital to them to preserve the situation which existed. They were cut off from an appeal to more than a limited section of the public in a society with a rigid social and economic structure.

Nor was that all. Until the twentieth century the white sector in the non-Hispanic Caribbean—not just in the English Antilles—continued to behave like transients. Their homes were in the islands, but their hearts were in a hallowed, idealized, imaginary Europe. As the situation in the French Antilles at the time of the Revolution revealed, these whites wanted to be at one and the same time Europeans and Antilleans. That could not be. Their failure to come to grips with history and reality precluded their ever developing that sense of nationalism and *patriachiquismo* which seemed so much a part of the Spanish-American empire.

Precisely for this reason it seems pointless to condemn the West Indian proprietor class for its chronic absenteeism during the nineteenth century. A large number of these proprietors had never been in the West Indies (having largely inherited their estates), and their presence would have made scant difference to the development of Caribbean nationalism. It would have made little difference, that is, unless they underwent a miraculous sea-change and ceased to be Englishmen. That was possible of course. Some American settler societies did cease to be English, in a long and subtle process.

But plantation societies in particular, and exploitation societies in general, were highly resistant to such change. To lose one's Englishness in a predominantly European society was forgiveable. To lose one's Englishness in a predominantly West Indian society was a fate equal to death. It was less a question of losing their cultural ideals, however, than of accepting the fact that they had lost such ideals.

Slight variations in administrative forms marked colonies even within the same imperial system. For example the older English colonies—Barbados, Jamaica, and the Leeward Islands—had local representative legislatures that reflected the interests of planters, merchants, and their attorneys. After 1763 the so-called "ceded islands" (lost by France during the Seven Years' War, 1756-1763) of Grenada, Dominica, and St. Vincent also established elected assemblies patterned after the older territories, although the conflicts and difficulties of the colonial experience forced the Board of Trade to attempt unsuccessfully to curtail their independence. The "newer colonies," which became British at the end of the eighteenth and beginning of the nineteenth century—St. Lucia, Berbice, Demerara, and Trinidad—retained most of their former laws and institutions under the virtual autocratic control of a governor appointed by the Crown. From the British metropolitan point of view, Crown Colony government was the most satisfactory, yet the bitter lesson of taxation without representation driven home on the North American continent between 1776 and 1783 made perpetuation of the administrative quiltwork preferable to revoking the tradition of assemblies. The major difference between the Crown Colonies and the Legislative Colonies, was that in the former the governors both ruled and governed, while in the latter the governors governed but did not rule.

Britain exhibited great indecision in its Caribbean colonial policy during the nineteenth and early twentieth centuries. Local legislative government collapsed in Jamaica, the Leewards, and the Windwards, except for Barbados, in the stormy period following the Morant Bay disturbances of 1865. Crown Colony government became the order of the day. This proved no more satisfactory than the old planter-controlled assemblies, and after the labor riots of the 1930's representative government with greater local responsibility was restored to the region. But there was a crucial difference. Under the old representative system, only a small proportion of the population could either vote or serve in the assemblies. Of the nearly half-million population in Jamaica in 1864, only 1903 had the vote. Barbados had an electorate of only 1016 on an island population of a little more than

100,000 in 1833. While the franchise was restricted to property-owning males, these figures represent truly small proportions of the adult male populations. Besides, not many nonwhites were included in the voter lists—only 75 nonwhites on the Barbados voter lists of 1832. The steady enfranchisement of the wealthy nonwhites under Crown Colony government did not bring about great changes in the number of voters. Before the Second World War only a small number of British West Indians had the vote—only 5000 in a 1937 Barbados population of about 200,000; and only 25,000 in a 1934 Trinidad population of 400,000.

The French political system operated as Crown Colonies with advisory bodies called *conseils soverains*. Between 1787 and 1815 the Saint-Domingue, Martinique, and Guadeloupe assemblies gained representation in the French National Assembly. This was in itself a revolutionary advance that converted the colonies into de jure integral administrative departments of the metropolis. With the Bourbon Restoration the political status returned to the earlier eighteenth-century system. The reduced imperial possessions—Martinique, Guadeloupe, Cayenne (made a penal settlement after 1852), and St. Bartholomew (bought from Sweden in 1877)—lost the power both of autonomous legislation and of direct representation in the metropolitan parliament. The revolution of 1830 created elected councils in Martinique and Guadeloupe from a rather limited electorate. Only 750 electors were in a Martinique population of well over 100,000, and not many more in the slightly larger Guadeloupe population. The revolution of 1848 restored direct representation to the overseas territories and greatly expanded the franchise. Although political representation was suspended between 1854 and 1871, the French Antilles moved forward on the path leading to their constitutional integration as Departments of France in 1946. The only significant feature of the political history was the dominant position of the nonwhite sector in the political structure after the later nineteenth century.

In the Danish Antilles a serious slave revolt in 1848 on St. Croix precipitated the immediate abolition of slavery by the governor-general. Denmark, then busily dismantling its overseas empire, offered the islands for sale to the United States at a price of $7,500,000. A treaty to this effect was agreed upon. The Danish legislature approved the price and the transfer, but the United States Senate rejected it in 1867. After numerous overtures to sell the small islands to Germany, the United States finally paid $25,000,000 for the group of islands, which became the United States Virgin Islands in 1917. The local population of about 25,000 had no influence on their collective sale and derived few benefits from the imperial transfer.

The century between roughly 1850 and 1950 saw a quiet, subtle change overcome those formerly glorious, valuable, and distinguished colonial possessions, suddenly *venido a menos*. From the metropolitan point of view they became charges—albeit charges that provided some economic benefits—and a ready outlet for the bureaucratic and administrative mediocrities crying out for recognition at home. Their political systems, in general, did not provide avenues for the cultivation and creative fertilization of sentiments of national consciousness and collective self-respect. Official imperial attitudes wavered between maudlin paternalism and exasperated contempt. With few exceptions—most notably John Jacob Thomas of Trinidad, author of two outstanding, if undeservedly unknown, books, *The Theory and Practice of Creole Grammar* and *Froudacity: West Indian Fables by James Anthony Froude*—West Indians succumbed to the alien notions of European social Darwinism, dissipating their energies in commercial pursuits and social climbing. To excel according to the criteria of the mother countries' culture became the ultimate achievement. The Caribbean populations became adept at imitation.

Apart from Haiti, the only clear contradiction to this trend occurred in the Spanish Antilles. There the political bankruptcy of the Spanish colonial system and the fiscal insolvency of the domestic government proved powerless in the face of the robust growth of a fierce nationalism—or at least separatism. The nineteenth century saw a great decline in Spanish military status and moral posture from the exalted days of the sixteenth century. By 1821 the Spanish flag had been replaced on the mainland. Spain lost the vast area from Texas and California in the north to Chile and Argentina in the south. It

sold Florida to the United States in 1821, and, with the exception of
the brief period from 1861 to 1863, lost the colony on the western
part of Hispaniola. Only Cuba and Puerto Rico remained loyal,
though restive, their loyalty flaunted by the artificially exaggerated
fear of the dismal aftermath of revolutionary Haiti, while the local
oligarchies expanded their plantations and their profits. Both in Cuba
and Puerto Rico, high profits and economic prosperity assuaged the
disgraceful perpetuation of the slave society.

Puerto Rico succeeded in greatly expanding sugar production without the massive African slave build-up that characterized the Cuban
effort, nor the elaborate curtailment of the mixed agriculture that
centuries of imperial neglect and the exigencies of self-sufficiency had
imposed on the island. Like Cuba, Puerto Rico made an abortive
attempt to declare its independence with the *Grito de Lares* on September 18, 1868. That was quickly suppressed. But a major slave
revolt the same year prodded the reluctant local "slavecrats" to abolish slavery in 1873. Spain granted major domestic autonomy in 1897,
engineered by the Puerto Rican autonomist party under Román Bal-
dorioty de Castro and Luis Muñoz Rivera. This charter of autonomy
conceded to Puerto Rico the right to elect a bicameral legislature,
make all laws except those reserved for the Spanish Cortes, send dep-
uties to the Cortes in Madrid, impose import duties, and establish
commercial relations with foreign states. These were the conditions
the Puerto Ricans had patiently pleaded for and negotiated since
1868.

Unfortunately 1898 was a very bad year to win concessions from
Spain. Although the island of Puerto Rico did not formally declare
war, the metropolis weakly ceded it to the United States at the Treaty
of Paris, which ended the Spanish-American War in December 1898.
The island endured two years of military government before the For-
aker Act instituted a civilian government that restored a colonialism
in Puerto Rico. This highly unpopular act established a quasi-republi-
can form of government in which the governor, the cabinet, and all
judges of the island's supreme court were appointed by the president
of the United States, while Puerto Ricans elected a lower house of

delegates of thirty-five members. Free trade with the mainland was established, but the entire tariff system of the island was merged with that of the more powerful United States.

Muñoz Rivera did not accept the derogation of the status of Puerto Rico lightly. He incorporated his own Federalist Party into an umbrella party called the Unión de Puerto Rico, and in 1910 was elected the resident commissioner for Puerto Rico in the United States Congress. Through skillful diplomacy, Puerto Ricans finally persuaded Congress to pass the Jones Act of 1917, which provided a bill of rights for Puerto Rico, conceded United States citizenship for residents of the island, and instituted popularly elected houses of the legislature. Moreover the governor was given greater freedom in appointing his cabinet.

The political victory of the Puerto Ricans was fundamentally a pyrrhic one. The social and economic price proved costly, damaging, and permanent. Puerto Ricans found themselves relegated to second-class citizens in their own land, and denigrated by the influx of a new people holding a different somatic norm image from themselves and arrogantly contemptuous of their culture and their inheritance. North American ingenuity rapidly destroyed the relatively diversified peasant economy and replaced it with seemingly endless fields of sugar cane, punctuated by efficient central sugar factories, and connected by ribbons of conveniently located railroads. For a few dazzling years Puerto Ricans enjoyed the chimerical euphoria of an economic success that disguised the malignant and painful side effects of their continuing colonialism. Then the bottom fell out of the sugar market, and the international depression of the 1930's hit savagely at every mono-cultural exporter. Between 1930 and 1932 the gross national product of the island plunged, dragging the per capita income from $122 to $86. Like everywhere else in the Caribbean, Puerto Ricans began to reexamine the bases of their society and their economy.

The lean years spawned intensive, often radical political activity. Pedro Albizu Campos and his Nationalist Party sought independence and a restructuring of the economic bases of the society. At political rallies marked by violence and fiery oratory he pointed out that Puerto

Ricans needed complete control of themselves if they were to attack the problems of overpopulation, illiteracy, unemployment, underemployment, and a dismally low adult life expectancy of forty-six years. Albizu Campos was imprisoned for conspiring against the United States and his party waned.

Between 1938 and 1964 Puerto Rico experienced the charismatic and effervescent influence of Luis Muñoz Marín, son of Luis Muñoz Rivera, and the cosmetic effects of "Operation Bootstrap." In 1938 Muñoz Marín founded the Popular Democratic Party, designed not to liberate Puerto Rico but to ameliorate the economic conditions of the island within the political status quo. Four times elected governor—in 1948, 1952, 1956, and 1960—Muñoz Marín converted the economy from agriculture to industry, forcefully attacked problems of health, housing, and education, and boosted the per capita income from a modest $121 in 1940 to $900 in 1965.

The major accomplishment of Muñoz Marín, however, was the modification of the political relationship with the United States, called the *Estado Libre Asociado* (Associated Free State, or Commonwealth Status). This relationship gave Puerto Rico complete autonomy in internal matters, and continues the equal use of the citizenship and federal services of the United States. On paper the relationship looked impressive enough to warrant a United Nations General Assembly resolution in 1953 that "the people of the Commonwealth of Puerto Rico have been invested with attributes of political sovereignty." Although the economic glitter faded rapidly after 1964, a referendum held in 1967 indicated that 60 percent of the voters preferred the commonwealth status, 39 percent wanted statehood, and less than 1 percent wished complete independence. But the glitter contained a severe dross. The attractive gross economic statistics of Puerto Rico, like the data for Saint-Domingue in 1789, Mexico in 1910, or Cuba in 1958, was the mirage that obscured the painful reality.

Neither North American colonialism before 1952, associated statehood since 1952, nor unstinted largesse since 1900 have genuinely revolutionized Puerto Rican society. "Operation Bootstrap" undoubtedly introduced many changes to Puerto Rico, and even—before 1959 —made Puerto Rico the envied half-sibling of the other Caribbean states. Few in those halcyon days bothered to look beneath the astounding figures of expansion and growth or made the distinction between quantitatively more and qualitatively better. Today in Puerto Rico it is becoming generally clear that more and different did not automatically amount to a better quality of life for Puerto Ricans. Although average per capita income ranks among the highest in the Caribbean, it falls far below the poorest state in the North American federation. More than 50 percent of all Puerto Rican families used federal food stamps and nearly 40 percent of the labor force was unemployed in 1976. Nor has "Operation Bootstrap" reduced the historical gap between the "haves" and the "have-nots." In 1953 it was calculated that the poorer 45 percent of Puerto Ricans shared a mere 18 percent of the total income. In 1970, despite the rapid expansion of material culture and material needs, that 45 percent shared only 16 percent of the total Puerto Rican income. Despite vast increases in home construction and home ownership, one-third of all Puerto Rican homes are deemed substandard by the United States Census Bureau, and 90 percent of these are owned by individuals who could not purchase a new home on the open market. Drug addiction in Puerto Rico has increased tenfold from approximately 1500 cases in 1961 to more than 15,000 in 1970. The educational system has seriously deteriorated at all levels, and an entire generation of Puerto Ricans are attaining adulthood without linguistic competence in either Spanish or English. These are some of the basic ingredients of contemporary Puerto Rican society. Associated statehood for a quarter of a century had made Puerto Rico different in degree but not in kind from the neighboring states of the Caribbean and circum-Caribbean—with the notable exception of Cuba. What is worse, massive expenditure and the positive benevolence of the most wealthy and powerful country in the world had not removed the fundamental conditions breeding discontent and revolutionary unrest in Puerto Rico, nor had it alleviated the political and social and cultural disorientation.

The Puerto Rican experience was not quite duplicated in Cuba during the late nineteenth century and the pre-Castro twentieth century. Cuba was colonized without the benefit of the formal colonialism which was a part of the Puerto Rican background.

The Cuban sugar revolution of the nineteenth century completely revolutionized the social, demographic, and economic structure of the island. Between 1792 and 1899 the population increased from 254,821 to 1,572,797. The slave sector made the most dramatic growth: during the period of the nineteenth-century slave trade, that is, between 1800 and 1860, Cuba imported more than 600,000 Africans. Despite the high mortality accompanying slavery and the trade, the slave population grew from about 39,000 in 1770, shortly after the onset of the sugar revolution, to more than 400,000 in 1840, when the major technical introduction of railroads, steam engines, and vacuumatic pans were about to propel the sugar industry to new levels of production. As elsewhere in the Caribbean, the major consequences of the emphasis on a monocultural export economy was a reexamination of attitudes toward race and color. In the Cuban case this was made more poignant by the notorious example of French Saint-Domingue after 1788. But prosperity meant sugar, and sugar demanded slave labor.

The expanding industry rapidly dominated the landscape from Havana eastwards to Puerto Principe, expelling or absorbing small farmers, destroying the majestic hardwood forests, and undermining the previously self-sufficient mixed economy. By 1850 sugar and sugar products accounted for more than 83 percent of all exports. By 1860 Cuba produced slightly less than 500,000 tons of sugar, the equivalent of one-third of the world's cane sugar production and one-fourth of the entire world sugar production. By 1895 Cuban production had surpassed 1 million tons, equal to 35 percent of the world's sugar cane and 14 percent of the total cane and beet sugar production.

The growing world beet sugar production was the nemesis of Caribbean sugar production, but to the Cubans, with relatively open areas of virgin sugar lands, that was merely a minor irritant. Their problem was a scarcity of low-wage-earning workhands. Nevertheless the industry had certain long-range problems, and beet sugar output was one of them. Beet sugar, developed during the period of the Napoleonic Wars at the beginning of the nineteenth century, did not come into its own until the second half of the century. Until 1857 the island of Cuba alone produced more cane sugar than all the world's beet sugar producers combined. But while Cuban sugar production stabilized at a little more than a half-million tons during the Ten Years War, beet sugar production increased from 474,719 tons in 1864 to 1,615,934 tons in 1878. By 1900 beet sugar production had exceeded 6 million tons, while Cuba, still recovering from the economic effects of the war of national independence, produced only 300,000 tons of cane sugar. While beet sugar production has not yet surpassed cane sugar output in the twentieth century, its proportion of world sugar has moved toward parity.

In Cuba the concomitant requirements of sugar production generated very big business and some major problems. Until the 1870's a new class of landed, sugar-producing, slave owners took over political control of the island. Some of these families, such as that of Julian Zulueta, were new arrivals to the island, having immigrated during the nineteenth century. But the majority were old, established creole Cubans: the Aldamas, Poeys, Iznagas, Arangos, Calvos, Montalvos, and O'Farrils. The insatiable demands of labor brought not only Africans but also Mexican Indians and Chinese to the island, diversifying the labor force as well as complicating the social and racial problems.

Spanish colonial administration in Cuba during the nineteenth century was corrupt, inefficient, and quite inflexible—reflecting the most salient features of metropolitan affairs. But that was not the major cause of the metropolitan-colonial friction, which came from economic roots based on the concentration on sugar. The demands of sugar production—laborers, capital, machines, technical skills, markets, consumer supplies—not only strained the internal racial relations in Cuba but aggravated the political and economic differences with Spain and thereby laid the foundation for the ultimate break in 1898. When the British consul at Havana ruefully remarked in the 1840's that Cuba was rapidly becoming Americanized, his remarks had an unintended double meaning. For Cuba was moving rapidly into both the economic orbit of the United States, and the regional pattern of exploitation colonies subject to all the economic vicissitudes and internal social contradictions of that type of society.

It was perhaps inevitable that the United States should have manifested a lively interest in Cuba during the nineteenth century. In 1823 the Monroe Doctrine had seemed an inflated boast, but by 1850 the insidious expansion of Manifest Destiny became a menacing threat. During the decade between 1848 and 1858 Cubans and United States citizens mounted filibuster expeditions to liberate Cuba and attach it, as was so successfully done with Texas, to the North American federation. The most determined of these filibusters were Narciso López, a gentleman with good social connections in Cuba and several southern states, and John Quitman. López was a Venezuelan-born adventurer who had fought for Spain against Simón Bolívar's army and in Spain on the Carlist side. A perpetual organizer with a penchant for supporting losing causes, and a rather dismal record as a merchant-entrepreneur in Cuba which he first visited in 1823 with the retreating Spanish army, López obtained semiofficial support—or something like benevolent neutrality, American style— for his 1850 expedition which landed at Cárdenas on May 19 with an almost exclusive North-American contingent. It failed dismally to arouse any local Cuban support. A similar expedition the following year ended in a rout and the execution of the leader. John Quitman, an exgovernor of Mississippi and an earlier supporter of López, organized a series of expeditions between 1852 and 1855, but they all failed to leave the mainland. Meanwhile the United States government made a number of bids to purchase the island from Spain between 1848 and 1868. Spain adamantly refused what were sometimes temptingly attractive offers of up to $100,000,000. Spanish honor could not be bought or sold.

But Spanish policy exasperated the colonists. The failure to grant some form of political autonomy, while relentlessly increasing taxes, fomented the outbreak of the first war of independence, the Ten Years War (1868-1878), and the short revolt that followed. The long war emphasized Spain's military and administrative weakness, even though the campaign ended in a stalemate. Neither the rich sugar producers of the western part of the island nor the vast majority of slaves—accounting for more than 28 percent of the population of the western sector and just over 25 percent of the island total in 1861 —rallied to the nationalist cause during the Ten Years War. Moreover, while nationalism was strong in the predominantly nonplantation eastern sector, the nationalists themselves were sharply divided on questions of slavery, political independence, autonomy within the Spanish empire, or annexation to the United States. Carlos Manuel Céspedes, the leader of the declaration of Yara, failed to unify his anti-Spanish forces. The first spark of independence died, but the lesson remained: a unified Cuba could defeat Spain. But a unified Cuba required the abolition of slavery and a mediating voice that could attract Cubans of any persuasion to a nationalist cause. Slavery was abolished in 1886. Shortly thereafter José Martí, one of the most remarkable poets, intellectuals, and political propagandists the Americas produced, began to attract all and sundry to the cause of "Cuba Libre."

Spain also realized that something had to be done. Cuba could not be restrained by force of arms. At the same time any metropolis which could only control 6 percent of a colony's export trade ran the risk of losing such a colony. Forced intervention had failed; therefore in 1878 Spain signed the Convention of Zanjón, promising to reform the political and economic relationship with the island of Cuba. Many Cubans envisaged a status resembling that held by Canada within the British Empire. But some Cubans, including the brilliant nationalist leader, General Antonio Maceo, refused to surrender and accept the Spanish conditions, and left the island to recruit foreign support. But Maceo's efforts failed and, transferring his family to Jamaica, the military leader then moved on to Costa Rica, where he successfully organized a group of exiles to pursue not war but farming.

During the fifteen years before 1895 Spain failed to make good on her promises of political and economic reform. The crisis and colonial alienation deepened. United States foreign investment in the island grew to about $50,000,000 and its annual trade with Cuba exceeded $100,000,000. From his base in the United States, José Martí wrote eloquently and movingly of a free Cuba, and recalled the magnificent heroism of the Ten Years War:

> That wonderful and sudden emergence of a people, apparently servile only a short time before, who made heroic feats a daily event, hunger a banquet, and the extraordinary, a commonplace. . . . That war that has been by foreign observers compared to an epic, the upheaval of a whole country, the voluntary abandonment of wealth, the burning of our cities by our own hands, the erection of villages and factories in the wild forests, the dressing of our ladies of rank in the texture of the woods, the keeping at bay, in ten years of such a life, the powerful enemy, with a loss to him of 200,000 men, at the hands of a small army of patriots, with no help but nature!

Martí also traveled widely to organize, coordinate, and excite those who were and would be patriots: the comfortably exiled in New York, New Haven, and Boston; the poor tobacco workers of Key West and Tampa; the redoubtable Mariana Grajales, mother of Antonio Maceo, in Kingston; Máximo Gómez in Santo Domingo; and Maceo himself in Costa Rica. Finally, after many moments of despondency, the second war for Cuban independence broke out with the *Grito de Baire*, on February 24, 1895. Spain confronted a nation in arms.

The fighting spread quickly and furiously throughout the island. Spain found no sector of support, as it had during the Ten Years War, and deployed more than 200,000 troops in a vain attempt to bludgeon the Cubans into submission. That was not the last time the lesson was to be taught that a nation in arms and willing to fight for its freedom can be destroyed but can never be defeated. Like Haiti, Cuba was almost destroyed; and like Haiti, Cuba prevailed.

Within three years Cuban commercial activity fell to a standstill. Sugar production declined from more than 1,500,000 tons in 1894 to 200,000 tons in 1897. The destruction of life and property was tragic and brutal. The sacrifices were great, including Martí, shot down in ambush in Dos Ríos on May 19, 1895, and Maceo, killed in battle in December of the following year. The defenders of the economic interests of the United States intensified their concern and demanded intervention. Excited by the "yellow press" and incensed by a mysterious explosion aboard the USS *Maine* in Havana harbor, the United States finally declared war against Spain on April 25, 1898. It was a short campaign, but long enough for some heroics and photography by the Americans. In August Spain signed a protocol in Washington ending the hostilities, and in December Cuba gained its nominal political independence under the military occupation of the United States.

The military occupation attempted to restore normalcy. Under Generals John Brooke and Leonard Wood the Americans built a number of schools, roads, and bridges, deepened the harbor at Havana, paved some streets, repaired and extended the telegraph system and the railroads, started sewer works, and made a significant advance against yellow fever and malaria. The Americans were primarily interested in preparing Cuba for eventual statehood, and American economic, cultural, educational, and values were imposed. Catholicism was denigrated; Protestantism—especially the southern fundamentalist strains—was encouraged; and even the electoral franchise was designed to eliminate Afro-Cuban political participation. Moreover the Platt Amendment (1901), reluctantly accepted by the Cubans, gave the United States the right to oversee international commitments, dominate the economy, intervene in internal affairs, and establish a naval station at Guantánamo Bay. The age of aggressive United States domination of, and interference in, the neighboring American states had begun. The Cuban republic became a feeble ward of its continental neighbor.

Both the Cuban state and the Cuban nation experienced considerable difficulties between 1902 and 1959, most stemming from the continued direct and indirect influence of the United States. Party politics did not begin auspiciously, and when the pro-United States annexationist Tomás Estrada Palma sought to return to power at the end of the second election in 1905, the political structure seemed

threatened. On September 29, 1906, the second United States occupation of Cuba began. The occupation, however, failed to resolve the
political discontent that already plagued the young republic. Charles
Magoon, who took over the administration of the island for the
United States in 1906, judiciously continued the Cuban constitution
and kept the Cuban flag flying over public buildings as a sign that the
island still remained nominally free. But the drive to Americanize
Cuba continued, as citizens of the United States poured into Cuba
in the wake of expanding capital investment, and Cubans traveled to
the mainland to be educated and trained. For the nonwhite sector
of the Cuban population, those were some very hard and trying days
as the North American influence sharpened the overt forms of racism
and color prejudice. The official American occupation ended on January 28, 1909, when Magoon handed the reigns of power to the second president, José Miguel Gómez.

Meanwhile political instability did not inhibit steady economic
expansion, as the price of sugar rose until the 1920's. Vast new cen-
trals were built in Oriente province, and the rate of production increased. To provide labor, seasonal immigrants came from Jamaica,
Haiti, and a number of other Caribbean islands. The income from
sugar was augmented by a vigorous tourist business based on hotels,
casinos, and the uninhibited peddling of sexual favors. Havana became especially attractive during the period of prohibition in the
United States as a place where the well-to-do could find ready liquors
and diverse pleasures.

Yet economic development remained plagued by the boom-and-
bust characteristics of the sugar business. The successive waves of
prosperity in the 1920's, 1940's, and 1950's enriched only a few Cubans—mainly politicians and their families. The majority of Cubans
continued in abject poverty and neglect, especially in the rural regions. Education, housing, consistent employment, and available
health care seemed to be subjects far removed from governmental
concern. As late as 1958, while the national per capita income was
$353, among the highest for Latin America and the Caribbean, the
conditions of life remained among the worst for the area. Even in

the sugar zones unemployment and underemployment were rife. The average rural worker earned merely $91 per year, was taught precious little, and as Fidel Castro lamented in 1953, knew virtually nothing about Cuban history. Foreign interests controlled the economy, owning about 75 percent of the arable land, 90 percent of the island's essential services, and 40 percent of the sugar-producing facilities in 1958.

The Cuban political scene was dismal before 1958. Graft, corruption, maladministration, fiscal irresponsibility, and social insensitivity —especially toward the Afro-Cubans—were the most outstanding characteristics. Public office became the major conduit for the acquisition of private wealth. During the Gómez administration (1909–1913), the Afro-Cubans, led by Evaristo Estenoz and Pedro Ivonet, organized a political party to secure better jobs and more political patronage and to protest the 1910 law prohibiting parties based on race or color. Estenoz and Ivonet had been political activists since 1905 and felt, with considerable justification, that the new Cuba was grossly unfair to some of its oldest citizens. They fomented a conspiracy based in Oriente. Under United States pressure, government troops moved against the rebels in 1912, killing an estimated 3000 Afro-Cubans. No major black demonstrations occurred again in Cuba. The lottery became more important than civil rights. The only distinguishing features of the presidencies of Gerardo Machado (1925-1933) and Fulgencio Batista (1940-1944; 1952-1959; the Cuban "strongman" since 1933) were their notorious use of political assassination, constitutional manipulation, and military power either to gain or maintain office. Machado had Julio Antonio Mella, the founder of the Cuban Communist Party, murdered in Mexico in 1929; Batista had Fidel Castro, the leader of the Moncada Barracks attack of 1953, imprisoned. The ideas of Mella and the leadership of Castro eventually produced the revolution in Cuba.

In the non-Hispanic Caribbean colonialism still flourished during the first half of the twentieth century in an economy still uneasily wed to the production and export of sugar. Attempts to diversify met with only partial success. After 1900 British Guiana exported rice, and

Jamaica began the regular export of bananas. The petroleum industry began a slow growth in Trinidad in 1910 and expanded during and after World War I. During the 1950's Canadian and American companies developed bauxite in Jamaica and British Guiana; Jamaicans expanded citrus production in British Honduras, and consumer-oriented manufacturing provided employment for a growing number in Jamaica and Trinidad. At about the same time the tourist industry expanded into the region with mixed, or at best, uncertain economic and social impact. But the principal banes of Caribbean life remained the woes of colonialism.

Until the Second World War the fluctuating fortunes of the sugar industry remained the chief barometer of the general economic condition of the English Caribbean. Until almost the end of the nineteenth century the Anglo-Caribbean producers resisted the type of technical innovations which had helped catapult sugar production upward in Cuba: innovations such as rail transportation and central factories. Goaded by the Colonial Office, the Caribbean producers seemed to think that the two aims of increasing laborers and increasing the yield per acre exhausted the possibilities of higher production. To effect the former they imported Asians, especially East Indians, to work on the estates. In some islands, Jamaica being the prime example, general revenues were used to subsidize the cost of importing the indentured laborers. In others, especially Trinidad and British Guiana, public funds supported up to one-half the cost. The use of general funds to subsidize the labor costs of private estates meant that everyone directly contributed to the profits of a few, including poor, struggling peasant farmers short of land, tools, transportation, and technical assistance.

British West Indian planters refuted the criticism that they failed to imitate the Cuban example by pointing, correctly, to the dissimilar terrain, and the discouraging experience of their initial efforts to upgrade their industry. Cuba had a gently rolling terrain throughout most of its provinces, facilitating the construction and utilization of rail transportation. The sharp and dissected valleys of most islands of the English Antilles made transportation costs virtually prohibitive in all except Antigua, Barbados, Trinidad, and the Guianese lowlands. But as a concession in the direction of the *central*, the British Antillean producers attempted the *métayage* system, successfully used to cushion the postemancipation labor impact in Martinique and Guadeloupe. This was another of those characteristically Caribbean approaches to a modified barter system, whereby small cane farmers had their sugar canes crushed and manufactured into sugar by the larger planters for a commonly agreed proportion of either the cane or the sugar.

In general the *métayage* system was unsatisfactory and unfair. A fixed proportion of the cane could not necessarily be correlated to the proportion of sugar; and the planters tended to end up with the valuable by-product of the rum distilled. Also, while the planter was relieved of the burdens of a cash flow for wages and sugar cane purchases, he still had the problems of marketing the small farmer's sugar, and the inconvenience of an irregular source of raw material. In return the individual grower found that sales commissions and transportation costs made the enterprise less than economically rewarding at best, and quite insecure at worst. In Tobago, the most successful example of the use of the *métayage* system, peculiar conditions explain its success, derived from the bankruptcy of the principal sugar producer, the house of Gillespie, in 1884, and the subsequent availability of a number of sugar estates to small landowners. Besides, the compact area of production and the small size of the island kept transportation costs reasonable. Barbados did not need the *métayage* system, and other colonies found it unfeasible or socially undesirable. In British Guiana it was identified—from the estates' point of view—as "tantamount to admission of failure of a sugar estate, and loss of prestige."

Until 1884 a large number of small or marginal producers continued to supply the British market. But the increased dumping of European beet sugar, particularly from Germany, forced sugar prices down in the London market. British Guiana sugar, considered the best on the market, fell from 26 shillings per hundredweight (112 pounds) to 15 shillings, and general muscovado fell from 20 shillings to 13 shillings per hundredweight in one year. The impact spread swiftly across the Caribbean, eliminating a number of smaller sugar producers, and forcing the larger producers to modernize or fail. A number modernized. In Grenada sugar production fell 60 percent during 1883-84. Two years later about two-thirds of the area previously under sugar cane cultivation in St. Vincent had been abandoned. In Jamaica a number of sugar estates went on the market or into bankruptcy or were abandoned. By 1900 the more efficient sugar producers had installed better mills to increase the quantity of juice extracted from the sugar cane, and used the centrifugal process of crystal separation to improve the quality of their sugar. But in the industry as a whole, technical improvements were introduced slowly, and too often the response to increased production costs or decreased profits was simply to lower wages.

The reduction of British Antillean sugar estates—from about 2200 in 1838 to about 800 in 1900—made more land available for peasant farming. Peasant farms, therefore, competed for labor on the estates. Nevertheless the main reasons for the shortage of labor on the sugar estates remained the discouragingly low wages paid. Despite the assertions of the sugar producers to the contrary, West Indian nonwhites were industrious and eager to work, as indicated by the constant stream of emigration to the canal works of Panama, the plantations of Costa Rica, the farms of the United States, and the sugar estates of Cuba.

Compared to Cuba and Puerto Rico, the manifestations of nationalism, or even of class consciousness, were slow to appear in the British West Indies. This is certainly surprising, given the enthusiasm the black populations showed for education and for cooperative associations, from the religiously organized free villages of the 1840's to the agricultural societies of the 1940's and 1950's. In any case workingmen's associations, such as that of the ports of Port-of-Spain, Trinidad, and Kingston, Jamaica (founded in 1907 and 1919, respectively), failed to survive owing to lack of economic and popular support. The same was true of political parties. Although Marcus Garvey enjoyed spectacular popularity throughout the region, his attempt to mobilize the Jamaican masses into a political party in the 1930's was far less successful than his efforts in the United States. The lack of political parties, however, should not be identified with an absence of political sentiment. Political sentiment found expression through individual radicals such as Sandy Cox and J. A. G. Smith in Jamaica and A. A. Cipriani in Trinidad.

Nationalism and class consciousness gained major impetus in the interwar years. Like the Bolivian Indians after the wars in the Gran Chaco, the West Indians who returned after service in the European war theater agitated for change. And their agitation coincided with a number of other factors which together contributed toward hastening the end of European colonialism in the Caribbean. These factors were—besides the experience and aroused self-consciousness of the war years—the Harlem Renaissance and the Garveyite United Negro Improvement Association; the economic impact of the great worldwide Depression beginning in 1929; the crisis of the West Indian sugar industry; and the cutoff of the outlets for emigration, especially to Panama, Cuba, and the United States. All these factors were related, becoming more acute as time passed. Political and economic conditions facilitated the success of Bustamante's Labor Party in 1944, when only fifteen years before, in 1929, Garvey's People's Political Party had failed to alter the system. The difference was that in 1944 the colonial system had collapsed, and the masses had the vote.

The Harlem Renaissance involved a number of expatriate West Indians—Claude McKay, Marcus Garvey, W. A. Domingo, Richard B. Moore—who were articulate, politically organized, and aware of the Caribbean position in world affairs. They gave support to a more vigorous local press by contributing fiery letters and provocative articles, and began the literary shift away from the Eurocentric romanticism of the nineteenth century to a type of work focusing on Caribbean society and its classes. This nationalism found expression in the poetry of Thomas Henry MacDermott, alias Tom Redcam; journals such as the *Jamaica Post, Jamaica Times,* and *Public Opinion*; novels such as W. Adolphe Roberts's *The Single Star*; and histories such as C. L. R. James's *The Black Jacobins* and A. H. Maloney's *After Eng-*

land We. These authors and their works were the precursors of the
literary torrent produced after the Second World War. They created,
with great difficulty, the closest works the British Caribbean had
ever had to a popular literature designed for the masses without
patronizing the masses.

From 1919 to 1929 labor discontent erupted into riots throughout
the Caribbean. Each was followed by a British Commission of Inquiry that toured the area, diagnosed, as best as it could, the source
of the grievances, and prescribed, often with British Fabian social
consciousness, palliatives parading as reforms. But the 1930's were
very serious years. The Depression hit hard at the local export economies. Sugar prices fell. Wages almost disappeared; and the usual
escape valves of emigrating to work rapidly closed as Panama, Cuba,
and the United States suddenly found black Caribbean laborers dis-
pensable and undesirable. Between 1935 and 1938 labor unrest raced
through the Caribbean like fire on a windy day. In 1935 the sugar
workers in St. Kitts and British Guiana went on strike, followed by a
coal strike in St. Lucia, and a strike against an increase in customs
duties in St. Vincent. In 1937 the oilfield workers in Trinidad went
on a strike that widened into a general strike and eventually merged
into widespread labor unrest in Barbados, St. Lucia, British Guiana,
and Jamaica. In 1938 Jamaican dock workers refused to work without
better pay and better working conditions. The colonial authorities
panicked. Military reinforcements rushed to the colonies to support
the local law enforcement officers. Order was restored at a cost of 115
wounded, 29 dead, and considerable property damage. Labor unions
sprang up like mushrooms to channel the workers' discontent: the
Bustamante Industrial Trades Union in Jamaica, the Oilfield Workers Trade Union in Trinidad, the Barbados Workers Union, and the
General Workers Union of British Honduras. These labor unions
rapidly spawned political parties, which rushed to accept passage of
the electoral reforms extended piecemeal throughout the region after
1944. Within a short time each territory had a more or less established two-party system, and a number of able, popular eminent
politicians: Norman Manley and Alexander Bustamante in Jamaica;

Robert Bradshaw in St. Kitts; Eric Gairy in Grenada; Grantley Adams in Barbados; Uriah Butler, Albert Gomes, and Eric Williams in Trinidad; Cheddi Jagan and Forbes Burnham in British Guiana; and George Price in British Honduras.

The political accession from the late 1930's and the parade of independence in the 1960's and 1970's had been relatively gradual and orderly. As British West Indians accepted more political responsibility they became increasingly aware of the position of the region in international relations in a postwar world heavily colored by the ideological gulf between the United States and the Soviet Union, as well as the rapid demise of their former metropolis as a world power. The latter was a realization the French and Spanish Antilles had experienced a century before. But perhaps the major lesson for the English Antilles was the political hegemony assumed by the United States in the Caribbean. For the United States had politically and militarily intervened in every independent state in the region—Cuba, Haiti, and the Dominican Republic—and stood ready to intervene again whenever it felt its interests threatened. The "Good Neighbor" policy of F. D. Roosevelt enunciated to put a soft glove on the heavy-handed efforts of the early decades, was designed not to foster political independence, but to control it. Unfortunately for the Caribbean, hemispheric subordination proved no more advantageous than nonhemispheric subordination. That is why the revolution occurred in Cuba after 1959; and that is why the Caribbean peoples are so self-consciously seeking identification with the Third World nations.

Nowhere was the failure of the proposed western hemisphere solidarity and subordination to the United States of America more evident than in the separate histories of Haiti, the Dominican Republic, and the United States Virgin Islands during the twentieth century. Haiti entered the twentieth century after a long period of political and economic turmoil. A succession of governments, usually headed by military men, had tried periodically to stabilize both the social chaos and the economic fluctuations. Some significant advances were indeed made. The system of education was expanded to include rural areas, but the quality remained poor. New export crops such as cacao and cotton joined coffee and logwood. Until 1915 the state managed to avoid foreign intervention, but had failed to maintain itself economically.

Haiti lacked either the political stability or the economic infrastructure to pull itself out of the spiraling squalor which threatened to engulf it. Like Mexico during the nineteenth century, economic improvement depended on reliable political leadership—and that was the most elusive aspect of Haitian history since 1804. Between 1804 and 1879 about seventy presidents spent varying periods of time manipulating the reigns of government and plundering the public treasury. Some ruled over a divided nation. Some, such as Faustin Soulouque (1847-1859) and Fabre-Nicolas Geffrard (1859-1867), had enough time to cultivate a popular following, and attempt some feeble public works. But Haiti produced no Porfirio Díaz and no modernizing revolution. Poverty, political discontent, and illiteracy became the hallmarks of the land once considered the richest colony in all the Americas. Illiterates aspired to the presidency because it was one certain way to escape poverty, even temporarily.

Between 1908 and 1915 the presidency changed hands seven times, and political unrest became endemic. Each president—and each faction—borrowed heavily abroad to meet the costs of arms and administration, pledging the declining customs receipts in repayment, or issuing unsecured paper money. By 1915 the country was utterly bankrupt. The United States, sensitive to the strategic location of Haiti near their recently opened canal across the isthmus of Panama, and preoccupied both with private investments in Haiti and the expanding World War, occupied the country until 1934.

The immediate explanation for the invasion was the standard one, enunciated by the United States with the Monroe Doctrine of 1823 and the Roosevelt Corollary of 1904, "to save American lives and property." It was a hollow pretext. On numerous occasions during the last decades of the nineteenth century the United States had tried to buy Haiti, or at least the strategic northwestern promontory called the Môle St. Nicolas, commanding the narrow windward passage opposite eastern Cuba. Haitians had adamantly refused to sell all or part of their territory. Contingency plans to invade and occupy Haiti were made during the summer of 1914, and in December a group of marines entered the national bank and removed a half-million dollars worth of gold, ostensibly for safekeeping in New York. In 1915 the United States investment in Haiti amounted to only $4 million, a sum equal to 1.8 percent of similar investments in Cuba, about one-half percent of the investment in Mexico, and an even smaller proportion of the total of $1.7 billion direct United States investment in Latin America. The two main United States business interests— W. R. Grace and Company and National City Bank of New York— could protect themselves; and no evidence exists, apart from the declaration of Woodrow Wilson, that American citizens were in jeopardy.

With the experience of Cuba, Puerto Rico, the Dominican Republic, and Nicaragua, the United States had established military intervention as a standard political procedure in its neighboring states. In all cases the modus operandi and the rationale were the same. In Haiti more than 2000 United States marines secured the towns, took over the customhouses and the administration, established a military system of justice, and began to dictate to Haiti what the foreigners felt were best for Haitians. But the subordination was camouflaged by the election of a puppet president, and the ratification of a treaty by both parties—reluctantly to be sure, on the part of the Haitians—legalizing the devolution of Haitian sovereignty. In the final analysis, the goals of foreigners were "to maintain order, to provide an atmosphere conducive to American investment, and to construct basic public works." As they did earlier in Cuba, the United States marines built roads, sewerage systems, telephone and telegraph service, irrigation canals, wharves, schools, prisons, and hospitals.

The occupation, however, did not dramatically change Haiti or Haitian life. The gross national statistics were more impressive than the every day conditions for the Haitians, especially the rural peasants. The expansion in exports and imports hardly exceeded the rate of increase in the local population. The United States administration achieved budgetary surpluses partly by efficiency, partly by the fortunate upswing in agricultural prices between 1917 and 1928, and by the reduction of the allocations for domestic education and other services. The actual annual expenditures for education, for example, remained at about the same budgetary figure during the period of occupation as it had in the years 1913 to 1915, in spite of a rise in both the general population and the school-age groups. The North Americans created their loyal, local police force and recruited their political lackeys, but they made no serious attempt to strengthen the social and political institutions, or the educational level and civil proficiency of the Haitians. Moreover, they accentuated racial prejudice, segregation, and prostitution.

The United States departed prematurely in 1934. Haitian resistance escalated after 1928 when a hurricane destroyed a major portion of the coffee crop, and after the 1929-30 world Depression undermined all export economies. Open rioting in 1929 coincided with United States President Herbert Hoover's attempt to implement a "good neighbor policy" toward Latin America by renunciating the Roosevelt Corollary. Finally, at the Inter-American Conference in Montevideo in 1933, President Franklin Roosevelt declared that his government had abandoned the right of unilateral intervention in the internal affairs of other American states. Thereafter, the powerful North American state observed the letter but not the spirit of that important announcement.

Haiti signed a reciprocity treaty with the United States in 1935, and entered the latter's commercial sphere. But neither economic nor political conditions improved measurably. Tens of thousands of Haitians left their country to work in Cuba, the Dominican Republic, the United States, and elsewhere. In 1937 about 20,000 Haitian citizens living and working in the western part of the Dominican Republic were massacred on the orders of Rafael Leonidas Trujillo, creating a major diplomatic crisis between the two neighboring states. Between 1934 and 1957 the political system was a return to the pre-occupation instability and corruption.

The immediate political beneficiary of the United States with-

drawal was Sténio Vincent (1874-1959), a Port-au-Prince-born law-
yer, member of the mulatto elite, and a leading politician during the
occupation. Elected president in 1930, Vincent was instrumental in
obtaining the release of his territory. With the help of the American-
created police force, and a skillful manipulation of the constitution,
Vincent kept himself in power until 1941, when he unexpectedly re-
signed, citing failing health and fading vision. The war years brought
a limited improvement in the economy, but the deterioration returned in the 1950's, and with it the return of political unrest. The
climactic year was 1957, which produced four provisional governments and many months of unrest, and ended with the election of
François Duvalier (1907-1971), a black country doctor who had dab-
bled in the renaissance literature of the 1940's, and had participated
in the antimalaria and antiyaws campaigns.

In terms of local politics, Duvalier distinguished himself by his
exaltation of black consciousness, subordination of the military police to his private arm of Tonton Macoutes, encouragement of Vo-
dun, elimination of free political expression, and restoration of the
life presidency, which he was able to pass on to his son in 1971. Duvalier brought a dictatorial, independent, and strong rule to Haiti,
but he failed to elevate the population from miserable poverty,
neglect, disease, and the scourge of malnutrition. The testimony to
the failure of the regime to improve the economy or create a social
climate conducive to the comfort of its citizens lay in the massive
exodus of Haitians in the late 1950's and throughout the 1960's. In
1970 the population of Haiti was estimated at 4.9 millions, and perhaps one million Haitians were legally and illegally living in Cuba,
the Dominican Republic, the Bahamas, Canada, and the United
States.

Like Haiti, the Dominican Republic entered the twentieth century
nominally independent, but in political chaos and economic bankruptcy. From 1882 until 1899 Ulises Heureaux dominated the state,
blending a Napoleonic political authoritarianism with a socially conscious, modernizing program of internal reforms. Like Francisco
Franco in post-Civil War Spain, Heureaux combined severe political

repression with the expansion of education, industry, internal communications, and improvements in the army and the bureaucracy. His assassination in 1899 left the country without the political apparatus or the fiscal solvency to attack its mounting domestic and foreign problems. The most pressing of these problems was an enormous foreign debt.

The United States involvement went through three stages, culminating in the military occupation of 1916. In 1905, partly at the request of some interested Dominicans, the United States took over the collection of customs duties, and the servicing of the enormous domestic and foreign debt amounting to nearly $30 million. For about twelve years the United States tried to manipulate the electoral process, and partly to ensure political stability, partly to secure the desired influence according to the Roosevelt Corollary and its conviction that failure to assert North American hegemony would result in the intervention of a European power.

The occupation brought the customary zeal to build roads, establish schools modeled on those in North America, and build bridges, hospitals, sewer systems, and telecommunications. Behind the marines went the usual brigades of capitalists dispensing North American techniques in just about everything from agriculture to morality. As elsewhere, the administrative efficiency reduced the national debt, but created profound resentment among the Dominican people at the economic and cultural dependency imposed from outside.

The withdrawal of the United States in 1924 failed to demonstrate that their occupation and rule could develop political democracy or increased social awareness on the part of the governing elite. Within six years the country plunged into a fragmented politics accentuated by the Great Depression of 1929-30. From this state it was rescued by Rafael Trujillo who completely dominated Dominican society, economy, and politics for thirty-one years.

Trujillo, a native of San Cristóbal, was a product of the occupation. Of modest education and humble class, he joined the quasi-military constabulary created by the United States marines in 1916. By 1924 he had, by shrewd politics and his own ambition, become head of the national army which succeeded the occupation forces, and which provided the power-base for his coup d'état in 1930. No other dictatorship was ever as strong and as pervasive as that established by Trujillo in the Dominican Republic. He controlled the army, the government, the judiciary, and the national economy, and made the state virtually his private domain. His political conduct combined elements of Spanish colonial corporatism, Italian fascism, and the popular, eclectic *justicialismo* of Juan Perón of Argentina. He used murder, torture, and terrorism with reckless abandon, while attempting to boost his vanity, paternalism, and peculiar nationalism. Along with his family and selected associates, he owned or controlled about 75 percent of all the economic activity in the state. He built schools, highways, cities, and factories less to develop a nation than to glorify himself.

The rule by force and coercion ended suddenly with a volley of bullets in 1961. It took nearly two restless years to establish viable political parties, and a national, as opposed to a personal, economy in which the general welfare prevailed. In 1962 Juan Bosch of the Partido Revolucionario Dominicano (PRD) won 62 percent of the presidential popular vote after a campaign to institute land reforms, expand education, and drastically restructure the society along socialist lines. Within a year the military, supported by a combination of landholders, businessmen, and foreigners, ousted Bosch, thereby forging an opposition from the peasants, students, and workers. Supported by the United States, a civilian-military junta ruled uneasily until April 1965 when civil war broke out. The United States sent in its marines to prevent the return of Juan Bosch, and to forestall another "Cuba" in the Caribbean. The Organization of American States later narrowly approved the intervention, and arranged a withdrawal in late summer and early fall. Supervised elections returned Joaquin Balaguer as president. The Dominican Republic gained a political leader acceptable to the United States of America. It also got a respite from the approaching chaos, but it lost an opportunity to initiate the political programs necessary to remove the debilitating legacies of Rafael Trujillo.

St. Thomas, St. Croix, and St. John (the United States Virgin Islands) came into the North American orbit by purchase, not by conquest, in 1917. Their peculiar geography and status forced an entirely different formal relationship from that of occupied territories such as Cuba, Haiti, or the Dominican Republic. The islands are small in physical size with a total area of 192 square miles. Despite an immigration boom during the 1960's, the estimated population in 1970 was about 70,000. Their commercial importance passed away along with the demise of the steamship, and the reduction of the tyranny of distance that steam-powered transportation facilitated. Between 1917 and 1931 the islands were administered by the Department of the Navy. Afterwards the Interior Department took over jurisdiction. In 1927 Virgin Islanders became citizens of the United States, but like citizens in Puerto Rico and the District of Columbia, they did not enjoy the full benefits of that status. In 1970 the governor of the Virgin Islands ceased to be the political nominee of the president of the United States, and was elected locally.

Until the 1950's the economy of the Virgin Islands rested on congressional largesse, the income from the United States sugar quota, and a local long-standing free port economy. It was a small, simple economy consonant with the neglected political status of the islands. The advent of tourism brought the winds of economic change. The hotel industry created a demand for servants, and boosted the curio and artisan suppliers. Then Congress permitted the duty-free importation of a number of articles assembled in the Virgin Islands; and with the construction of a Crown oil refinery and Harvey Alumina, the territories have taken off on a course reminiscent of the "Operation Bootstrap" in Puerto Rico during the 1940's and 1950's.

That the economic developments have brought considerable changes to the islands is beyond doubt. Much of the change, however, remains superficial, temporary, and cosmetic. As in the Bahamas or Bermuda, tourism shapes both the economy and political consciousness. Despite the munificent economic returns from industry, it is a form of national prostitution which has subordinated local social and political considerations to the comfort of an increasing number of tourists. The economic incentives that attach the islands to the North American mainland create a sharp dichotomy and ambivalence on the local scene. On the one hand, the islands attract or produce a group that tries to be acceptable to their mainland hosts. On the other hand, the islands remain part of the Caribbean culture area, and this reality is constantly reinforced by the flow of immigrants, often illegal entrants, from the nearby Leeward Islands chain. This ambivalence between North American aspirations and Caribbean traditions undermines the growth of a local *patriachiquismo* which might eventually merge into a larger Caribbean nationalism, and remains yet another factor fragmenting regional cooperation.

Chapter 8 • The Cuban Revolution and the Contemporary Scene, 1959-1976

I have travelled everywhere in your sea of the Caribbean . . . from Haiti to Barbados, to Martinique and Guadeloupe, and I know what I am speaking about. . . . You are all together, in the same boat, sailing on the same uncertain sea . . . citizenship and race unimportant, feeble little labels compared to the message that my spirit brings to me: that of the position and predicament which History has imposed upon you. . . . I saw it first with the dance . . . the merengue in Haiti, the beguine in Martinique and today I hear, de mon oreille morte, the echo of calypsoes from Trinidad, Jamaica, St. Lucia, Antigua, Dominica and the legendary Guiana. . . . It is no accident that the sea which separates your lands makes no difference to the rhythm of your body.

Père Labat, 1743

In his book, *From Columbus to Castro: The History of the Caribbean*, Eric Williams wrote that "the Castro Revolution in 1958 was a belated attempt to catch up with the nationalist movement in the rest of the Caribbean." Such an assertion seems to have little histori-

189

cal substantiation. Rather than belatedly joining the nationalist movement of the Caribbean, the Cubans seem to have been in the vanguard of Caribbean nationalist movements. If the argument made in chapter three is valid, and a *conciencia de sí* becomes a clear manifestation of proto-nationalism, then the Cubans have a record of self-assertion going back a century and a half.

This proto-nationalism may be seen in the aggressive self-confidence of the Havana Economic Society; the conspiracies of the 1820's and 1830's; the novels and poems of Domingo Del Monte's group in the 1830's; the Ten Years War (1868-1878) against Spain; the War of Independence of 1895-1898; and in various muted forms throughout the twentieth century. This is the basis for the assertion of a student of Cuban history that

> the Castro Revolution represented the final political phase in a process of revolutionary change whose antecedents stretch back to the early nineteenth century. . . . The establishment of the plantation society symptomized a metamorphosis, the social and economic implications of which were already complete by the middle of the nineteenth century. The achievements of Fidel Castro in the middle decades of the twentieth century merely completed the political aspects of a process of on-going social revolution which had profoundly altered the relationship of the island to the wider world of international politics and economics.

With the possible exception of Haiti, no other Caribbean region had experienced such a swift or such a spectacular economic success. This economic success possibly accentuated the normal social imbalances and fostered the early growth of Cuban nationalism. In any case no other Caribbean colony had the articulate prophets of this *patriachiquismo* type of nationalism as did Cuba. None produced a Francisco Arango y Parreño, a José Antonio Saco, a Rafael María de Labra, or a José Martí. Without these, it would have been hard to produce a Fidel Castro.

The Castro Revolution began inauspiciously with the abortive attack by a group of idealistic young men and women on the Moncada military baracks in Santiago de Cuba. The purpose of the attack was to secure arms to overthrow the corrupt political regime of Fulgencio Batista, the most detested leader since Gerardo Machado. Fidel Castro started in 1953, like Francisco Madero did in 1908 in Mexico, with a simple, popular, political goal: throw out bad government and replace it with good. The lesson the Cubans learned—as the Mexicans had before them—was that true political change encompasses every facet of society. The revolution, therefore, began as a simple political personnel change and ended as a monumental and thorough social reconstruction as all revolutions do.

The group of 150 to 170 which executed the suicidal attack in Santiago on July 26, 1953 (thereafter called the 26th of July Movement), was a motley crew of diverse social background. Only a few were students, approximately 10 had some form of higher education, and only 5 had finished formal university training. Most of the group were factory workers, builders, agricultural workers, or truck drivers. But just about every occupation was represented: accountants, bakers, bank workers, barmen, bus drivers, businessmen, bookstore attendants, butchers, carpenters, chimney sweepers, cooks, mechanics, nurses, office workers, photographers, plumbers, printers, sailors, shoemakers, sugar workers, tailors, tanners, and teachers. Only one person admitted to being unemployed, and the occupations of about 23 could not be ascertained. Surprisingly not many came from the province of Oriente, the scene of the attack. About 60 came from Havana, but of this group nearly one-half were not native to the city. Twenty were from Artemisa, and 5 from Guanajay. Of the 87 whose ages were known, 28 were under 20 years old; 36 were between 20 and 29; 14 were between 30 and 39; and 9 were more than 40 years old. The group, consonant with the occupations listed, was predominantly white, mulatto, or mestizo. Few were married; and most had some radical, activist political past. The main political persuasion was the Ortodoxo political party once led by Eduardo Chibás. No member of the Moncada group of 1953 was an avowed communist. Nor was there any representative of the Communist Youth Movement among the ranks of those who supported the attack.

Cuban middle-class youth in 1953, like most middle-class youth throughout Latin America at that time, were quite politicized. Castro's program, however, was neither exceptionally radical, nor ideologically specific. He sought a return to the constitution of 1940, agrarian reform, profit sharing by workers, educational reform, and housing reform. Violence in Cuba had been widespread, at least since 1868; and although Castro's movement was audacious, it was not especially unusual to "pronounce" against the government and seek to overthrow it. Moreover 1953 was the centenary of the birth of José Martí, and a year when Batista was still plagued by military dissatisfaction over his coup d'état of March 10, 1952.

The Moncada attack failed miserably. Many of the participants were killed or murdered in cold blood afterwards. But Moncada made Castro a hero and further discredited the illegal Batista regime. Castro and the survivors of his group were sentenced to prison on the Isle of Pines, but gained their liberty under the general amnesty granted by Batista. They left the Isle of Pines on May 15, 1955. Castro went to Mexico, where he trained a small band of guerrilla fighters to challenge the mighty army and the secure presidential position of Fulgencio Batista. That is the group that returned to Cuba in December 1956, aboard the 58-foot yacht, *Granma*. Almost wiped out early in the campaign, the fighters of the 26th of July Movement retreated to the Sierra Maestra mountains and fought a two-year guerrilla war, which culminated in the victory of the Fidelistas in January 1959.

The problems that facilitated the downfall of Batista were legion. Some were recent; some were long-term; all were deep-seated. Cuban society in 1958, in common with so many Caribbean and Latin American societies, bore the sad and bitter scars of the hasty process of social construction. Deep divisions and patent injustice were rife with crime in high places, political corruption and ineptitude, and misery and poverty amid great abundance. The statistics of development given for Cuba fail to portray the massive maldistribution inherent in such figures. For example Cuba had one of the most highly developed cattle industries in all Latin America, but the price of meat was high, and only an estimated 41 percent of the rural population (about three and a half million or 45 percent of the total population) ate meat regularly. Cuba had many daily papers, but the illiteracy rate was 46 percent among the adult population.

By Latin American standards Cuba ranked among the top five in the following statistics: railroad mileage; radios, newspapers, motor cars, and television sets per capita; energy consumption; life expectancy at birth; and proportion of the population not engaged in agriculture. The statistics only indicate that Cuba was comparatively a modern society. It was, too, a society in which the extremes of wealth and poverty stood out starkly behind gross national statistics. At one extreme Batista's police chief, Rafael Solas Cañizares, extorted $730,000 per month from gambling interests in Havana. At the other extreme, the peasants earned an average of $91 per month. Thirty percent of the Cuban labor force were either unemployed or only partially employed—a figure that fluctuated between 200,000 workers during the *zafra* and 500,000 individuals during the *tiempo muerto*. Thirty-six percent of those employed full-time in 1957 were in service occupations. Despite the apparent prosperity of the island, most workers without government jobs in 1957 were facing some form of economic hardship.

Greater Havana, which had about 17 percent of the Cuban population, had a disproportionate share of everything in Cuba: 60 percent of the dentists; 66 percent of all nurses; 60 percent of all chemists; and an equal proportion of doctors. But even in Havana the contrast between the affluent of Miramar, Vedado, and El Country Club and the poor of Old Havana and Pogolotti was remarkable.

More remarkable, however, was the contrast between urban and rural Cuba. Rural Cuba remained, in 1958, a country apart, almost forgotten and abandoned in its neglect. Well over 90 percent of rural Cubans did not eat fish, meat, bread, or milk regularly. About 50 percent of the rural folk were completely illiterate, and about 44 percent had never been to school. In 1957 more than 60 percent of children under fourteen years of age were not attending schools either because they could not afford to attend or because there were no schools. Housing was inadequate, with 50 percent of rural houses having no bathroom facilities; 85 percent without running water, and 91 percent without electricity; and 99 percent were picturesques *bohíos* and *caneyes* with palm-leaf roofs, adobe walls, and earthen floors. Health care was virtually nonexistent in the countryside.

Nor was the Cuban economy as healthy as the figures indicate. With almost 80 percent of its land cultivable, Cuba utilized less than 30 percent, and planted about 25 percent in sugar cane. The result was the massive importation of food to feed a population which, with planned agriculture, could have been self-sufficient. Cuba spent a large proportion of its income on the purchase of foodstuff, while much land went fallow.

Latifundism was widespread, although, unlike other parts of Latin America, the land was owned more by giant corporations than individuals. The United Fruit Company owned 93,000 acres; the Punta Alegre Company owned 112,000 acres and leased another 43,000 acres. The Vertientes-Camagüey Company owned or leased 800,000 acres. The Cuban Atlantic Sugar Company had 400,000 acres and the Cuban-American Sugar Company had 500,000 acres. The Manatí Sugar Company owned or leased 237,000 acres, mostly in sugar lands, and Julio Lobo owned or otherwise controlled 1,000,000 acres, and was the world's largest single sugar vendor. The *Administración de Negocios Azucareros*, owned by the heirs of the Spaniard Laureano Falla Gutierrez, had 300,000 acres. While the sugar industry was predominantly Cuban-owned, foreign interests, particularly from the United States, virtually controlled the Cuban economy. Foreigners owned or controlled 75 percent of all arable land, 90 percent of the essential services, and 40 percent of the sugar industry. In 1959 the major business of Cuba involved the production and export of sugar.

Both economic and social structure, therefore, dictated the pattern of the Cuban Revolution. The coalition that provided the popular base of the 26th of July Movement came from among the poor peasants, the urban workers, the politically disenchanted and idealistic of all classes, the young, and the nonwhite. The revolution did not set out initially to take from the rich to feed the poor, but indirectly ended up doing just that. Under Castro's personal direction, the government gradually adopted a form of pragmatic socialism designed to bring equality and social justice via agrarian, educational, and social reforms.

The course of the revolution, perhaps indicative of its eclectic and pragmatic concepts, has often been unclear, and often stormy. It has acquired administrative skills, and by the late 1970's has exhibited four clearly designed, though sometimes concurrent stages: the liquidation of capitalist enterprise between 1959 and 1963, and the introduction of socialist institutions modeled on some type of Soviet socialism; a period of flux from 1963 to 1965; a period of radicalization both abroad and at home from 1966 to 1970; and a period of evaluation and institutionalization after 1970.

The years between 1959 and 1963 were confusing and difficult ones for the revolution. The first order of business for the new government was the elimination of the remnants of Batista's army, as well as the previous political parties, labor unions, and professional and farmers' associations. A new set of institutions replaced the old: the National Institute of Agrarian Reform (INRA, founded in 1959), the Cuban Institute of Cinematic Arts (ICEAC, 1959), the Central Planning Board (JUCEPLAN, 1960), the Federation of Cuban Women (FMC, 1960), the Committee for the Defense of the Revolution (CDR, 1960), the National Association of Small Farmers (ANAP, 1961), the Revolutionary Armed Forces (FAR, 1961), the Ministry of the Interior (MININ, 1961), the National Union of Cuban Writers and Artists (UNEAC, 1961), the Young Communist League (UJC, 1962), and the Integrated Revolutionary Organizations (ORI, 1961-1963).

The nationalization of hundreds of millions of dollars of property owned by citizens of the United States brought about the undisguised hostility of the North American government. The United States reduced the sugar quota in 1960, which adversely affected the Cuban economy, declared a total trade embargo and broke diplomatic relations in January of 1961, supported an unsuccessful invasion by Cuban exiles armed and trained by the Central Intelligence Agency in April 1961 at Playa Girón, or the Bay of Pigs in south-central

Cuba, and voted for the expulsion of Cuba from the Organization of American States in January 1962. In addition the Central Intelligence Agency has supported dozens of expeditions designed to overthrow the Castro government, while encouraging anti-Castro Cubans to harass the operations of that government abroad. As the hemispheric hostility to the revolution increased, the Cuban government became more popular at home, while drifting toward communism and economic and military dependence on the Soviet Union. This development divided the country at large, and alienated some of the early supporters of the 26th of July Movement. A great number of Cubans, especially among the wealthy and the skilled, emigrated, mainly to the United States of America, Mexico, Spain, and Venezuela. The loss of this sector further diminished the efficiency of the administration and increased the frustration and discontent of some otherwise friendly supporters of the revolution. An attempt to diversify the economic base under the auspices of the National Institute of Agrarian Reform disrupted sugar output without producing the desired results. The constant mobilization for war, coupled with the ad hoc nature of the government, created havoc among the numerous organizations, and frustrated attempts at long-term planning. Notwithstanding these setbacks, INRA had, by the end of 1962, ended rural unemployment, and built fifty new hospitals, thousands of houses and shops, and more than a hundred new schools, including the large primary boarding school city built in the Sierra Maestra, and named after the revolutionary, Camilo Cienfuegos, who disappeared in an air crash in 1959.

For much of the 1960's Cuba remained alienated from most of the neighboring Latin American countries as a result of Cuban attempts to export revolution—as Castro characteristically put it, to "make the cordillera of the Andes, the Sierra Maestra of Latin America." But attempts to influence the internal affairs of the Dominican Republic, Venezuela, Bolivia, and elsewhere did not produce tangible results. Only Mexico, among members of the Organization of American States, maintained full diplomatic and commercial relations with Cuba throughout the revolutionary period. However, with the election of Salvador Allende in Chile in 1970 and the return of Juan Peron in Argentina in 1973 the hemispheric diplomatic isolation of Cuba began to crumble.

Under Castro Cuba began to extend its diplomatic ties in the early period, despite the reciprocal disaffection with the Organization of American States. Cuba and the Soviet Union achieved full diplomatic relations early in 1960, and eventually that country replaced the United States as the major trading partner and source of investment capital and military supplies. Beginning in July 1960 the Soviets bought the greater part of the Cuban sugar harvest, and began to spend more money in Cuba than anywhere else. The Castro government concluded an economic agreement which set the quantity of sugar purchased, and extended a loan to Cuba of $100,000,000 at an annual interest rate of 2.5 percent. The Russians also promised to supply Cuba with crude and refined petroleum, iron, steel, aluminum products, chemicals, fertilizers, newsprint, factories, and machinery as well as the technicians to set them up and train Cubans to operate them. Soviet influence became dominant in Cuba at this time. The installation of Soviet missiles in the summer of 1962 brought the world to the brink of war, as the United States forced the Russians to remove their warheads or face a full-scale nuclear war. The Soviets complied.

It was during this period, too, that the celebrated ideological dispute took place between the Soviet Union and China. Many high-ranking members of the Castro government, including Ernesto "Ché" Guevara, remained fascinated by Mao Tse-tung's revolutionary methods; they traveled to China and were impressed by the achievements there since 1949. China, along with many of the Soviet bloc countries, had become an important trading partner of the Cubans. But in the light of the hostility of the United States and the activities of exiled counterrevolutionary Cubans, Soviet military support was crucial for the defense of the revolution. The Cubans continued their close relationship with the Soviet Union.

The early years were extremely difficult for the domestic economy. INRA had failed to boost industrial production, despite—or maybe because of—the widespread nationalization of private property and private industry. INRA had initiated large-scale agrarian reform, but shortages of everything became marked. Meat, milk, eggs, vegetables, and most basic consumer articles were rationed. Part of the problem grew out of the lack of technical evaluation of the agrarian reform structure. Part of the problem stemmed from the rapid changes in the program during its first three years. And part of the problem was beyond the control of politicians and economists. Bad weather, especially hurricanes and floods, seriously affected farming, particularly in 1963 and 1964. The unavailability of manpower, particularly to cut canes, adversely affected the harvest forecasts. Meanwhile the general shortage of skilled persons, accentuated by the exodus, greatly reduced efficiency and productivity. By 1963 these shortcomings were becoming clear. Temporary booms in 1961 foreshadowed some hard times ahead. In late 1961 the Cuban government announced its first five-year plan.

The second stage of the revolution opened with Castro's first visit to Russia during April and May of 1963. The next two years witnessed a period of flux and reassessment. The revolution had been much more secure as a result of the fiasco at Playa Girón, but the country could not relax its vigilance. External threats had been a valuable component in consolidating internal cohesion, and whether the threats were real or imagined, mass mobilization instilled a form of discipline and boosted revolutionary morale.

One lesson had been learned. Cuban economic strength could not be built on the promotion of industry at the expense of sugar production. Despite a potential abundance of raw materials, the island still lacked the energy supplies, the technical capacity, and the requisite administrative cadres to boost industrial production to the point where Cuba could sell on the world market an adequate amount of goods to enable the state to make the necessary purchases it required.

During 1963, therefore, Cuba not only instituted compulsory military service but also inaugurated the second agrarian reform. The implementation of this extensive military service went hand in hand with the increase in the professionalization of the armed forces and a decline in the role and importance of the militias that had been the main instruments of national defense. It also reflected the general awareness at the higher echelons of government that in order to succeed and maximize efficiency the state needed a larger pool of trained, competent managers.

The second agrarian reform reinstituted sugar production and agriculture as the mainstay of the economy. Heavy industrialization went on the back burner. No single commodity could be produced as quickly and as easily as sugar in Cuba. The technical requirements were simple and were already available. The returns came with the harvest of the sugar cane twelve to fifteen months after planting. No other item sold on the world market could compete with the monetary return from sugar sales, so the Cubans returned to sugar production. Along with sugar, other agricultural production was boosted: citrus production, mango, cacao, coffee, and vegetables were given much attention, along with more scientific management of the cattle industry. Labor productivity that had fallen at the end of the first stage was attacked by transfering the surplus labor pool to agriculture and introducing the Soviet system of wage scales, work quotas, and production incentives in the form of bonuses and flattering honors.

It was during this period, too, that the influence of "Ché" Guevara peaked. In late 1964 he went on an extended tour of Asian and African countries, visiting Vietnam and Angola among other countries. The following year, after Castro's long speech attacking the Sino-Soviet dispute, Guevara quietly left Cuba for an unknown destination. In 1965 the Cubans formed the Cuban Communist Party and Central Committee. It was dominated by pro-Castro and pro-Soviet individuals, had a very small membership, and kept a low profile. The Young Communist League was reorganized and merged with the other youth organizations. Guevara's ideal Cuban "New Man" policy, modeled after the Chinese norm, was attempted briefly, with considerable modification, and largely without Guevara's direction.

The replacement of moral incentives by material ones pumped a lot of money into the economy, which upset the attempted equilibrium between supply and demand. The result was not only a rapid extension of black market activity but a reluctance to work mainly because the rewards of working hard—the accumulation of income—brought little satisfaction if the extra income could not be translated into a more comfortable style of life and the pursuit of pleasures. Labor absenteeism, therefore, became marked and often disruptive.

The four years between 1966 and 1970 comprised the third stage of the revolution. The meeting of Latin American communists in November 1964, and the civil war in Santo Domingo in April 1965, culminating in the United States military intervention, rekindled the Cuban desire to export their revolution to certain targeted areas. In January 1966 a tricontinental congress was held in Havana, and 1967 was declared to be the year of "One, Many Heroic Vietnams." These years were the most radical ones for revolution both at home and abroad, with significant changes in organization and direction.

The state moved to eliminate private property and, in 1968, nationalized the hundreds of small businesses ranging from shoemaking to car repairing, from carpentry to night clubs, which had been allowed to coexist with the state operations. The major exemption remained the approximately one-third of the agricultural sector that continued to be in the hands of individual private concerns. An attempt was made to produce a harvest of 10 million tons of sugar in 1970. The goal was never attained, and the massive effort made to meet that goal resulted in severe dislocation in other sectors of the economy and a significant decline in general productivity. Nevertheless the 1970 crop was a record one, and by 1970 Cuban sugar production had achieved a considerable quantitative growth over the prerevolution pattern.

This third stage included a great campaign against bureaucracy. In a number of spheres managerial skills and technical talent were replaced by revolutionary fervor. Military personnel moved into the top ranks of the government, the party, and industry. Workers were organized into brigades and microbrigades, and additional emphasis was placed on nonmaterial incentives as a desirable prerequisite for the revolutionary society of new individuals. Quite unobtrusively, the party assumed command of the government as the duplication of individuals and overlapping of functions made actions by the party indistinguishable from actions of the government. The new military permeated all sectors of the society: workers, soldiers, teachers, writers, and artists.

But while the mass mobilization in brigades facilitated political indoctrination and national self-consciousness, it tended to polarize factions into camps of ideologues and pragmatists. The discomfort of some who conformed may be gleaned in Nicolás Guillen's great poem, "I Declare Myself an Impure Man," which ends (in the excellent translation by Robert Márquez) deploring:

> In short, the purity
> of anyone who never was sufficiently impure
> to know what purity is.

In practice the struggle turned around competing politicoeconomic systems based on either the Soviet or the Chinese model. The Cubanized version of the Soviet model won out.

The fourth phase of the revolution began around 1970 with some sobering realities. The political concept of exporting revolution via tightly organized *focos* had lost its appeal with the untimely death of Guevara in the Bolivian jungles in 1967. The Cuban model of socialism had failed dismally to meet established goals of production and required levels of productivity. Ad hoc fiscal planning and revolutionary fervor had proved poor substitutes for central planning and conventionally organized, realistic structure and coordination. Above all, an independent Cuba—that is without massive Soviet support— was unrealistic and unviable. The fourth stage, therefore, brought a return to orthodoxy. Sugar production was again deemphasized, and in sugar as in other sectors of the economy, more realistic levels of production were set and some were attained. The return to orthodoxy bore fruit. Long-term planning, plus the use of computer techniques to measure labor and capital efficiency, resulted in marked increases in availability of food, and consequently in consumption. Along with the restoration of material incentives went manipulated pricing systems designed to reduce the money glut by encouraging spending for

"luxury" items, additional food, and vacations. But return to orthodoxy also meant a return to the emphasis on training, managerial
skills, and established minimal standards. Hierarchical organization
returned to the army, management, and political organizations.

The structure of the revolution was formally institutionalized. Reorganization took place at all levels from the party down to the National Association of Small Farmers and the Young Communist
League. Party activities became distinct from the government, and
its membership and visibility increased, culminating in the first congress in 1975 and general elections in October 1976. The general elections followed local union elections in 1971, and partial or regional
elections in 1973.

Return to orthodoxy also meant a significant increase in the influence and assistance of the Soviet Union. Castro paid two visits to
Russia during the period, reciprocated by top Soviet officials, including Premier Leonid Brezhnev. Russia signed a number of trade agreements with Cuba, increasing the price paid for sugar and nickel, increasing technical aid, deferring repayments of previous loans and
interests, and allowing Cuba to have more access to international markets. Agreements negotiated with Canada and Argentina increased
significantly the availability of consumer durables, and brought the
first long run of prosperity to the island—a prosperity that became a
temporary boom afer the dramatic increase of sugar prices in 1973
and 1974. In keeping with Soviet-American détente, Cuba reduced
its manifest support of worldwide revolution, but did not retreat
from specific intervention. In the mid-1970's, Cuban military assistance made the difference in the political resolution of the postin-
dependence Angolan civil war. At the same time, Cuban technical
missions have been active in friendly countries, building schools, hospitals, and mass housing from neighboring Jamaica to far away Chile.
(The Cubans were expelled from Chile after the overthrow and assassination of Chilean President Salvator Allende.)

After nearly two decades, the Cuban revolution has made significant progress. Education, health care, social services, and housing
have been extended to all the population regardless of social status

and geographical abode. Not all Cubans are well-fed, well-housed, well-cared-for, and well-educated. Political prisoners still remain an issue of international importance. But the vast majority of the population has access to facilities their ancestors would never have dreamed about. Despite the strong position of the Soviet Union in Cuban affairs, Cubans feel a greater sense of nationalism, personal freedom, and identification with their country than ever before. The government, for the first time in the history of the republic, is honest, popular, and genuinely concerned about the general welfare. Cubans have become socialists without being any less Cuban. Above all the Cuban Revolution has become respectable internationally, and its advice and assistance are welcome in areas where only shortly before they were despised.

One reason for the growing popularity of the Cuban Revolution within the Caribbean area may be the recent growth of nationalism—or at least statism—in the region. The Caribbean zone, like Africa and Asia, felt the centrifugal winds of political decolonization. To new independent states seeking to establish some form of identity and independence, the Cuban model seemed attractive, if not totally acceptable. At least it showed that a small Caribbean state, with some luck, some sacrifice, and some outside goodwill, could ameliorate the conditions of life for its rapidly growing masses. But success hinged on local control of the political apparatus. To secure the nation, it was first necessary to constitute the state.

In the English Antilles, no consensus existed among the intelligentsia concerning the exact nature of such a state. But both in Great Britain and in the West Indies there was a small, vocal support for a federation of the British islands and the two mainland enclaves of British Guiana and British Honduras. The ideas go back to the middle of the nineteenth century, when British officials were looking for some way to reduce the mounting administrative costs and embarrassment of small colonies which seemed economically unviable. There were also some hesitant steps toward confederation. In 1871 the Leeward Islands Confederation was constituted. An attempt to incorporate with Canada failed, but the talk of a federation of some sort continually haunted discussions about the political future of the English Caribbean. While individuals from the region often participated in these discussions, the most serious proposals came from a series of reports sponsored by the British Parliament: the Royal Commission of 1882; the Royal Commission of 1897; the Major Wood Report of 1922; and the Royal Commission of 1938.

After 1920 a number of shared organizations or common associations lent some practical experience to the idea of confederation. By 1958 the English Caribbean had common participation in labor unions, trade and commerce, bar associations, a Civil Service Federation, cricket teams, and, the most federal of all, the Imperial College of Tropical Agriculture, the University College of the West Indies, and the West Indian Meteorological Service. All these associations, however, were weaker than the local units, had a less coherent view of the West Indies than their names and functions suggested, and were often out of touch with the masses locally or regionally. Finally, in a series of conferences between 1944 and 1958—with almost indecent haste toward the end of the period—the concept of political federation was brought to fruition. With British Guiana and British Honduras abstaining, Jamaica, The Leeward Islands, the Windwards Islands, Barbados, Trinidad, and Tobago became federated.

The federation lasted four years. It was born in strife and rivalry over a number of issues, such as the geographical location of the capital, imposition of federal taxation, freedom of travel, a federal constitution, and a federal custom's union. As soon as the paeans to the resolution of these factors had appeared, they were deluged by the obituaries and postmortems of a noble idea that passed with the fleeting fascination of a tropical storm. For in 1961 in the midst of renewed squabbling between the federal government and its major component units—Jamaica, Trinidad, and Barbados—Jamaica held a referendum which voted itself out of the federation. Prime Minister Eric Williams of Trinidad had made a laconic prophecy of axiomatic political astuteness: "One from ten leaves nothing," meaning that the defection of any of the ten member states would destroy the federal idea. The West Indian Federation collapsed in 1962.

Many reasons have been proposed for the impromptu termination of the federal experience. All have some merit; none is singularly persuasive; and some are rather farfetched. Insular political squabbling among the politicians, the weakness of the constitutional structure, the great distance between the islands, the inability of West Indians to rule themselves, and the alien imposition of the political form itself have all been put forward with varying degrees of seriousness as primary causes of the collapse. But the fundamental failure of the West Indian Federation went beyond the superficial reasons advanced above.

Its failure stemmed from the essential conflict between competing forms of nationalism, or rather, more specifically between the incipient *patriachiquismo* of Trinidad and Jamaica, and the nationalism or internationalism of the included units as a whole. Because the federal government lacked either the authority or the military might to restrain the centrifugalism of the core units—such as the northerners had in the United States Civil War against the South—it had to accept its own demise.

Nationalism at the level of a grand federated system was alien to the Caribbean. But it was no more alien than European colonialism was to the region in 1500. There were some historical facts that had to be confronted if the federal structure were to be given a fair chance of success.

Both Jamaica and Trinidad and, to a lesser extent, Barbados, had achieved some measure of internal self-government within the British colonial system between 1944 and 1956. Jamaica and Trinidad, with their bauxite and petroleum, thought that they had the potential for a diversified industrial base, toward which they were advancing with a series of industrial incentive laws that proved long on promises but short on achievement. Before the shallowness of this industrial potential became patent, both islands insisted on measures to protect their fledgling industries. In short their insular economic interests took precedence over their sense of common identity. In order to protect these particular interests, both islands insisted on measures that would limit the power of the federal government to impose taxation on their incipient industries, or, in the case of Trinidad, restricted the free flow of citizens of the federation from one region of limited opportunities to another of less restricted opportunities. So the very fears which had caused British Honduras and British Guiana to sit on the sidelines led to the creation of a weak federal center where each unit tried to yield as little power and autonomy as it could in order to retain as much as was possible. It was an impossible situation from the start, compounded by a penchant to postpone discussion and resolution of the difficult issues, or merely to divide equally, if ambiguously, the powers between the central government and the component units. *Primus inter pares* is a great slogan but an unwieldy basis for procedure. Federal nationalism ran headlong into unit nationalism and lost.

Gordon K. Lewis has proposed another very perceptive analysis of the failure. He suggests that the West Indies (as well as their English sponsors) were too preoccupied with the form of the federation. In their myopic concern for form they created a structure which accentuated the worst features of Caribbean societies. A federation, therefore, "was in itself a grossly misconceived structure to impose upon West Indian society" because "it assumed the almost permanent divisibility of the society." Lewis then goes·on to argue that the assumption should have been that the regions comprised one unit, and a political prescription should have been made for a unified state. Such an assumption, however, could only have been generated by a people with more *conciencia de sí* than was evident in the British West Indies between 1944 and 1962.

The failure of the West Indies Federation paved the way for the national independence of the separate states. Jamaica and Trinidad and Tobago gained their independence in 1962, Barbados in 1966, along with British Guiana (which became the Republic of Guyana in 1970), and Grenada and the Bahamas in 1974. The other units began to move either toward independent statehood, or associated statehood with Great Britain.

Political independence created the states in which Caribbean nationhood could develop. The fact of statehood became certified by acceptance and representation in such international bodies as the

United Nations and the Organization of American States. But the establishment of the state and its structured paraphernalia does not make the process of creating a nation any easier. In some cases it may even become more difficult. For statehood was achieved without the coalescing hostility of an external enemy. No vicious civil war of national purification such as the British North American war of 1776 to 1783, or the Spanish American wars of independence between 1810 and 1823, or the Haitian civil war between 1788 and 1804, or the Cuban struggle for independence between 1868 and 1898 accompanied British West Indian statehood. Area leaders in the 1960's and 1970's found a metropolitan government enthusiastic in its desire to surrender the burdens of imperialism in the region. British West Indians would willingly have transferred their subordination to the United States—as Alexander Bustamante publicly offered after Jamaican independence in 1962. But times had changed. The United States preferred imperialism without colonialism, and took its hegemony in the area for granted anyway. It offered fiscal aid and negotiated some agreements with Trinidad and Tobago that gave back, in 1967, the naval base at Chaguaramas granted by the British in 1941 offered $30 million in grants from the Agency for International Development, and released to local control in late 1971 the missile tracking station operated locally by the United States Air Force. Agreements with Jamaica have facilitated tens of millions of dollars in grants from the Agency for International Development and the Export-Import Bank and the American Peace Corps. Agreements with Guyana have resulted in the entry of more than $55 million of public United States funds between 1964 and 1971. Only Barbados had not benefited from the benevolence of the United States between 1964 and 1976.

But political independence also had other consequences. Colonialism had, like a tattered glove, partially insulated the ruling classes from the realities and handicaps of an agricultural export economy with a population expanding with socially explosive force. The new governments had to find some new ways to deal with old problems. The annual population growth rate hovers around 3 percent in the

Caribbean, and most governments have considerable difficulty in providing the social services required by their citizens. The fiscal problems confronting the states after the British government decided to
enter the European Common Market, and sterling ceased to be one
of the world's reliable currencies, have been immense. In some cases,
especially in Jamaica, Trinidad, and Guyana (though not in Barbados
as late as 1970), the United States has taken up the decline in the
British Antillean sector of the export trade. For example, before independence in Trinidad and Tobago, Great Britain handled about
33 percent of the Trinidadian import and export trade. In 1971, however, British trade had declined to about 12 percent of the total, while
trade with the United States had grown to 41 percent. Similarly the
United States handled more than 50 percent of Jamaica's exports and
43 percent of its imports in 1970. Without exception all the Caribbean states import far more than they export, although the recent increase in petroleum prices has altered that situation for Trinidad and
Tobago after 1973.

The economic necessities have forced some common action. In
1968 the English Antilles joined Guyana and Belize to form the
Caribbean Free Trade Area (CARIFTA) in an attempt to pool their
individually small domestic markets and enhance their appeal to industry. In 1970 the Caribbean Development Bank (CDB) was established, and in 1973 CARIFTA turned into a common market of sorts.
Nevertheless the English Antilles have not moved much in the direction of incorporating the other free states in the area, despite some
recent rhetoric to that effect. Members of the Commonwealth Caribbean, as the political leaders of the British West Indies like to call
themselves, have been loathe to broaden their vision and their identity to include the non-English-speaking members of their Caribbean
community.

The economic problems in the Caribbean—and this is by no means
restricted to the English Antilles—are more than increasing a gross
national product or securing adequate public funding for the costs of
public projects and public administration. The economic problem
also entails the redistribution of resources within the state. This has

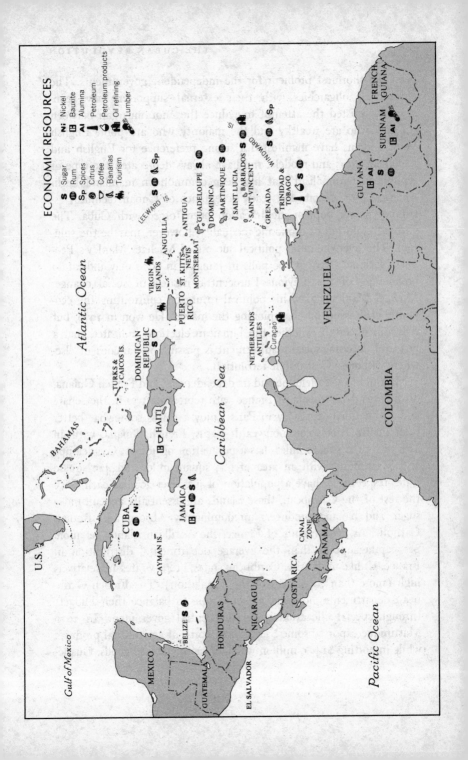

ECONOMIC RESOURCES

S   Sugar
🥃 Rum
Sp Spices
☕ Coffee
🍌 Bananas
🌴 Tourism
Ni Nickel
▣   Bauxite
Al Alumina
🛢   Petroleum
⛽ Petroleum products
⛽ Oil refining
🌲 Lumber

been the thorniest problem for the independent governments. The entrenched oligarchies with their external supporters have consistently resisted the attempt to reduce the enormous gap between the few who are wealthy and the majority who are poor. English West Indians have manifested a strong preference for English and American ideas and models, and have always deprecated the type of republican nationalism that has been common on mainland Latin America. Nor, despite the ready acceptance of Cuban technical assistance, has a popular identification been forged with Cuba. The Cuban resolution of economic inequality, however, may be the solution. The overwhelming political success of Michael Manley's People's National Party at the polls in Jamaica in 1976 may indicate a broadening of the previous Eurocentric models of social change. Michael Manley staked his political future on confronting the economic class issue, on championing the masses. He won in 1976, but it is still uncertain whether the Jamaican elections indicated that a peaceful, internal social readjustment is possible in Jamaica or elsewhere without a Castro-style revolution.

Martinique, Guadeloupe and its dependencies, and French Guiana, as overseas departments of France with representatives in the senate and the national assembly in Paris, enjoy a status somewhat better than Puerto Rico's commonwealth status. French Guiana, with an area of 35,100 square miles, has a population of 40,000. Guadeloupe and Martinique, with an area of 689 square miles and 425 square miles respectively, have a population of just over 300,000 each. Like the rest of the Caribbean, these islands are essentially agricultural—sugar and banana producers, predominantly African and Roman Catholic. As departments of France, the Antillean islands get more per capita support than the average departmental distribution in France. Unlike most other Caribbean states, literacy rates are relatively high (more than 70 percent of the population). The French Caribbean departments, however, are only able to balance their budgets through special allocations from the central government. In 1970 Martinique exported some $30 million worth of agricultural produce, while importing $145.9 million worth of manufactured goods. Guadeloupe exports that same year amounted to $34 million, and its imports to $150.0 million. Despite criticism from time to time of the status of territories, no strong separatist sentiments currently exist in any of the French regions. However, with a growing population, a high unemployment rate, and a fluctuating international economy, the status of the territories may change in the future.

This was the experience in the Netherlands Antilles and Surinam. A charter in 1954 conceded equality of status between the Netherlands and its overseas territories, the latter being internally autonomous. By the late 1960's public unrest began in Aruba and Curaçao, which brought down the government, while Surinam began a series of political crises that ended in complete independence on November 25, 1975.

The contemporary scene in the Caribbean is one of superficial diversity, accentuated by the historical fragmentation remaining as a legacy to the days of imperialism and colonialism. But a great deal of commonality, if not a patent community, underlies this diversity. The most common and most profound aspect of Caribbean life is a strong dependence on the outside world. Cuba depends on the Soviet Union, Puerto Rico on the United States, The Commonwealth Caribbean on Britain, Canada, and the United States, Martinique, Guadeloupe, and Guiana on France, Curaçao and Surinam on the Netherlands. This trend is unlikely to cease in the immediate future. The economic situation, while not hopeless, cannot be termed encouraging. With the exception of Cuba, throughout the region the increases in per capita income seem to have been accompanied by increases in the unemployment rate and a decline in the real standard of living of a significant sector of the population. Incentives to attract new industries have not been successful in reducing economic ills. The Puerto Rican "Operation Bootstrap," once highly hailed, proved eventually to have more style than substance. Elsewhere the belief still prevails that external prescriptions best solve internal problems, and the stream of consultants from the industrialized nations has perhaps been the single most serious handicap to Caribbean social development. If the early Caribbean societies manifested a dichotomy between the settler and the exploiter colonies, the legacy of that dichotomy can only be removed by a unified inward-looking, self-generated regional action.

No ideology imported to the Caribbean will thrive without modification. This was true of capitalism, mercantilism, "Black Power," and communism. The challenge of the future will be to produce new and creative solutions to local problems, not to import, mimic, and adapt. The circumstances of the Caribbean force it to be a revolutionary society, not to destroy or disturb, but to survive. And that is a reality the rest of the world will have to accept sooner or later.

Political Chronology

1492   October 12, Christopher Columbus, sailing under the Spanish flag, sights land on Guanahani in the Bahamas, and begins the subsequent integration of America, Europe, and Africa. The Atlantic World takes shape.
October 28, Columbus lands in Cuba.
December 6, Columbus lands in Santo Domingo and, after the wreck of his flagship, the *Santa Maria*, establishes the first European settlement in the New World.

1493   Second voyage of Columbus. Between November 3 and November 19, sights a number of islands between Dominica and Puerto Rico. On November 14 the first sea battle takes place in Caribbean waters between the Spanish *flotilla* and a group of Indian canoes.

1494   May 5, Jamaican north shore explored.

1498   Third voyage of Columbus. Discovers Trinidad on July 31, and lands on the continent across the Gulf of Paria on August 5. First gold rush on Santo Domingo.

1501   Nicolás de Ovando named governor of Santo Domingo, effectively revoking the original Columbus charter.

1502   April 3, Columbus's fourth and last voyage begins at Seville, and after a delay, lands at Martinique on June 15. Battered by storms, the fleet explores the islands and the coast from Honduras to Panama. Ovando arrives in Santo Domingo.

1503-4   Columbus marooned on north shore of Jamaica with 115 men. *Casa de Contratación* established in Seville to regulate shipping and trade to the New World, as well as collect the "royal fifth" of gold, pearls, and trade goods. Spanish expansion to Puerto Rico begins.

1508   Juan Ponce de León officially settles Puerto Rico and finds gold. Indians on Santo Domingo rapidly diminishing.

1509-10   Juan de Esquivel settles Jamaica. First sugar mills begun on Santo Domingo.

1511   Diego Velazquez settles Cuba. Council of the Indies established. Fray Antonio de Montesinos preaches a sermon against ill-treatment of Indians which converts an *encomendero* of Santo Domingo, Bartolomé de las Casas.

1512   Laws of Burgos, first European colonial charter, attempts to establish proper official relations between Spanish and non-Spanish society in the Americas.

1515   First samples of Caribbean sugar sent to Spain.

1516   Las Casas appointed Protector of the Indians.

1518   August. Charles V grants permission for 4000 African slaves to be sent to the Antilles to relieve the labor shortage, especially in the mines.

1519   Hernán Cortes sails from Cuba to conquer Mexico.

1542   New Laws of the Indies. Spanish begin convoy system to protect their silver fleet from pirates, privateers, and envious European rival powers.

1517-1600   Challenges to Spanish hegemony in the Caribbean lead to expansion of escorted *flotillas* and retrenchment of enclaves.

1595   Spain begins formal grant of *Asientos* to supply slaves to the
              Indies.

1604   Spanish concede inability to monopolize the Americas in
              Treaty of London. Dutch developing salt industry off Vene-
              zuelan coast.

1609   Spanish concede limitations of their American possessions at
              Truce of Antwerp.

1604-1620   Attempts by English and Dutch to plant permanent colonies
              on periphery of Spanish possessions in Eastern Antilles and
              Guianas. Dutch succeed in Essequibo in 1616.

1621   Dutch West India Company formally established.

1624   English settle Barbados and St. Kitts. Dutch settle Berbice.

1625   English and Dutch settle St. Croix.

1628   Dutchman Piet Heyn captures Spanish treasure fleet off
              Matanzas Bay, Cuba. Nevis settled by English.

1630-1697   Age of the buccaneers.

1630-1640   Dutch establish themselves on Curaçao, Saba, St. Martin,
              St. Eustatia. English settle Antigua, Montserrat, St. Lucia;
              French settle Martinique and Guadeloupe.

1640   Population of Barbados estimated at 30,000.

1647   First Barbados sugar sent to England.

1649   First slave revolt in Barbados.

1652   Navigation Ordinance attempts to implement mercantilism,
              leads to series of naval wars between English and Dutch.

1652   First Anglo-Dutch War.

1655   Jamaica captured from the Spanish.

1666-1667   Second Anglo-Dutch War.

1672-1678   Third Anglo-Dutch War. Royal Africa Company organized by English.

1685   French systematize their slave system by promulgation of the *Code Noir*.

1692   Earthquake destroys city of Port Royal, Jamaica.

1697   Spain cedes Western Santo Domingo to France at the Treaty of Ryswyck.

1702   French Guinea Company gains *Asiento*.

1713   England exacts from France and Spain transfer of the *Asiento* to a semiofficial commercial front, the South Sea Company.

1739   Spanish government suspends *Asiento*, leading to War of Jenkins' Ear.

1739-1763   Wars between European powers over Caribbean commerce and possessions. Capture of Havana by English. French lose all possessions except for Saint-Domingue during the war.

1734   First Maroon War in Jamaica.

1740   Real Compañía Mercantil de la Habana, or Havana Company, formed to develop Cuban slave trade and agriculture.

1754   Moravian Missions established in Jamaica.

1755   Barcelona Company chartered to trade with Puerto Rico and Santo Domingo.

1767   French sugar exports exceed British in Caribbean.

1772   English Chief Justice, Lord Mansfield, declares slavery illegal in England.

1774   Census puts population of Cuba at 171,620.

1766-1776   Expansion of Free Trade in Caribbean.

1778   Ackee fruit tree introduced to Jamaica from West Africa.

1788   Outbreak of the French Revolution. *Societé des Amis des Noirs* founded in France.

1789   Cuba begins free trade in slaves. Methodists begin missions in Jamaica.

1791   Havana Economic Society formed by 27 creoles. Slave revolt begins in Saint-Domingue.

1793   Breadfruit tree introduced to Jamaica from Tahiti. British Navy captures Martinique, Guadeloupe, and St. Lucia.

1795   Second Maroon War in Jamaica. Carib War in St. Vincent.

1797   Trinidad captured by British.

1798   Toussaint Louverture establishes the domination of the slaves.

1799   Toussaint made governor-general of Saint-Domingue and captures Spanish Santo Domingo.

1800   Scottish Missionary Society begins work in Jamaica.

1801   Toussaint announces first constitution of Saint-Domingue.

1802   Napoleon Bonaparte decides to reconquer Saint-Domingue, and kidnaps Toussaint.

1804   Jean-Jacques Dessalines declares independence of Haiti. Denmark abolishes its trans-Atlantic slave trade.

1808   British trans-Atlantic slave trade abolished. United States follows suit.

1811   Act of British Parliament declares slave trading felony.

1813   Sweden abolishes slave trade.

1814   Holland abolishes slavery. First English Baptist missions
            in Jamaica.

1815   End of Napoleonic Wars. British purchase Demerara, Esse-
            quibo, and Berbice from the Dutch.

1816   Cuban sugar planters gain right to deal in real estate.

1818   France declares slave trade officially illegal. Holland abolishes
            slave trade.

1820   Spain, on receipt of £400,000, declares the slave trade
            illegal.

1823   Grenada grants full citizenship to free nonwhites. Large slave
            revolt in British Guiana.

1827   British Parliament declares slave trading piracy, therefore
            punishable by death.

1828   Order in Council abolishes all civil and military distinctions
            in Crown Colonies.

1831-1832   Antimissionary riots in Barbados, Jamaica, and British
            Guiana. Jamaica and Barbados grant full citizenship to free
            nonwhites. Tax on manumission abolished in French An-
            tilles, and free persons of color granted full citizenship.

1833   Emancipation Act passed by British Parliament initiates ap-
            prenticeship system in British Antilles. Grande Anse slave
            revolt in Martinique. Compulsory registration of slaves in
            French Antilles.

1834   Havana-Güines railroad begun. British Guiana imports la-
            borers from Madeira. Antigua abolishes slavery without ap-
            prenticeship. Elected colonial councils on restricted franchise
            begin in Martinique and Guadeloupe. French Society for the
            Abolition of Slavery founded to replace *Amis des Noirs*.

1836   Slavery declared illegal in France.

1838   Havana-Güines railroad completed. Slavery finally abolished in British Antilles.

1840   Codrington College completed in Barbados.

1846   Sweden abolishes slavery. Peasant revolt in Haiti crushed. Act of British Parliament removes preference on colonial sugar imported into mother country.

1848   Slavery abolished in French and Danish Antilles. French Antilles given direct representation in National Assembly.

1849-1852   Narciso López expeditions against Cuba.

1854   French Antillean representation in National Assembly suspended until 1871. Plans by the U.S. to purchase Cuba fail.

1863   Holland abolishes slavery.

1865   Morant Bay "revolt" in Jamaica. Crown Colony reestablished. Santo Domingo declares its independence.

1868-1878   Ten Years War in Cuba.

1873   Puerto Rico abolishes slavery. 53 members of cruiser *Virginia* shot in Santiago harbor for aiding Cuban insurgents.

1878   Pact of Zanjón ends Cuban Civil War.

1895-1898   Cuban War of Independence.

1897   Spain grants autonomy to Puerto Rico.

1899   Spain cedes Puerto Rico to the U.S. at Treaty of Paris. U.S. military occupation of Cuba begins (until 1902).

1900   Puerto Rico becomes U.S. territory.

1902   Platt Amendment gives the U.S. the right to intervene in Cuban affairs, and to establish a naval station at Guantánamo Bay.

1902   Republic of Cuba established. Major volcanic eruptions of
            Souffrière in St. Vincent kills 2000 persons, and of Mont
            Pelée in Martinique. Virgin Islands Legislative Council
            abolished. Danish legislature refuses to sanction sale of An-
            tillean Islands to the U.S. Urban riots in Montego Bay, Ja-
            maica, and Port-of-Spain, Trinidad.

1906   Second U.S. intervention in Cuba (until 1909).

1907   U.S. intervenes in Dominican Republic by control of
            customs.

1908   Riots in St. Lucia.

1912   Demonstrations by Afro-Cubans in Oriente led by Estenoz
            and Ivonet, leading to loss of approximately 3000 black lives.
            Riots in Kingston, Jamaica. Revolt in the Dominican Re-
            public.

1915   Revolt in Haiti. U.S. occupies Haiti (until 1934).

1916   U.S. occupies the Dominican Republic (until 1924).

1917   Puerto Ricans become citizens of U.S. Danish Antilles sold
            for £25,000,000 to U.S. East Indian migration to English
            Antilles ceases.

1919   Riots in Belize. British Honduras, and San Fernando, Trini-
            dad.

1921   Imperial College of Tropical Agriculture opened in Trinidad.

1925   Isle of Pines issue settled in favor of Cuba. Gerardo Ma-
            chado becomes president of Cuba.

1926-1935   Several hurricanes sweep through the Caribbean, while
            earthquake tremors are felt on Montserrat for two years.

1928   British Guiana abolishes old constitution and establishes a
            Legislative Council.

1930   Pedro Albizu Campos elected president of Puerto Rican
            Nationalist Party. Trujillo assumes power in Dominican
            Republic.

1933   Machado overthrown in Cuba. Fulgencio Batista emerges.

1935   Riot in St. Vincent.

1936   Constitutional change in British Honduras, British Wind-
            ward, and British Leeward Islands provides for elected mem-
            bers to the Legislative Councils, with a majority elected in
            the Windwards.

1937   Riots in Barbados and Trinidad. Trujillo massacres 20,000
            Haitian cane cutters in Dominican Republic.

1938   Riots in Jamaica. British appoint the Moyne Commission
            to investigate the conditions in the British West Indies.

1940   Luis Muñoz Marin becomes senate president in Puerto Rico.
            Cuba gets new constitution. Dominica separated from Lee-
            ward Islands and included in Windward Islands. Develop-
            ment and Welfare Organization established for all British
            Antilles.

1941   Anglo-American Agreement gives bases to U.S. throughout
            the English Antilles.

1942   Anglo-American Commission established.

1943   Caribbean Regiment reestablished in English Antilles. Brit-
            ish Guiana gets elected majority.

1944   Universal adult suffrage in Jamaica, with limited self-govern-
            ment. Women given vote in Barbados, British Guiana, and
            Bermuda.

1945   Expansion of electoral franchise in British Guiana and Brit-
            ish Honduras.

1946   Universal adult suffrage introduced to Trinidad. First British
            Antilles census. Puerto Rico gets first local governor, Jesús T.

Piñero. Martinique and Guadeloupe made Overseas Departments of France.

1947   Conference held at Montego Bay, Jamaica, to discuss British West Indian Federation. Puerto Rico allowed to elect its own governor.

1948   Colonial Development Corporation established for English Antilles. British Honduras threatened by invasion from Guatemala. Luis Muñoz Marín becomes first elected governor of Puerto Rico.

1949   Royal Charter granted for the University College of the West Indies.

1950   Universal adult suffrage introduced to Barbados. Trinidad gets new constitution. Widespread riots in Puerto Rico over constitutional issue.

1951   Universal adult suffrage introduced to Leeward and Windward Islands. Riots in Antigua and Grenada.

1952   Batista coup d'état in Cuba. Commonwealth status established for Puerto Rico. Universal adult suffrage granted to British Guiana. Dutch constitution amended to alter status of colonial possessions.

1953   Fidel Castro leads unsuccessful Moncada attack in Santiago de Cuba. British Guiana constitution suspended.

1954   Surinam and Dutch Antilles made autonomous and equal with the Netherlands.

1956   Eric Williams forms People's National Movement in Trinidad.

1957   François Duvalier elected president of Haiti; writes new constitution.

1958   Federation established among 10 territories of the British Antilles (dissolved in 1962).

1959   Fidel Castro comes to power in Cuba.

1961   Trujillo assassinated. Abortive U.S. invasion of Cuba. Racial
            violence in British Guiana.

1962   Jamaica, Trinidad, and Tobago become independent. First
            free elections in 38 years in Dominican Republic won by
            Juan Bosch.

1965   U.S. invades Dominican Republic with OAS troops.

1966   Barbados and British Guiana become independent.

1967   Trinidad and Tobago and Barbados, join the Organization
            of American States. "Che" Guevara dies in Bolivia.

1968   Caribbean Free Trade Area formed.

1969   Jamaica joins Organization of American States. Armed
            clashes between Guyana and Surinam. Riots in Curaçao.

1970   Guyana becomes a republic. Riots in Trinidad.

1973   Fidel Castro makes two-month tour of Eastern Europe, Rus-
            sia, and Africa.

1974   Castro visits Guyana and Trinidad en route to West Africa,
            Algiers, India, and North Vietnam. Jamaica, Trinidad and
            Tobago, Guyana, and Barbados form Caribbean Community
            and Common Market (CARICOM). Grenada and the Ba-
            hamas gain independence. Riots in Surinam.

1975   OAS foreign ministers vote to alter its 9-year boycott of Cuba
            and allow individual states to reestablish normal diplomatic
            relations. Surinam becomes independent as the Republic of
            Surinam.

A Selected Guide to
the Literature on the Caribbean

The historical literature of the Caribbean is abundant in quantity and varied in quality. Some periods and some themes have received more attention from scholars than others, especially themes dealing with slavery and the Cuban Revolution. The range of questions examined and the methodological sophistication of the best works compare most favorably with those in any other field of history. The major handicap is the frequent restriction of these themes to a single island, nation, or cultural area. Few authors have tried to integrate the events in a common history, although the anthropologist, Sidney Mintz, has been advocating this approach for the past twenty years. The reader willing to pursue a number of parallel studies will find the activity as richly rewarding as the sources.

The best of the general histories to date is John Parry and Philip M. Sherlock, *A Short History of the West Indies* (London, 1956), although its Anglo-Caribbean slant is strong. Eric Williams, *From Columbus to Castro. The History of the Caribbean 1492-1969* (New York, 1970), is rich in figures for the English Caribbean, and tries to bring in the non-English region. John E. Fagg, *Cuba, Haiti and the Dominican Republic* (Englewood Cliffs, N.J., 1965), provides a useful, if somewhat superficial account for those three places. Elsa Goveia, *A Study on the Historiography of the British West Indies to the End of the Nineteenth Century*

(Mexico, 1956), is a superb evaluation of the writings on the region, and recognizes many of the non-English writers whose works were relevant to the English Antilles.

The following provide good introductions to the regional geography: W. M. Davis, *The Lesser Antilles* (New York, 1926); Salvador Massip, *Introducción a la Geografía de Cuba* (Havana, 1942); G. Canet, *Atlas de Cuba* (Cambridge, Mass., 1949); Harold Wood, *Northern Haiti: Land Use and Settlement* (Toronto, 1963); Robert T. Hill, *Cuba and Puerto Rico, with the Other Islands of the West Indies* (New York, 1898); Robert C. West, *Middle America: Its Lands and Peoples* (New Jersey, 1966); Colin G. Clarke, *Kingston, Jamaica. Urban Growth and Social Change, 1692-1962* (Berkeley, 1975); R. M. Bent and E. L. Bent-Golding, *A Complete Geography of Jamaica* (London, 1966); Helmut Blume, *Die Westindischen Inseln* (Braunschweig, 1968).

Population figures for the pre-Hispanic period vary widely. I have looked at Angel Rosenblat, *La Población Indígena y el mestizaje en América*, 2 vols. (Buenos Aires, 1954); Carl Sauer, *The Early Spanish Main* (Berkeley and Los Angeles, 1966); Alejandro Lipschutz, "La Despoblación de las Indias Después de la Conquista," *America Indigena*, 26 (1966), 229-247; Sherburne F. Cooke and Woodrow Borah, *Essays in Population History: Mexico and the Caribbean* (Berkeley and Los Angeles, 1971); H. Thomas, *Cuba, the Pursuit of Freedom* (New York, 1971); and, Ramiro Guerra y Sanchez, *et al.*, eds., *Historia de la Nación Cubana*, 10 vols. (Havana, 1952). Cook and Borah's estimate (p. 396) of "not less than 2,500,000 nor more than 5,000,000" persons in Hispaniola in 1496 defies credulity; while Hugh Thomas's inclination (p. 1512) to accept a population of 16,000 for Cuba in 1492 seems extremely cautious. It should be borne in mind that the population of all Spain in 1530 barely exceeded 3 million.

The pre-Hispanic cultures can be followed in: Julian Steward and Louis Faron, *Native Peoples of South America* (New York, 1959); Fernando Portuondo, *Historia de Cuba* (6th ed., Havana, 1965); Mark Harrington, *Cuba before Columbus*, 2 vols. (New York, 1921); Cornelius Osgood, *The Ciboney Culture of Cayo Redondo, Cuba* (New Haven, 1942); Irving Rouse, *Archaeology of the Maniabon Hills* (New Haven, 1942); and by the same author, "The Caribbean Area" in Jesse Jennings and Edward Norbeck, eds., *Prehistoric Man in the New World* (Chicago, 1964), 389-418; "The Caribbean," in Gordon Willey, ed., *Prehistoric Settlement Patterns in the New World* (New York, 1956); *Culture of the Fort Liberté Region, Haiti* (New Haven, 1941); *The Entry of Man into the West Indies* (New Haven, 1960); and, "The Inference of Migrations from Anthropological Evidence," in R. H. Thompson, ed., *Migrations in New World Culture* (Arizona, 1958), 64-68. Also useful are Manuel Rivero de la Calle, *Los Aborígines de Cuba* (Havana, 1963); William C. Sturtevant, *The Significance of Ethnological Similarities between Southeastern North America and the Antilles* (New Haven, 1960); J. A. Bullbrook, *On the Excavation of a Shell Mound at Palo Seco, Trinidad* (New Haven, 1953); Marshall B. McKusick, *Aboriginal Canoes in the West Indies* (New Haven, 1960); and Eric Wolf, *Sons of the Shaking Earth. The People of Mexico and Guatemala—Their Land, History and Culture* (Chicago, 1959).

The early interchange between Europeans and Americans is dealt with by: Cristóbal Colon, *Los Cuatro Viajes del Almirante y Su Testamento* (Edición y prólogo de Ignacio B. Anzoátegui, 4th ed., Madrid, 1964), or the uneven English translation of J. M. Cohen, ed., *The Four Voyages of Christopher Columbus* (Penguin Books, 1969). Samuel E. Morrison, *Admiral of the Ocean Sea: A Life of Christopher Columbus*, 2 vols. (Boston, 1942), is the most majestic and readable of the many Columbus biographies which are excellently treated in Martin Torodash, "Columbus Historiography since 1939," *Hispanic American Historical Review*, 46 (Nov. 1966), 409-428. No better treatment of the medical and biological impact exists than Alfred W. Crosby, Jr., *The Columbian Exchange. Biological and Cultural Consequences of 1492* (Westport, 1972). Richard B. Moore, *Caribs, "Cannibals" and Human Relations* (New York, 1972), persuasively argues that the Caribs were not savage eaters of human flesh. The most detailed description of early Carib society comes from R. P. Jean-Baptiste Du Tertre, *Histoire Général des Iles . . . des S. Cristophe, de la Guadeloupe, de la Martinique, et Autres dans l'Amérique*, 3 vols. (1667-1671), and the monumental work of the Abbé Raynall, *History of the Settlements and Trade of the Europeans in the East and West Indies*, 6 vols. (London, 1798, reissued Conn., 1969).

The general literature on the expansion of Europe in the fifteenth and sixteenth centuries is essential background reading. Among the best works are: William H. McNeill, *The Rise of the West* (Chicago, 1963); Boies Penrose, *Travel and Discovery in the Renaissance, 1420-1620* (Cambridge, Mass., 1952); John H. Elliot, *The Old World and the New, 1492-1650* (London, 1970); C. R. Boxer, *The Portuguese Seaborne Empire 1600-1800* (London, 1965); Charles Verlinden and Florentino Pérez-Embid, *Cristóbal Colon y el Descubrimiento de América* (Madrid, 1967); Ralph Davis, *The Rise of the Atlantic Economies* (Ithaca, 1973); John H. Parry, *The Age of Reconaissance* (New York, 1963); T. Bentley Duncan, *Atlantic Islands. Madeira, the Azores and the Cape Verdes in*

Seventeenth Century Commerce and Navigation (Chicago, 1972). The travails of the fledgling Spanish settlements are set forth in: Troy S. Floyd, *The Columbus Dynasty in the Caribbean, 1492-1526* (Albuquerque, 1973); Ursula Lamb, *Fray Nicolás de Ovando, Governador de las Indias* (Madrid, 1956); Guillermo Céspedes del Castillo, "La Sociedad Colonial Americana en los Siglos XVI y XVII," in J. Vicens Vives, ed., *Historia de España y América* (2nd ed., 5 vols., Barcelona, 1971); Sherburne F. Cook and Woodrow Borah, *Essays in Population History: Mexico and the Caribbean*, vol. 1 (Berkeley, 1971); and Irene A. Wright, *The Early History of Cuba, 1492-1586* (New York, 1916; reissued New York, 1970). Wright's study must be used with some caution. She is patently incorrect in saying that Cuban *vecinos* owned the land. They had usufructal tenure of some very large plots, but Diego Velasquez could not alienate what in effect was the king's land. But she is useful in outlining the careers of some of the early Cuban *vecinos* who became distinguished in the later history of the Americas. Bartolomé de las Casas shared an *encomienda* of Indians with Pedro de la Rentería in Trinidad (then located on the present site of Casilda). Bernal Díaz del Castillo, the famous chronicler of the conquest of Mexico, as well as a number of defectors from Pedrarias Dávila's Darien colony settled in Sancti-Spíritus. Vasco Porcallo de Figueroa began a farm in central Camaguey province. Hernán Cortés was an *alcalde* of Santiago de Cuba, the leading Spanish-American port city in 1515. Other valuable sources for the period and the colonial activity include: Bernal Díaz del Castillo, *The Conquest of New Spain* (translated by J. M. Cohen, 4th printing, Baltimore, 1969); Pierre Chaunu, *L'Expansion Européenne du XIIIe au XVe Siècle* (Paris, 1969); Frédéric Mauro, *L'Expansion Européenne 1600-1870* (Paris, 1964); Victorino de Magalhães Godinho, *Os Descubrimentos e Economia Mundial*, 2 vols. (Lisbon, 1963); James Lockhart, *Spanish Peru, 1532-1560* (Madison, 1968), and *The Men of Cajamarca. A Social and Biographical Study of the First Conquerors of Peru* (Austin, 1972), by the same author. Also useful is Silvio Zavala, "The Frontier of Hispanic America," in W. D. Wyman and C. B. Kroeber, eds., *The Frontier in Perspective* (Madison, 1957); and Richard Morse, "The Heritage of Latin America," in Louis Hartz, ed., *The Founding of New Societies* (New York, 1964).

The Spanish background can be followed in Vicens Vives, ed., *Historia*, as well as J. H. Mariéjol, *The Spain of Ferdinand and Isabella* (translated and edited by Benjamin Keen, New Brunswick, N.J., 1961); and George Foster, *Culture and Conquest* (Chicago, 1964).

The intellectual and legal conflicts have a very rich bibliography: Lewis Hanke, *The Spanish Struggle for Justice in the Conquest of America*

(Philadelphia, 1949); *Aristotle and the American Indians. A Study in Race Prejudice in the Modern World* (Bloomington, 1959, 1970); John L. Phelan, *The Millennial Kingdom of the Franciscans in the New World* (Berkeley and Los Angeles, 1956, 1970); *The Kingdom of Quito in the Seventeenth Century* (Madison, 1967); E. N. van Kleffens, *Hispanic Law* (Edinburgh, 1968); and C. A. C. Carter, "Law and Society in Colonial Mexico: Judges in Mexican Society from the Tello de Sandoval *Visita General*, 1543-1547," Ph.D. dissertation, Columbia University, 1971. Peter Boyd-Bowman, *Indice Geobiográfico de Cuarenta Mil Pobladores Españoles de América en el Siglo XVI*, vol. 1 (Bogota, 1964), describes the regional origins of Spaniards coming to the New World before 1519. Other volumes look at later arrivals.

The administrative and economic structure is dealt with in: Charles Gibson, *Spain in America* (New York, 1966); Enriqueta Vila Vilar, *Historia de Puerto Rico, 1600-1650* (Seville, 1974); John Parry, *The Spanish Seaborne Empire* (New York, 1966); Ruth Pike, *Enterprise and Adventure. The Genoese in Seville and the Opening of the New World* (Ithaca, 1966); Clarence H. Haring, *Trade and Navigation between Spain and the Indies in the Time of the Hapsburgs* (Cambridge, Mass., 1918); Robert F. Smith, *The Spanish Guild Merchant. A History of the Consulado, 1250-1700* (Durham, North Carolina, 1940); while the developments of the seventeenth and early eighteenth centuries may be consulted in a wide range of works including C. R. Crone, *Maps and Their Makers* (New York, 1962, 1966); P. M. Ashburn, *The Ranks of Death. A Medical History of the Conquest of America* (New York, 1947); Richard S. Dunn, *Sugar and Slaves. The Rise of the Planter Class in the English West Indies 1624-1713* (Chapel Hill, 1972); Carl and Roberta Bridenbaugh, *No Peace Beyond the Line. The English in the Caribbean 1624-1690* (New York, 1972); Cornelius Ch. Goslinga, *The Dutch in the Caribbean and on the Wild Coast* (Gainesville, 1971); Van Cleaf Bachman, *Peltries and Plantations. The Economic Policies of the Dutch West India Company in New Netherland, 1623-1639* (Baltimore, 1969); C. R. Boxer, *The Dutch Seaborne Empire 1600-1800* (London, 1965, Pelican, 1973); Nellis M. Crouse, *French Pioneers in the West Indies, 1624-1664* (New York, 1940); W. A. Roberts, *The French in the West Indies* (New York, 1942); J. H. Parry, *Europe and a Wider World 1415-1715* (rev. ed., London, 1969); Richard Ligon, *A True and Exact History of the Island of Barbados* (London, 1657); J. Saintoyant, *La Colonisation Française sous l'Ancien Régime (du XVe siècle à 1789)*, 2 vols. (Paris, 1929); Edward Long, *History of Jamaica*, 3 vols. (London, 1774); Jean Baptiste Labat, *The Memoirs of Père Labat, 1693-1705* (translated and abridged by John Eaden, London, 1931); L. B. Simpson, *The Encomienda in New Spain* (Berkeley, 1950); Ward Barrett, "Caribbean Sugar Production Standards in the Seventeenth and Eighteenth Centuries," in J. Parker, ed., *Merchants and Scholars* (Minneapolis, 1965); Ward Barrett, *The Sugar Haciendas of the Marqueses del Valle* (Minneapolis, 1970); Richard Sheridan, *Sugar and Slavery. An Economic History of the British West Indies, 1623-1775* (Baltimore, 1974); M. L. E. Moreau de Saint-Méry, *Description Topographique, Phisique, Civile, Politique et Historique de la Partie Française de L'Isle Saint-Domingue*, 2 vols. (Philadelphia, 1797-98).

Slavery and the slave trade have produced some of the finest scholarship for the area. Philip D. Curtin has revised some of the figures that he originally set forth in *The Atlantic Slave Trade. A Census* (Madison, 1969, in "Measuring the Atlantic Slave Trade," included in that very fine collection of essays edited by Stanley Engerman and Eugene D. Genovese, *Race and Slavery in the Western Hemisphere: Quantitative Studies* (Princeton, 1975), 107-128. Other important and relevant contributions from that volume are Roger Anstey, "The Volume and Profitability of the British Slave Trade, 1761-1807" (3-31), and Johannes Postma, "The Origins of African Slaves: The Dutch Activities on the Guinea Coast, 1675-1795" (33-49). Further revisions of the original Curtin figures may be found in, Enriqueta Vila Vilar, "Los Asientos Portugueses y el Contrabando de Negroes," *Anuario de Estudios Americanos*, Vol. XXX (1973), 557-599; David Eltis, "The Traffic in Slaves between the British West Indian Colonies, 1807-1833," *Economic History Review*, 25:1 (2nd ser. February, 1972), 55-64; Eric Williams, *Capitalism and Slavery* (Chapel Hill, 1944); Perry Viles, "The Slaving Interest of the Atlantic Ports, 1763-192," *French Historical Studies*, 7 (1972), 529-543; *Revue Française d'Histoire d'Outre-Mer*, 62 (1975) provides a number of articles on the slave trade in the issues of the first and second trimesters. Figures may also be found in Noel Deerr, *The History of Sugar* (London, 1949); V. T. Harlow, *A History of Barbados* (New York, 1969); as well as in the readable but not very reliable B. Davidson, *Black Mother: The Years of the African Slave Trade* (Boston, 1961); and Daniel Mannix and Malcolm Cowley, *Black Cargoes: A History of the Atlantic Slave Trade* (New York, 1962).

The ramifications of the slave society are detailed in: Mervyn Ratekin "The Early Sugar Industry in Española," *Hispanic American Historical Review*, 34:1 (1954), 1-19; Elsa Goveia, *Slave Society in the British Leeward Islands at the End of the Eighteenth Century* (New Haven, 1965); Edward Brathwaite, *The Development of Creole Society in Ja-*

maica, 1770-1820 (Oxford, 1971); Orlando Patterson, *The Sociology of Slavery* (London, 1967); Gaston Martin, *Histoire de l'Esclavage dans les Colonies Françaises* (Paris, 1948); Shelby T. McCloy, *The Negro in the French West Indies* (Lexington, Ky., 1966); François Girod, *La Vie Quotidienne de la Société Créole. Saint-Domingue au XVIIIe Siècle* (Paris, 1972); Gabriel Debien, *Les Esclaves aux Antilles Françaises (XVIIe-XVIIIe Siècles)* (Basseterre, etc., 1974); Manuel Moreno Fraginals, *El Ingenio: El Complejo Económico-Social Cubano del Azúcar. 1760-1860* (Havana, 1964; English version, New York, 1976); José Antonio Saco, *Historia de la Esclavitud de la Raza Africana en el Nuevo Mundo*, 4 vols. (Havana, 1938); Roland T. Ely, *Cuando Reinaba Su Majestad el Azúcar: Estudio Histórico-Sociológico de una Tragedia Latino-Americana* (Buenos Aires, 1963); Raul Cepero Bonilla, *Obras Históricas* (Havana, 1963); Luis Díaz Soler, *La Historia de la Esclavitud Negra en Puerto Rico* (Rio Piedras, 1975); Ramiro Guerra y Sánchez, *Azúcar y Población en las Antillas* (Havana, 1927), English translation, *Sugar and Society in the Caribbean* (New Haven, 1964).

The planters and propertied classes expressed their views in Edward Long, *The History of Jamaica*, 3 vols. (London, 1774); Bryan Edwards, *The History, Civil and Commercial of the British West Indies*, 5 vols. (London, 1819, reprinted, New York, 1966); W. J. Gardiner, *A History of Jamaica* . . . (New York, 1909); M. L. E. Moreau de Saint-Méry, *Description* . . . *de la Partie Française de L'Isle Saint-Domingue*, 2 vols. (Philadelphia, 1797-98); J. G. F. Wurdemann, *Notes on Cuba* (Boston, 1844); Antonio de las Barras y Prado, *Memorias La Havana a Mediados del Siglo XIX* (Madrid, 1925); and Francisco de Arango y Parreño, *Obras* (new ed., Havana, 1952). The most remarkable work from the perspective of the enslaved may be found in that curious biography, Estebán Montejo, *Biografía de un Cimarrón*, Miguel Barnet, ed. (Havana, 1967). The best studies of plantations are J. Harry Bennett, *Bondsmen and Bishops. Slavery and Apprenticeship on the Codrington Plantations of Barbados, 1710-1838* (Berkeley, 1958), and M. Craton and J. Walvin, *A Jamaican Plantation. The History of Worthy Park, 1670-1970* (London, 1970).

For the disintegration of the system, see Lowell J. Ragatz, *The Fall of the Planter Class in the British Caribbean, 1753-1833* (New York, 1928; new ed., 1969); Barry W. Higman, *Slave Population and Economy in Jamaica, 1807-1834* (New York, 1976); Franklin W. Knight, *Slave Society in Cuba during the Nineteenth Century* (Madison, 1970); Gwendolyn M. Hall, *Social Control in Slave Plantation Societies: A Comparison of St. Domingue and Cuba* (Baltimore, 1971); Arthur F. Corwin, *Spain and*

the Abolition of Slavery in Cuba, 1817-1886 (Austin, Texas, 1967);
W. L. Burn, *Emancipation and Apprenticeship in the British West Indies* (London, 1937); Reginald Coupland, *The British Anti-Slavery Movement* (London, 1933); D. J. Murray, *The West Indies and the Development of Colonial Government, 1801-1834* (Oxford, 1965); William A. Green, *British Slave Emancipation: The Sugar Colonies and the Great Experiment, 1830-1865* (Oxford, 1976); Claude Levy, "Barbados: The Last Years of Slavery, 1823-1833," *Journal of Negro History*, 44 (1959), 308-345; Robert William Fogel and Stanley L. Engerman, "Philanthropy at Bargain Prices: Notes on the Economics of Gradual Emancipation," *The Journal of Legal Studies*, 3 (1974), 377-401; Victor Schoelcher, *Des Colonies Françaises. Abolition Immédiate de L'Esclavage* (Paris, 1842; new ed., Basseterre, Guadeloupe, and Fort-de-France, Martinique, 1976); Charles Frostin, *Les Revoltes Blanches à Saint-Domingue aux XVIIe et XVIIIe Siècles. (Haiti avant 1789)* (Paris, 1975); C. L. R. James, *The Black Jacobins* (London, 1934); T. O. Ott, *The Haitian Revolution, 1789-1804* (Knoxville, Tenn., 1973); D. B. Davis, *The Problem of Slavery in the Age of Revolution, 1770-1823* (Ithaca, 1975).

Marronage and slave resistance contributed substantially to the gradual erosion of the system of slavery. The growing literature on marronage may be sampled in Richard Price, ed., *Maroon Societies* (New York, 1973), and examined more fully in Pedro Deschamps Chapeaux, "Cimarrones Urbanos," *Revista de la Biblioteca Nacional José Martí* 2 (1969), 145-164; Gabriel Debien, *Les Esclaves aux Antilles Françaises (XVIIe-XVIIIe Siècles)* (Basseterre, Guadeloupe, and Fort-de-France, Martinique, 1974); as well as "Le Marronage aux Antilles Françaises au XVIIIe Siècle," *Caribbean Studies*, 6 (1966), 3-44; Mavis C. Campbell, "The Maroons of Jamaica: Imperium in Imperio?," *Pan-African Journal*, 6 (1973); and perhaps the most sophisticated work to date on marronage, Barbara K. Kopytoff, "The Incomplete Polities; an Ethnohistorical Account of the Jamaica Maroons," Ph.D. dissertation, University of Pennsylvania, 1972. Francois Girod, *La Vie Quotidienne de la Société Créole. Saint-Domingue au XVIIIe Siècle* (Paris, 1972), presents a long general description of Maroons as well as other aspects of slave society. Slave revolts are looked at in various ways. Some contrasting treatments are Orlando Patterson, "Slavery and Slave Revolts: A Socio-Historical Analysis of the First Maroon War, 1665-1740," *Social and Economic Studies*, 19 (1970), 289-325, and the articles by Monica Schuler, Stuart Schwartz, and R. K. Kent in the *Journal of Social History*, 3 (1970).

The free persons not incorporated into the white upper structure are studied by Jerome S. Handler, *The Unappropriated People. Freedmen in the Slave Society in Barbados* (Baltimore, 1974), Mavis C. Campbell, *The Dynamics of Change in a Slave Society. A Socio-Political History of the Free Coloreds of Jamaica, 1800-1865* (New Jersey, 1976), and a number of authors in D. W. Cohen and J. P. Greene, eds., *Neither Slave nor Free. The Freedom of African Descent in the Slave Societies of the New World* (Baltimore, 1972).

Between the sixteenth and the eighteenth centuries, the moving frontiers facilitated the rise of transfrontier groups such as the buccaneers. The classic on the buccaneers is Alexander O. Exquemelin, *The History of the Bucaniers* (London, 1678). See also C. H. Haring, *The Buccaneers in the West Indies in the XVII Century* (London, 1910; reprinted, Hamden, Conn., 1966); Richard Hill, *The Picaroons; Or, One Hundred and Fifty Years Ago* (Dublin, 1869; reprinted, New York, 1971); Frank R. Stockton, *Buccaneers and Pirates of Our Coast* (New York, 1897); James Burney, *History of the Buccaneers of Jamaica* (London, 1816; New York, 1891); and a new sympathetic account of one of the most notorious English buccaneers, Sir Henry Morgan, written by a descendant, Hubert R. Allen, *Buccaneer Admiral Sir Henry Morgan* (London, 1976).

A valuable source of commercial data for the nineteenth century is John MacGregor, *Commercial Statistics. A Digest of . . . Shipping, Imports and Exports of all Nations*, 5 vols. (London, 1850). Social adjustments are dealt with in Verena Martínez-Alier, *Marriage, Class and Colour in Nineteenth-Century Cuba: A Study of Racial Attitudes and Sexual Values in a Slave Society* (New York, 1974); Philip D. Curtin, *Two Jamaicas: The Role of Ideas in a Tropical Colony* (Cambridge, Mass., 1955); Douglas Hall, *Free Jamaica, 1838-1865: An Economic History* (New Haven, 1959); Gisela Eisner, *Jamaica, 1830-1930* (Manchester, 1961); Donald Wood, *Trinidad in Transition: The Years after Slavery* (London, 1968); Alan Adamson, *Sugar Without Slaves: The Political Economy of British Guiana, 1838-1904* (New Haven, 1972); H. Hoetink, *El Pueblo Dominicano, 1850-1900: Apuntes Para su Sociología Histórica* (Santo Domingo, 1971), and his provocative and wider-ranging *Slavery and Race Relations in the Americas: An Inquiry into Their Nature and Nexus* (New York, 1973); and Robert I. Rotberg and Christopher Clague, *Haiti. The Politics of Squalor* (Boston, 1971).

Works dealing with the twentieth century have varied in quality, quantity, and focus. Some of the best works are: Trevor Munroe, *The Politics of Constitutional Decolonization: Jamaica, 1944-1962* (Mona, Jamaica, 1972); A. W. Singham, *The Hero and the Crowd in a Colonial Polity* (New Haven, 1968); Gordon K. Lewis, *The Growth of the Mod-*

ern West Indies (New York, 1968), as well as *Puerto Rico* (New York, 1968); and *The Virgin Islands. A Caribbean Lilliput* (Evanston, Ill., 1972); Selwyn Ryan, *Race and Nationalism in Trinidad and Tobago: A Study of Decolonization in a Multiracial Society* (Toronto, 1972); T. Draper, *The Dominican Revolt: A Case Study in American Policy* (New York, 1965); Abraham F. Lowenthal, *The Dominican Intervention* (Cambridge, Mass., 1971); Howard Wiarda, *Dictatorship and Development: The Methods of Control in Trujillo's Dominican Republic* (Gainesville, Fla., 1970); G. Pope Atkins and Larman C. Wilson, *The United States and the Trujillo Regime* (New Brunswick, N.J., 1972); Edwin A. Weinstein, *Cultural Aspects of Delusion: A Psychiatric Study of the Virgin Islands* (Glencoe, Ill., 1962); Darwin D. Creque, *The U.S. Virgins and the Eastern Caribbean* (Philadelphia, 1968); H. E. Lamur, *The Demographic Evolution of Surinam, 1920-1970. A Socio-Demographic analysis* (The Hague, 1973); C. A. M. Smith, *The Making of Modern Belize. Politics Society and British Colonialism in Central America* (Cambridge, Mass., 1976); James Leyburn, *The Haitian People* (new ed., New Haven, 1966); Rayford Logan, *Haiti and the Dominican Republic* (New York, 1968); Peter Newman, *British Guiana: Problems of Cohesion in an Immigrant Society* (London, 1964); Raymond T. Smith, *British Guiana* (London, 1962); Truman R. Clark, *Puerto Rico and the United States, 1917-1933* (Pittsburgh, 1975); Robert Hoernel, "Sugar and Social Change in Oriente, Cuba, 1898-1946," *Journal of Latin American Studies,* 8 (1976), 215-249. The bibliography on the Cuban Revolution is enormous and rapidly expanding. The first phase can be gauged by Nelson P. Valdés and Edwin Lieuwin, *The Cuban Revolution: A Research-Study Guide, 1959-1969* (Albuquerque, N.M., 1971). See also Hugh Thomas, *Cuba. The Pursuit of Freedom* (New York, 1971); Richard R. Fagen, *The Transformation of Political Culture in Cuba* (Stanford, 1969); Carmelo Mesa-Lago, *Revolutionary Change in Cuba* (Pittsburgh, 1971); and *Cuba in the 1970s: Pragmatism and Institutionalization* (Albuquerque, N.M., 1974); Archibald R. Ritter, *The Economic Development of Revolutionary Cuba: Strategy and Performance* (Berkeley, 1974); Maurice Halperin, *The Rise and Decline of Fidel Castro* (Berkeley, 1972); and Jaime Suchliki, *University Students and Revolution in Cuba, 1920-1968* (Coral Gables, Fla., 1969).

Roland Perusse has edited a group of highly informative essays on Caribbean dependency patterns in *Revista/Review Interamericana,* 6 (Spring, 1976), and George Beckford has edited a number of stimulating essays, *Caribbean Economy* (Mona, Jamaica, 1975), which examine the economic situation of the English Caribbean in the 1960's and 1970's.

Tables

TABLE 1. AFRICANS SUPPLIED TO BARBADOS, 1673-1684.

Year	Number of Cargoes	Slaves	Estimated Average Delivery Price in Pounds Sterling
1673	1	204	18
1674	4	1006	20
1675	6	1506	17
1676	7	1833	15
1677	4	886	15
1678	8	2053	15
1679	5	569	15
1680	6	1340	15
1681	11	1501	12
1682	8	1033	14
1683	18	2963	13
1684	6	1380	14

TOTAL:

12	84	16,274	

Average cargo: 194 slaves
Average annual importation: 1356 slaves

Note: Estimated average delivery prices rounded to nearest pound sterling, and based on the recalculation of Harlow's average price per cargo.

TABLE 2. SLAVE IMPORTATION DISTRIBUTION BY PERCENTAGES, 1600-1870.

Region	1600-1700	1701-1810	1811-1870	Percent of Entire Trade, 1500-1870
Br. N.A./USA	?	5.8	3.0	4.5
Brazil	41.0	31.0	60.0	38.0
Br. Antilles	20.0	23.0	—	
Sp. America	21.8	9.6	32.0	
French Antilles	12.0	22.0	5.0	
Dutch Antilles	3.0	7.6	—	
Danish Antilles	0.3	0.4	—	50.0
Est. total imports	1,400,000	6,000,000	2,000,000	9,500,000

TABLE 3. SUGAR PRODUCTION AND SLAVE POPULATION FIGURES
IN SELECTED COLONIES, 1643-1860.

	Year	Sugar in Tons	Slave Population
A. Barbados	1643	—	6000
	1680	—	38,400
	1712	6343	42,000
	1757	7068	63,600
	1792	9025	64,300
	1809	6062	69,400
	1834	19,728	82,000
B. Jamaica	1703	4782	45,000
	1730	15,972	74,500
	1754	23,396	130,000
	1775	47,690	190,000
	1789	59,400	250,000
	1808	77,800	324,000
	1834	62,812	311,070
C. Guadeloupe	1674	2106 (metric tons)	4300
	1730	6230	26,800
	1767	7898	71,800
	1790	8725	85,500
	1820	22,300	88,400
	1838	35,124	93,300
D. Saint-Domingue	1720	10,500	—
	1739	?	117,411
	1764	ca. 60,000	206,000
	1776	76,000	240,000
	1789	70,313	452,000
	1791	78,696	480,000
	1836	8	—
E. Cuba	1774	10,000	44,300
	1792	18,571	85,900
	1817	43,415	199,100
	1827	ca. 70,000	286,900
	1841	162,425	352,483
	1860	447,000	367,400
F. St. Croix	1754	ca. 730	7566
	1770	8230	
	1780	12,100	
	1800	15,700	figures not available
	1821	23,000	for subsequent years
	1840	7000	
	1860	7600	

TABLE 4. CARIBBEAN POPULATION BY CASTES, EARLY 19TH CENTURY

Colony	Year	Total Population	Slave Population			Free Non-White Population				White Population		
			Slave Population	As % of Colony's Total	As % of Non-White	No.	As % of Total	As % of All Non-Whites	As % Free	No.	As % of Colony's Total	% Free
BRITISH ANTILLES												
Anguilla		?										
Antigua	1832	35,412	29,537	83.4	89.3	3,531	10.0	10.7	64.0	1,980	5.6	36.0
Bahamas	1810	16,718	11,146	66.7	87.4	1,600	9.6	12.6	29.2	3,872	23.0	70.8
Barbados	1834	100,000	80,861	80.6	92.5	6,584	6.5	7.5	33.9	12,797	12.7	66.1
Barbuda		?										
Berbice	1811	25,959	25,169	97.0	99.0	240	1.0	1.0	30.3	550	2.0	69.7
Bermuda	1812	9,900	4,794	48.4	91.4	451	4.6	8.6	8.7	4,755	48.0	91.3
Demerara	1811	57,386	53,655	93.5	96.0	2,223	3.9	4.0	51.3	2,108	3.6	48.7
Dominica	1811	26,041	21,728	83.4	87.9	2,988	11.4	12.1	69.3	1,325	5.2	30.7
Essequibo	1811	19,645	18,125	92.3	96.0	757	3.9	4.0	50.0	763	3.9	50.0
Grenada & Carriacou	1811	31,362	29,381	93.6	96.0	1,210	3.9	4.0	61.0	771	2.5	39.0
[Br.] Honduras	1790	2,656	2,024	76.2	84.5	371	14.0	15.5	58.7	261	9.8	41.3
Jamaica	1800	340,000	300,000	88.2	89.5	35,000	10.2	10.5	70.0	15,000	4.4	25.0
Montserrat	1812	7,383	6,537	88.5	94.2	402	5.4	5.8	47.5	444	6.1	52.5
Nevis	1812	10,430	9,326	89.4	93.9	603	5.8	6.1	54.6	501	4.8	45.4
St. Christopher	1812	23,491	19,885	84.6	90.9	1,996	8.5	9.1	55.4	1,610	6.9	44.6
St. Lucia	1810	17,485	14,397	82.3	88.5	1,878	10.7	11.5	60.8	1,210	7.0	39.2
St. Vincent	1812	24,253	22,020	90.8	94.0	1,406	5.7	6.0	62.9	827	3.4	37.1
Tobago	1811	17,830	16,897	94.8	98.0	350	2.0	2.0	37.5	583	3.2	62.5
Tortola		?										
Trinidad	1811	32,664	21,143	64.7	73.8	7,493	22.9	26.2	63.3	4,353	13.3	36.7
Virgin Islands												

	Year											
DANISH ANTILLES												
St. Croix	1841	—	20,000			?				3,200		
St. John		?				?				?		
St. Thomas	1841	7,000	5,000	71.4	76.9	1,500	21.4	23.0	75.0	500	7.2	25.0
DUTCH ANTILLES												
Saba		?	?			?				?		
St. Eustatia	1850	2,500	2,000	80.0	95.2	100	4.0	4.8	20.0	400	16.0	80.0
St. Martin	1850	3,600	3,000	83.3	—	?	—	—	—	600	16.6	—
Curaçao	1833	15,027	5,894	39.2	47.4	6,531	43.5	52.6	71.4	2,602	17.3	28.6
Surinam	1830	56,325	48,784	86.6	90.6	5,041	8.9	9.4	66.8	2,500	4.4	33.2
SPANISH ANTILLES												
Cuba	1827	704,487	286,942	40.7	32.9	106,494	15.1	27.1	25.5	311,051	44.1	74.5
Puerto Rico	1860	583,181	41,738	7.1	14.8	241,037	41.3	85.2	44.5	300,406	51.5	55.5
Santo Domingo	1791	125,000	15,000	12.0	?	?						
SWEDISH ANTILLES												
St. Bartholomew	1840	7,000	?	?								
FRENCH ANTILLES												
Guadaloupe	1836	107,810	81,642	75.7	94.0	5,235	5.4	6.0	33.3	10,636	11.0	66.7
Martinique	1789	96,158	83,414	86.7	94.0	28,000	5.3	6.0	41.0	40,000	7.6	59.0
Saint-Domingue	1791	520,000	452,000	86.9								
Guiana												
St. Martin (part)	1836	3,869	2,925	75.6								
Marie Galante	1836	13,188	10,116	76.7								
Saintes	1836	1,139	569	49.9								
Desirada	1836	1,568	1,070	68.2								

TABLE 5. CARIBBEAN SUGAR PRODUCTION AND EXPORTS, 1815-1894.

Colony	1815	1828	1882	1894
Antigua	8032	8848	12,670	12,382
Barbados	8837	16,942	48,325	50,958
Br. Guiana	16,520	40,115	124,102	102,502
Dominica	2205	2497	3421	1050
Grenada	11,594	13,493	1478	3
Jamaica	79,660	72,198	32,038	19,934
Montserrat	1225	1254	2314	1801
Nevis	2761	2309	16,664	16,901
St. Kitts	7066	6060		
St. Lucia	3661	4162	7506	4485
St. Vincent	11,590	14,403	8175	2727
Tobago	6044	6167	2518	599
Tortola	1200	663	—	—
Trinidad	7682	13,285	55,327	46,869
Total Br. Antilles	168,077	202,396	315,138	260,211
Martinique	15,814 (1818)	32,812	47,120	36,353
Guadeloupe	20,792 (1818)	35,244	56,592	43,041
Surinam	5,692 (1816)	11,728 (1825)	5410 (1885)	8023 (1895)
St. Croix	20,535 (1812)	10,576 (1830)	8482 (1890)[1]	8000 (est.)
Puerto Rico	—	31,714 (1843)	65,000 (1886)	48,500 (est.)
Cuba	39,961	73,200 (1829)[2]	595,000[2]	1,054,000[2]

[1] average for years 1880-90
[2] production figures

TABLE 6. HAITIAN EXPORT BEFORE AND AFTER THE REVOLUTION

Commodity	1789	1801	1818	1820	1826	1836	1841
Sugar	141,089,831	18,535,112	5,443,765	2,517,289	32,864	16,199	1,363
Coffee	76,835,219	43,420,270	26,065,200	35,137,759	32,189,784	37,662,672	34,114,717
Cotton	7,004,274	2,480,340	474,118	346,839	620,972	1,072,555	1,591,454
Cacao	—	648,518	434,368	556,424	457,592	550,484	640,618
Indigo	758,628	804	—	—	—	—	—
Dyewoods	—	6,768,634	6,819,300	1,919,748	5,307,745	6,767,902	45,071,391
Tobacco	—	—	19,140	97,600	349,588	1,222,716	3,219,690
Castor Oil	—	—	121	157	—	—	265
Cigars	—	—	—	—	179,500	33,000	728,650
Hides	—	—	—	—	—	14,891	27,126
Old Rags	—	—	—	—	—	275	44,596
Wax	—	—	—	—	—	15,620	43,413
Ginger	—	—	—	—	—	15,509	15,822

Note: All commodities in lbs. except castor oil measured in gallons, and cigars and hides in numbers.

Index